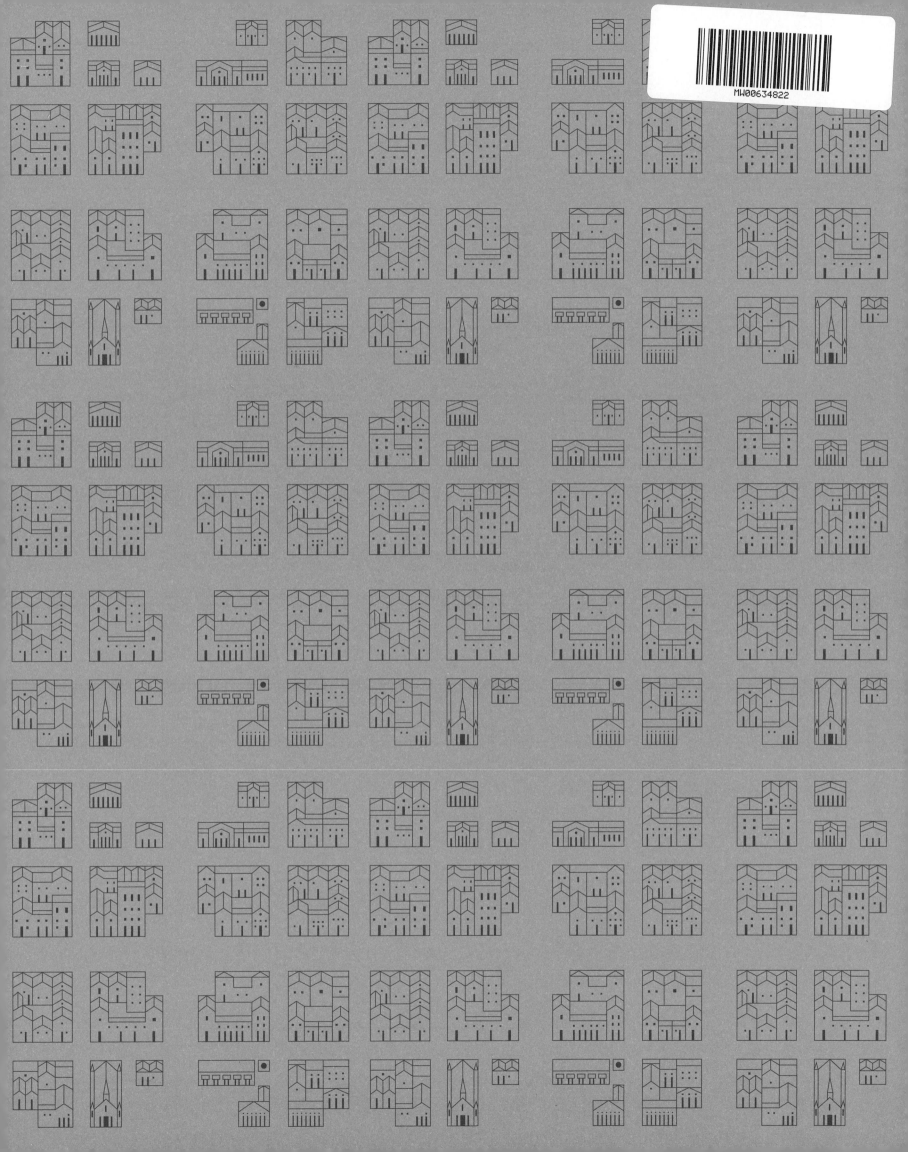

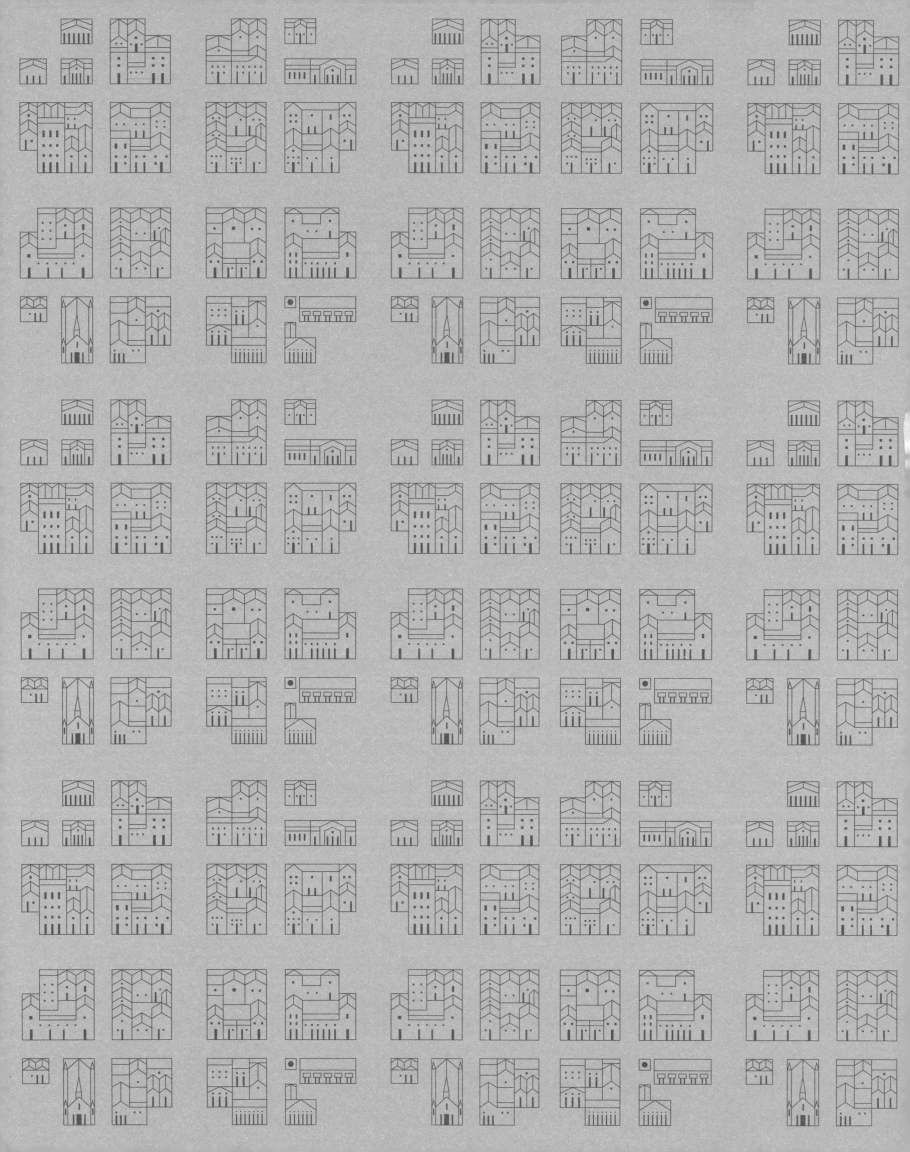

ARCHITECTS OF COMMUNITY

TORTI GALLAS + PARTNERS

FOREWORD

Elizabeth Plater-Zyberk
and Andrés Duany

INTRODUCTION

John Francis Torti *and*

Thomas M. Gallas

ESSAYS and DESCRIPTIONS

Edited by

Cheryl A. O'Neill

VENDOME
NEW YORK

+ Methodologies

Our goal is to elevate the quality of everyday environments, bringing new dignity to housing and more power to the places they make. Our work is about making the background buildings that line ordinary streets and squares of the city and in which daily life unfolds. Simply put, we are the designers of the fabric of the city and strive to make the most beautiful things out of the simplest clay.

+ Buildings

More Americans are living in metropolitan areas today than a decade ago, replacing years of decline with new growth. This section examines the rebirth of the city as a place of residence, exploring the architecture and urbanism of the mixed-use apartment building. Public/private development ventures, prescient re-zonings, and public transport have all fueled an urban residential building boom.

+ Neighborhoods

As a microcosm of the city, the neighborhood encapsulates all of its constituent parts. Our challenge is to act both as planners—establishing the pattern of streets and open spaces, the size and geometry of the block, its subdivision into lots and housing parcels—and as architects, creating the dwellings that respond to the needs of everyday life and give character to public spaces.

+ Places

The scale of our endeavors shifts from buildings to towns and cities. It is about the creation of new places and about fulfilling the policy objectives that will transform existing ones. Their time frame is not the here and now of today, tomorrow, or this decade, but the distant future of the next fifty or one hundred years. Our place-based approach is both cross-cultural and transnational.

+ FOREWORD

ELIZABETH PLATER-ZYBERK

& ANDRÉS DUANY

How to adequately describe the surprise and pleasure that we experienced when seeing all this work collected in one volume? Many of us have long known of this powerhouse architectural firm—so busy building wherever a pedestrian urbanism is to be supported. But reviewing this book has allowed us to understand why so few of us have known of the quantity of work, and of its quality. It is the essence of what makes the buildings of Torti Gallas + Partners so rare and important: they are designed to be almost invisible. The firm is not interested in calling attention to itself—none of that tiresome "look at me" search for some measure of immortality. Torti Gallas buildings blend in; they participate in their context—whether existing or future—fully committed to the collective endeavor that is urbanism.

The talented members of the firm are so good at this, and have been at it for so long, that one must admire the multigenerational culture. Torti Gallas transmits expertise the old way—through apprenticeship. Indeed, we might ask whether any current American architecture school is so dependably capable of teaching what we call "plain old good architecture." This know-how is now so rare that it is nearly lost—even as it is so necessary to a society confronting the limits of the twenty-first century.

OPPOSITE: Firm logo, designed by Robert S. Goodill, based on the Renaissance plan of Avola, Italy.

> "Torti Gallas buildings participate in their context, whether existing or future."

ELIZABETH PLATER-ZYBERK
& ANDRÉS DUANY

The Upton at
Rockville Town
Center, Rockville,
Maryland.

Other aspects of the firm's skill are worth noting. It practices in a great range of scales, from overall community planning, as in the excellent King Farm; to urban design at the scale of the retail street with all its components, as at Baldwin Park; to the scale of the urban building, the firm's unmatched expertise, as in the Upton apartment building; and even to the careful detail, as in the Georgetown Safeway. The best firms deliver expertly only at one or two of these scales of design. Torti Gallas dominates all four—and in the very difficult world of commercial development, which they have the courage to engage.

Evidence of this expertise is that the buildings are universally well liked whether they are small or large. In a culture of public participation that much prefers the small and usually opposes the large, their large apartment buildings are beloved by all—even by their immediate neighbors. Such is the power of design when dedicated to the common, intelligible language that is the essence of traditional architecture.

And the buildings, large or small, are not only contextual and popular—they are also quite beautiful. Torti Gallas has produced elegant designs for affordable housing, including for HUD's HOPE VI program, such as Belmont Heights, which incites the pride of residents. They are culturally responsive, too, to the families they serve, such as the neighborhoods of houses that provide a sense of normalcy for U.S. military personnel. Responsive also to other cultures: in Turkey, the Emirates, and China, Torti Gallas avoids the transplantation of the passing fashions of Anglo-American academies.

There is little need to say much more. The work presented is perfectly understood by those untrammeled by avant-garde concerns. The firm provides a great service to society, not only to its developer-clients but also to the inhabitants of the buildings; and not only to the cities where they set their superb standard but also to the generation of young architects, demonstrating to them how it should be done.

+ INTRODUCTION

"Every building increment must help to form
at least one larger whole in the city, which is both
larger and more significant than itself."

CHRISTOPHER ALEXANDER

The work of Torti Gallas + Partners is about making the most beautiful things out of the simplest clay. Passionate about designing places and buildings that quietly transform cities, suburbs, and people, the members of the firm are the designers of the fabric of the city—the houses, shops, and workplaces where daily life unfolds. Our world is about making cities whole.

The Torti Gallas portfolio now extends to thirty-six states, seventy-eight cities, and twelve foreign countries. With one hundred people headquartered in the Washington, D.C., area and offices in Los Angeles and Istanbul, we practice urban design and architecture as an inextricable whole. Developers, government officials, and members of the community turn to us for a partner who thinks beyond the building and plans for the positive, sustainable impact these places will have on the surrounding communities.

The firm's logo is taken from the plan of Avola, Italy (page 6). This Sicilian medieval hill town was destroyed by an earthquake and rebuilt on safer ground in the form of a Renaissance plan. The idea of destruction and rebirth—of transformation—is very much a part of Torti Gallas's philosophy.

OPPOSITE: Park Place, Washington D.C.

Founded by Jack C. Cohen, AIA, in 1953, the firm helped to build Washington's suburbs. As the name of the firm evolved from Cohen & Haft to CHK Architects and Planners in 1973, its success in residential design was validated in a 1972 *Washington Post* article that proclaimed the firm the "Architects of the Suburbs." For the next two decades, the firm enjoyed continued success in residential, commercial, senior living, and educational architecture. The 1990s, however, brought both professional and personal hardships. The recession in the early part of the decade reduced the firm from 165 to 37 employees. And in 1993, the firm's president, Jack Kerxton, the "K" in CHK, passed away.

Architect John Torti, FAIA, who joined the firm in 1973 and succeeded Kerxton as president, knew something had to be done. Along with Tom Gallas, the firm's chief financial officer, he changed the course of the firm "180 degrees," turning it into the "reformer of the suburbs." It became a firm dedicated to cleaning up the mess that it had helped create. With a commitment to the principles of New Urbanism, Torti remade the firm in the image of his beliefs. In 1998 the firm name was changed to Torti Gallas + Partners to reflect not only a new era of leadership but also a new dedication to urban design and architecture that resembled that of the best traditional American cities and towns.

With this change in leadership and ideology, the firm has combined the best aspects of new conceptual thinking drawn from academia with a well-run design business, building on lessons about real estate, the marketplace, and excellent construction documents from its earlier history. Torti and his creative partners have built a firm that understands the inextricable ties between urban design and architecture, between great cities and great buildings, and between conceptual thinking and creating value within buildings, neighborhoods, and places.

A key component of Torti Gallas's practice is the integration of its residential work with large-scale planning and urban design. Addressing projects as commissions that involve both architecture and urban design, the firm has expanded its scope from creating "projects" to creating "place." Its commissions are not "one-off" elite houses but the many types of buildings that form the fabric of the city. The firm is dedicated to combining this architecture and urban design into an inextricable whole where the creation of a strong public realm supports the architecture around it by giving it place, as the architecture supports the public realm by giving it a beautiful container. This is what good cities and places have been in history and can be again.

"Either a building is part of a place or it is not. Once that kinship is there, time will only make it stronger."

WILLA CATHER

Torti Gallas's work covers a broad range of the built environment, including urban infill, suburban repair, and to a lesser degree, responsible greenfield neighborhoods. The following beliefs are central to our practice and inform all projects, regardless of their scale or density:

1 The belief in a broad starting point, called the "Spectrum"—a 360-degree approach to the design task that simultaneously considers nature, the built environment, and people (pages 30–33).

2 The understanding that urban design informs architecture.

3 The conviction that cities must have a great public realm, a vital mix of uses, diverse populations, and strong connections, locally and regionally.

4 The belief that architecture must connect and be appropriate to the character of the place and not be self-conscious.

5 The recognition that design is a continuum and that the design must find a place to connect to when coming to a place and leave a place of connection for the next designer.

6 The commitment to design with multiple stakeholders in mind: the client, the community, and the city.

7 The knowledge that people complete the places they inhabit, as the places shape their inhabitants' lives.

DISCOURSE

To accomplish change in a firm of more than a hundred people, Torti Gallas created a platform called a "discourse." These discourses, which occur every other Friday, involve the entire firm and have a defined topic. Sometimes presentations are made; sometimes the discourse is just "pure" discussion, that is, discussion without rules or constraints, the only goal being the best, "purest" outcome. Since the firm's ideological rebirth there have been four major discourses: 1—Urbanism vs. Suburbanism, 2—Architectural Design, 3—Sustainability, and 4—the Language of Architecture. Some of these discourses took several weeks; others took months. Each has been a great success for the firm, resulting in a common set of principles around the given subject and, most important, a language in which to communicate those principles and beliefs. The most provocative of all the discourses was the one on Architectural Design, which produced the Design Charter (pages 292–93), a written set of principles on Architecture, Urbanism, Social Justice, and Sustainability in which the firm believes. Signing the charter is not mandatory.

2016 Torti Gallas principals.

CHANGE AGENTS

Torti Gallas believes that its practice is about transformation and that its primary work is to be a change agent to make a better world. This may sound ambitious or even naïve, but the results prove otherwise: the revitalization of the Capper/Carrollsburg housing complex in Southeast Washington, D.C., for instance, transformed public housing for 700 residents into a vibrant new mixed-income neighborhood for 1,600 families, including the original 700. By changing this neighborhood so profoundly, Torti Gallas helped create a continuous, secure, walkable connection between Capitol Hill and the Yards, the new waterfront development on the Anacostia River in the nation's capital.

The similarly profound effect that the firm's work has had on 34 HOPE VI communities across the country and on 25,000 military-family homes in more than 120 neighborhoods speaks to its being a change agent in the buildings and neighborhoods it creates and for the people that inhabit these places. The happy irony of this experience is that most of these neighborhoods are National Design Award winners. This book is full of such stories at the building, the neighborhood, and the place level.

GOOD DESIGN IS GOOD BUSINESS

From the outset, the idea behind Torti Gallas + Partners has been that "Good Design is Good Business." Though this may seem self-evident, it was a novel idea for the firm. Our successful predecessor firm, CHK Architects and Planners, followed a more service- and delivery-oriented business model that had a long and rewarding history of business success. The shift to a design-oriented focus represented a fundamental change in the firm's culture and ideology— one that recognized the value of maintaining high-quality design all the way through construction documents and construction administration. The New Urbanism design ideology enabled the firm to wrap our successful service and delivery methodology in a principle-based framework. By embracing this broader view of our abilities as design leaders and innovators, we were creating a foundation for a strong business model from which we could build a more successful firm.

As with any business decision, the more comprehensive and well thought out it is, and the fewer the unknowns, the less risk there is and the higher the probability for success. Having added a principled design ideology that was supported by a distinctive point of view about sensitive infill and neighborhood making, Torti Gallas was able to create a platform for business success beyond anything we had been able to achieve in our previous forty-year history. In essence, the philosophical belief system enabled us to craft a business strategy for realizing the value.

> "We are one hundred percent design and one hundred percent business. That is the pact Tom and I made."
>
> JOHN FRANCIS TORTI, FAIA

A SINGULAR FIRM

The business strategy for Torti Gallas became clear—to become "Singular." Though we acknowledge many very fine firms that do exemplary work, our goal has always been to be singular in the combination of strengths and attitudes we bring to each of our projects. This unique blend of skills and expertise, applied in different combinations and in different situations, defines our work and enables us to be important contributors to the success of our projects.

+ METHODOLOGIES

JOHN FRANCIS TORTI

The Architecture of
Real Estate

Great cities are made up of great neighborhoods. The rowhouse communities of Boston or the West End of London, New Orleans' French Quarter, and the railroad suburbs of New York City are but a few examples of fine neighborhoods. Most were built in a relatively short period of time in response to housing pressures generated by rapid population growth. Commissioned by private landowners or developers, they were constructed in a speculative process, producing housing to be rented or sold in the marketplace. Those neighborhoods built before World War II in the United States are among the country's finest, and the architects responsible for them, many unknown today, prospered from numerous commissions for often very modest housing and contributed to making places of great beauty. The architect Grosvenor Atterbury, for instance, worked hand-in-hand with the Olmsted Brothers landscape architecture firm on the design of Forest Hills Gardens in Queens, New York. Atterbury established the vision for the town's architecture, which, together with the Olmsted Brothers' layout, resulted in a garden suburb of uncommon beauty.

OPPOSITE: Centergate at Baldwin Park, Orlando, Florida.

Forest Hills
Gardens, Queens,
New York.

Aerial view of
Levittown,
Pennsylvania.

The post–World War II suburban building boom in the United States likewise created new neighborhoods over a short time span. A perfect storm of economic, political, and social factors—soldiers returning from the war, the easy availability of G.I. Bill mortgages, the passage of the National Defense Highway Act creating the first interstate highways—led to the rapid growth of suburban communities. This growth was also largely the result of a developer-driven, speculative process. With few exceptions, however, the resultant neighborhoods are distinguished by housing of poor quality. Unending repetition, kitschy design features, and lack of architectural integrity are but a short list of their failings.

The scale and power of these suburban speculative operations were much larger than that of their pre–World War II predecessors. They were dominated by large-scale home builders responsible for the development of roads and finished lots, as well as for the construction of housing. Absent was the empowered voice of either the city or design professionals. As a result, the focus shifted from the neighborhood as a whole to the individual house, which over time was reduced to the status of a mere "product," a commodity to be bought or sold in the marketplace. Site arrangements did little more than provide road access and a street address. The quality of the public realm degenerated from a place for people to a place for cars. After fifty or so years, with few exceptions, the balance between architecture and real estate was weighted heavily toward the latter.

THE MISSION OF TORTI GALLAS

We entered this speculative housing world focused on a simple mission—to raise the level of developer-driven housing production and reestablish equilibrium between architecture and real estate. Our aim is to resuscitate the practice of our pre–World War II forebears, creating ordinary housing of fine quality and neighborhoods of great beauty. We understand that to do this, we must fully engage in the developer world, taking into account both its intricacies and its essential role in the creation of neighborhood.

Our first approach to standard developer-driven housing production is to introduce site and place, as well as larger ideas of neighborhood, as active protagonists in the design equation. It is through the collective lens of urban design and housing design that we address speculative housing, understanding the power of the aggregation of buildings, even if just a few, to create place. This often requires mixing a wide range of demographics and income levels in the same neighborhood, bringing equal quality, and no differentiation, to them.

Our aim is also to reinvigorate the architecture of speculative housing, elevating its quality by aggressively inserting the voice of the architect—our voice—into its production. We strive to replace the banality of suburban housing with the architectural traditions of the cities and towns in which we work. Our early commissions, largely in greenfield sites, focused on reinvigorating the deadening suburban triad of multifamily, single-family attached, and single-family detached units, often finding inspiration in the rich architecture of local vernaculars and regional types. Urban infill projects have stimulated investigations into pre–World War II apartments and the ins and outs of urban façade making. In all of these cases, we have discovered that when the architecture and the urbanism are addressed collectively, the whole becomes much greater than the sum of its parts.

The Garlands of
Barrington,
Barrington, Illinois.

THE ARCHITECTURE OF REAL ESTATE

The formula of a developer-driven suburban neighborhood is a relatively simple one. Building types and parking requirements are designed in response to the demands and needs of the perceived market. Quality pertains to the features of the "product"—its curb appeal and whatever bells and whistles might attract the likely consumer. A successful real estate equation is one in which the cost to build the product is less, preferably substantially less, than the selling or renting price. The "product" is the central focus, and with large-scale developers, it is honed down to the selection of the bathroom faucets.

Introducing fit and context into the equation elevates the idea of site design from one of pieces to one of place. The design problem this generates is considerably more complicated than its developer-driven suburban equivalent, but in our minds far more fruitful. Adding the concept of fit and context to the variables of the suburban equation—building type, parking requirements, and the market—can be thought of either as a simultaneous equation of multiple variables (if you can remember your high school algebra) or a sandwich. In the middle of the sandwich are the variables of the suburban equation. They are framed by the "bread" of cost and quality, of fit and context. Our process begins with the site, analyzing its yield and taking cues on density and type from the context. What follows is a constant yin and yang, adjusting one variable to another and back again, to produce an end result where both context/fit and cost/quality are at their optimum.

The town center at
Fort Belvoir, Fairfax
County, Virginia.

Neighborhood green at Fort Belvoir, Fairfax County, Virginia.

The goal of this process is to find the intersection where architecture and urbanism yield a greater whole—a powerful idea of place—and greater value to the whole equation: the architecture, the urbanism, and the real estate. Place was not initially perceived by the development community as an important component of real estate, but over the two-and-a-half decades that we have been implementing this approach, we have seen that change. In developer-ese, place adds value to product, and the leaders of the developer world have come to recognize that. The motivations of many have shifted from a build-it-and-flip-it mentality to that of the great patrons of an older world—the builders and stewards of the city. As a repository of culture, memory, and permanence, the idea of the city is a powerfully motivating thing.

The to-and-fro between architecture and urbanism in our design process engages us in a constant dialogue between the housing type and the lot on the architecture side, and the block and the street on the urban side. The process is not a linear one, with the big urban decisions coming first and the design of the architecture following, but a continuous back and forth. Construction types and parking strategies have a huge impact on costs, housing types, and block dimensions, and consequently factor greatly in both architectural and urban decisions. The resolution of all of these demands is ever more challenging in today's world, where high land values, especially in urban areas, demand ever-greater site yields. In the end, the assemblage of the unit, the type, the lot, and the block is often crafted with the intricacy and precision of a Swiss watch.

It is also important to say that the equation that yields the highest real estate value, as well as the right fit between site and context, reaps enormous benefits for the architecture. We have mined this, becoming expert at the architecture not of the individual building but of its assemblage into the larger urban order of the street or square. Apartment buildings along a city street, a string of rowhouses, or single-family houses on a tree-lined boulevard—the ideas that belong to these, which somehow reside in between architecture and urbanism, are our forte.

ARCHITECTURE + BIG ARCHITECTURE

We practice our craft across many different density scales. When the project involves a single building in the city, we try to understand the greater place, both the place that is fully formed and the place that may just be emerging. Our goal is to find key points of connection and build from them, creating a larger and better whole, and leaving a place for the next designer to connect to.

When our commissions are large and involve multiple neighborhoods and hundreds of dwellings, we borrow a strategy from standard product design and develop a basic set of building "chassis" with multiple variations in style, massing, materials, and color schemes. A single neighborhood may consist of eight chassis, four styles, and ten color schemes. This approach marries the efficiency of high-volume real estate production with the variety of building types and nuanced architectural expression necessary to support a finely crafted urban plan. It represents the best value equation for the community and its future inhabitants, achieving the beauty of pre–World War II neighborhoods at the lowest possible prices. Efficiencies like these are important in the United States and around the world; the urgent need for shelter constantly demands large quantities of housing at affordable prices.

A BETTER WORLD

As our internal process has expanded in scope from the individual building to the collective of the neighborhood, so has our external process. It has enlarged from a focus on single sites to whole towns or cities, and from conversations

with a single client to discussions with an ever-expanding cast involved in the making of the city. We no longer make design decisions alone in a room with a roll of drafting paper and a pen, and the concomitant closed-door meetings have all but disappeared, replaced by interactive processes involving municipalities, city agencies, neighborhood stakeholders, and the local citizenry.

This shift began for us in the early days of the firm with several large greenfield projects. Utilizing charrette techniques developed by Duany Plater-Zyberk and other New Urbanists, we developed our master plans with large groups in an open-door creative process. And we loved it. We brought the process to many inner-city revitalization projects and learned a lot about brokering neighborhood change. It is very difficult to walk into a room and tell someone you are going to take away their house for a while, but that it is a good thing. What we learned is the importance of the conversation. And time. Lots of time—at the site, in the neighborhood, learning about the things that are loved and those that are hated.

No longer dominated by private developers, our client base has likewise changed, often involving joint ventures between private developers and municipal agencies—housing or transportation authorities, departments of economic development, or any combination thereof. These public/private projects are typically instigated by a broader public agenda: to bring new services to an underserved area of the city, to revitalize a distressed community, to maximize transit investments, to create a 24/7 downtown with new residential construction. In these instances, our project is a change agent, providing the catalyst that stimulates a broader transformation and helps to improve the city.

CONCLUSION

We understand that developer-driven real estate production is one of the entities that give form to the city. And we recognize the power of the ordinary dwelling. Absent a sense of place, however, its impact is very limited. Our goal is to elevate the quality of everyday environments, bringing new dignity to housing and more power to the places they make. Our work is about making the background buildings that line the city's ordinary streets and squares, in which daily life unfolds. Simply put, we are the designers of the fabric of the city and strive to make the most beautiful things out of the simplest clay.

T H O M A S   M .   G A L L A S

Neighborhood Transformation

Neighborhood transformation is about more than just a single design project on a site. It's about a spark or catalytic set of actions that leads to other positive planned and unplanned activities initiated by that project. It's about dramatic and comprehensive change to the physical, social, cultural, and economic aspects of a neighborhood. And it requires trust, vision, cooperation, consensus, partnership, and investment to be successful.

Vision for the transformation of Route 1, Crystal City, Arlington, Virginia.

Neighborhood transformation must start with a common will. Communities must first want it to happen and believe that it can happen. For it to be successful, the facilitators of change must earn the trust of the community and garner their support for change. Even for those who are convinced that neighborhood transformation is needed, it may still be hard to agree to participate as a "change agent" because "the devil you know is better than the devil you don't know." We all know that change can be frightening. People in the lower income brackets have seen promises go unfulfilled time and time again. And any constituents, rich or poor, private sector or public, must understand that change cannot happen if they are the only ones who want it. Real and successful neighborhood transformation requires the support of many. Cooperation and forming a consensus centered on finding "win-win" solutions are critical elements of change.

During the design phase of the Master Plan for Crystal City in Arlington County, Virginia (pages 238–41), Torti Gallas worked closely with existing neighborhood associations, holding a week-long charrette, three community forums, and more than forty task force meetings. Shortly after coming on board, Torti Gallas organized a community walking tour that included not only Crystal City but the neighboring areas of Pentagon City and Aurora Heights. Led by architects and planners from the firm, the tour provided an opportunity for two-way communication between the designers and interested community members while demonstrating interest in nurturing cooperation and consensus for the project. The citizens and the planners got to see the neighborhood through each other's eyes.

Establishing a common will must be paired with creating a common vision. This usually entails gaining community-wide cooperation and encouraging the stakeholders to listen to one another and express their ideas in a safe and non-hostile environment. If the community members feel that they can openly and candidly voice their wants and needs for neighborhood transformation, the probability of arriving at consensus and acceptance of change increases. And when the community can share ownership for change, the likelihood of success is more assured.

The Torti Gallas project at Salishan in Tacoma, Washington (pages 164–67), serves as a prime example of this type of community participation. The multigenerational residents from five different countries and the United States share a deep appreciation for the people and traditions of Salishan. When Torti Gallas architects asked the residents, "How can we help to better this neighborhood?" one man stood up to speak for his neighbors, asking

Salishan, Tacoma,
Washington.

in turn, "My question is, what can we do for you?" This attitude of mutual cooperation between designers and residents led to the hugely successful transformation of the Salishan neighborhood from a collection of dilapidated structures into a vibrant community of beautifully crafted homes combining subsidized, Habitat for Humanity, and market-rate (for purchase and rental) housing options.

Not all aspects of neighborhood transformation can or should be planned. Just as neighborhoods and cities evolve organically over time, neighborhood transformation can and should spark other creative and entrepreneurial activities and events that generate broader and more constructive change. Once there is agreement on the level of quality and the overall desired outcome, the actual responses can often materialize in idiosyncratic ways. In effect, the chemical reaction of both planned and unplanned activities initiated by the catalyst must be encouraged to provide a positive and healthy result. After the Torti Gallas–designed revitalization of the Capper/Carrollsburg housing development (pages 214–19) under HOPE VI, the entire southeast quadrant of Washington, D.C., between Capitol Hill and the Anacostia River went from undesirable to a place of rapid growth, reconnecting with Capitol Hill and the waterfront and becoming attractive as the home of the new stadium for the Washington Nationals baseball team.

Comprehensive neighborhood transformation starts with a successful first step—a single project or action reflecting a common vision—that is followed by other steps by other parties that feed off that first step. Such aspects of the first step as its strategic location and the level of quality it achieves are critical

determinants in establishing the degree of success of the ensuing transformative activities. And for the desired catalytic effect to occur, the first step must be successful, attracting follow-on financial and communal investment that will ensure the desired positive results. This initial successful investment must be considered as leverage toward other future transformative developments that will lead to comprehensive returns to the entire community.

Philadelphia has reaped this type of benefit with the comprehensive neighborhood transformation of the Martin Luther King Plaza public housing complex (pages 158–61). The area had become an island in the midst of the city, unconnected to surrounding neighborhoods, a place to avoid. Its failed high-rise towers were imploded and replaced by rowhouses, corner stores, and an urban square more in tune with the city of Philadelphia. Infill projects for additional housing and community retail were directed toward the

14th Street in
Columbia Heights,
Washington, D.C.,
prior to revitalization.

art-centered Broad Street to the west. The successful transformation of the MLK neighborhood has spurred private development, further connecting it to surrounding high-end parts of the city such as Society Hill to the east.

Public/private partnerships are often essential for realizing successful and comprehensive neighborhood transformations. The larger footprints associated with neighborhood transformations usually require the involvement of public partners to assemble land and garner neighborhood-wide participation. Private partners are then called upon to supply their expertise and capital to create innovative and economically viable outcomes.

Torti Gallas was involved in the public/private partnership that revitalized Columbia Heights in Washington, D.C. (pages 44–51). In that case, it took the efforts of city politicians and staff, working with local residents and community groups over many years, to keep the neighborhood intact. Its central commercial core had been burned out in the 1968 riots, and although the surrounding neighborhood had managed to remain strong, it was unable to rebuild by itself. Decades after the riots, residents fought to have the proposed Metro line include Columbia Heights, and eventually the city initiated redevelopment projects that brought together public and private investment to create housing and retail in this underserved area. The newly transformed

14th Street, after
revitalization.

neighborhood now boasts a mixed-use, transit-oriented development that caters to its residents with ground-floor restaurants and commercial space, as well as a variety of housing options for all income levels and ages.

True neighborhood transformation addresses not only the physical imprint of a neighborhood but its social, economic, and cultural aspects as well. As the mix and makeup of a neighborhood change, these less tangible factors all enter into the picture, with the overall result being the transformation of the lives of the people who live, work, shop, and play there. Social and cultural benefits can be derived from the services, amenities, and opportunities that take root in the community. And the economic transformation of the neighborhood must be available to a broad spectrum of the community's residents—not through displacement but through enrichment. True, positive neighborhood transformation cannot happen without all of this occurring in a balanced fashion.

Torti Gallas + Partners' success in transformation starts with its relationship with all of the stakeholders in the neighborhood. We are often called upon to assist communities in forming a shared vision for positive change in neighborhoods that have experienced serious disinvestment.

The array of concerned parties includes not only residents and community leaders but also city officials and their staff, churches, business people, developers, and designers. Torti Gallas has led hundreds of community-based design workshops and charrettes, using our skills to draw the "hopes, dreams, and fears" of the stakeholders in an open environment. People want to know that they have been heard and want to see their concerns addressed in the drawings. The designers draw multiple alternative solutions for each problem. Everyone in the audience can see aspects of their suggestions reflected in one or another of the alternatives. The alternatives are discussed in an open forum with 100 percent transparency. And through this discussion of good alternatives, bad alternatives, and foolish alternatives, Torti Gallas then narrows the options and repeats the process, ending up with one or two choices. This journey, which everyone including the designers goes through, produces the magic and allows successful, dramatic change to happen.

When neighborhood transformation is successful, the "rising tide lifts all boats"—one step feeding the next, with exponential impact over time. Torti Gallas + Partners' commitment to community education and to listening to stakeholders to facilitate consensus about the need for and the direction of change has resulted in catalytic developments that have sparked dozens of successful neighborhood transformations.

Implosion of the Lafayette Courts public-housing project, Baltimore.

Main Street in Shirlington Village, Arlington, Virginia.

ATUL SHARMA

The Spectrum

We live in a critical moment in history. Rapidly approaching what many have called the "peak carrying capacity" of our planet, we are facing increasing pressures on our current environmental, economic, and social frameworks. Surpassing 7 billion in October 2011, the global population is projected to reach 10 billion by 2035, creating what geologists are now calling the Anthropocene, or "Age of Man."

Aerial view of New York City.

Through such explosive growth, humans are irreversibly impacting the way our planet works. In our attempt to provide even basic needs for the global population, we are consuming natural resources at a much faster rate than the earth's ability to replenish them. This is simply not a sustainable model and demands that we take on the mantle of global stewardship with a holistic approach to sustainability.

Globalization is likewise radically impacting the world. In its early years, it focused mainly on global financial centers such as London, Tokyo, and New York, and subsequently spread to other megacities such as Dubai, Shenzhen, and Rio. The "first wave" catered primarily to the global elite and manifested itself as residential enclaves for the wealthy and corporate parks, often sequestered from the rest of the city. The next wave is expected to be focused on the middle and lower classes in the mid-tier cities of Africa, Asia, and Latin America. Such cities severely lack the infrastructure development and planning frameworks required to support sustainable development. There is a great need to provide affordable housing, create diverse economies, and address social equity in terms of access to jobs, resources, and education for all.

The digital age, with its technological advances, enhanced mobility, and global trade networks, has ushered in an era in which the lines between distinct cultures are fast being blurred. Economic growth today is inevitably followed by cultural transformation, which is often accompanied by disappointment over loss of character. Across the globe, the tension between the aspiration to enter the global middle class and the desire to preserve the heritage and the living culture of a place is splintering communities along economic and demographic lines. At the same time, communities now have the wherewithal to engage a global pool of professionals to craft and implement designs aimed at securing their future. This evolution of the design profession itself into a global undertaking involving various stakeholders at all stages, presents its own set of challenges related to culture and context.

THE SPECTRUM APPROACH

The trends outlined above pose unprecedented challenges for architects and urban planners. As we have confronted them in our practice, we have looked for new tools to aid our investigations. This has prompted the creation of a process that we call the "Spectrum," which addresses the design task through analysis of three key components: Natural Systems, the Built Environment, and People. A framework that extends from the dwelling to

"What is the use of a house if you haven't got a tolerable planet to put it on?"

HENRY DAVID THOREAU

Street in Delhi, India.

the region, Spectrum is a holistic approach that allows us to connect our work to the bigger whole.

To gain a broad understanding of a project, we begin by organizing our analysis around the three components of the Spectrum Matrix. "Natural Systems" analyzes how the ecology and natural resources within and around a

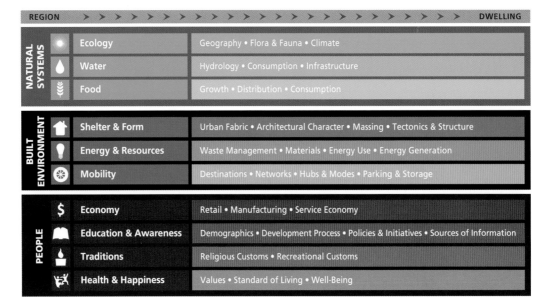

The Spectrum Matrix.

REGION ⟩⟩⟩⟩⟩⟩⟩⟩⟩⟩⟩⟩⟩⟩⟩⟩⟩⟩⟩⟩⟩⟩ DWELLING		
NATURAL SYSTEMS	Ecology	Geography • Flora & Fauna • Climate
	Water	Hydrology • Consumption • Infrastructure
	Food	Growth • Distribution • Consumption
BUILT ENVIRONMENT	Shelter & Form	Urban Fabric • Architectural Character • Massing • Tectonics & Structure
	Energy & Resources	Waste Management • Materials • Energy Use • Energy Generation
	Mobility	Destinations • Networks • Hubs & Modes • Parking & Storage
PEOPLE	Economy	Retail • Manufacturing • Service Economy
	Education & Awareness	Demographics • Development Process • Policies & Initiatives • Sources of Information
	Traditions	Religious Customs • Recreational Customs
	Health & Happiness	Values • Standard of Living • Well-Being

Illustration of the Neighborhood Model, Albemarle County, Virginia.

project are likely to influence its design. The "Built Environment" investigates the physical, man-made context of a project and the resources required to maintain and operate its infrastructure. "People" explores the culture of a place and the way of life of the people that will ultimately use the buildings and communities we create. Each of these three components is further divided into a set of ten subcategories, derived from our experience working on architecture and planning projects around the globe. These include tangible topics such as analysis of prevalent building types and streetscapes, as well as more abstract ideas like determining the factors that augment the health and happiness of a given community, given its social norms and traditions.

Because we work on projects that vary greatly in scale, our analysis is calibrated to highlight the most pertinent issues within the three components and their subcategories. For example, a regional analysis of Natural Systems may entail examining watersheds and local agricultural practices (Albemarle County, pages 258–59), whereas for an urban block or a single building we may focus on green roofs with native vegetation (360° H Street, pages 58–59) or community gardens in public spaces (Westlawn, pages 176–79). Addressing the Built Environment at the regional level, we may look at the area's transportation infrastructure or building material production (King Farm, pages

260–63); on the individual building level, we may analyze the structure's potential for adaptive reuse and the architectural character of the immediate neighborhood (College Park, pages 168–71). Analysis of the People aspect of a project ranges from how people trade goods and services and what festivals they celebrate at a regional level to their social norms regarding privacy at the level of the layout of a house (Arabian Canal, pages 146–49). These are all questions we pose before we begin to design solutions.

Such comprehensive analysis is especially critical for us because our practice regards planning and architecture as inextricably linked. When fully executed, a Spectrum analysis enables us to understand the issues quickly and craft design solutions that drill deeper and tap into a project's unique opportunities. Spectrum also enables us to communicate clearly with our clients and stakeholders in a language that they can understand. Its basic, tripartite organizational framework—Natural Systems, the Built Environment, and People—is simple and easily grasped. The issues it addresses, such as water use, energy use, climate, traffic, cultural traditions, and food production, are universal. And when we cast such a wide net at the beginning of a project, we are more likely to form partnerships—whether with other professional disciplines on our side or other organizations and agencies on our client's—that amplify the impact of our designs.

The success stories featured on the following pages are a testament to our unwavering commitment to make buildings and places that enhance the everyday lives of the people who inhabit them. It is our true hope that through such dedication to the building blocks of our society, we can indeed make a better world.

Community garden in Westlawn, Milwaukee.

Rendering of courtyard homes, Arabian Canal, Dubai.

Mixed-income housing, College Park, Memphis.

+ BUILDINGS

SARAH ALEXANDER & CHERYL A. O'NEILL

Urban Buildings

"Paris is so very beautiful that it satisfies
something in you that is always hungry in America."

ERNEST HEMINGWAY

A Moveable Feast

"You can't rely on bringing people downtown,
you have to put them there."

JANE JACOBS

The Death and Life of the Great American City

According to the latest census, more Americans are living in metropolitan areas today than a decade ago. Across all demographics, people are increasingly moving to urban centers, replacing years of decline with new growth. Character-rich neighborhoods, myriad cultural amenities, diverse populations, car-free lifestyles, and above all, the activity of the street—Americans have once again demonstrated their hunger for the places that provide these qualities. This growth has prompted substantial residential development, especially in the boomtowns of the East Coast (Washington, D.C., Boston, New York) and their surrounding metropolitan areas.

OPPOSITE: The Upton at Rockville Town Center, Rockville, Maryland.

Lyon Place at
Clarendon Center,
Arlington, Virginia.

This section examines the rebirth of the city as a place of residence, exploring the architecture and urbanism of the mixed-use apartment building. The Washington metropolitan region, where the majority of the projects featured in the section are located, has been fortunate to have public administrations focused on bringing residential building into neighborhoods that were previously limited to daytime business or were still languishing from the devastation of the 1968 riots. Myriad public/private development ventures, prescient re-zonings, and the completion of several of the last planned legs of the District's subway system, have all fueled an urban residential building boom that has transformed neighborhoods in and around the city.

LESSONS FROM PARIS

For Hemingway and his fellow ex-pats in the Paris of the 1920s, it mattered little that you lived in a tiny garret because when you lived in Paris, you lived *in* Paris. The minimal accommodations of the *res privata* were more than balanced by the opulence and exquisite urbanity of the *res publica* and the rich public life it offered. Though current apartments are larger than those of Hemingway's attic, they increasingly tend toward the minimal, especially with recent innovations such as the micro-unit. Embellishing the apartment and its inhabitants' life with the amenities of the public world—whether the street outside, common rooms inside, or a restaurant on the ground floor—is re-creating in contemporary apartment design the formula of Hemingway's Paris. Bigger is not better, more urban is.

One of the greatest impacts this has had on our apartment commissions has been their almost universal inclusion of ground-floor retail. We have become expert at deftly integrating the vertical alignment of apartments, with their small rooms and high degree of repetition, over the large floor plates and flexibility requirements of retail space. This is particularly challenging when the ground floor is a large-format grocery store. Some of the projects in this chapter record the transformation of grocery stores from freestanding buildings surrounded by parking lots into anchors of urban neighborhoods, sustaining existing communities (Georgetown Safeway, pages 66–67) or creating the catalyst for neighborhood regeneration (City Vista, pages 62–65).

The shift from single-use residential commissions to mixed-use projects has had a tremendous impact on neighborhoods in the District and surrounding inner-ring suburbs. Prior to the 1990s, active street retail in the District was confined to a handful of neighborhoods—portions of the central business district, Dupont Circle, and Georgetown. The shift in residential commissions to include ground-floor retail combined with the push, beginning with the administration of Mayor Anthony Williams, to place residential building in downtown neighborhoods, have radically altered that landscape, enriching the city with numerous neighborhoods that have a vibrant street life. The 14th Street corridor, Columbia Heights, NoMA (North of Massachusetts Avenue, a residential neighborhood that did not exist before the 1990s), and H Street NE have all been reinvigorated socially, physically and programmatically by new mixed-use buildings.

Residents' increased desire for public interaction has also influenced the communal spaces in our apartment commissions, resurrecting the lavish public rooms of pre–World War II residential hotels such as Alban Towers (pages 72–75). Our Park Van Ness project in upper Northwest (pages 76–79) includes an elaborate set of common rooms, all with spectacular views of Soapstone Valley Park at the rear of the building. The development of the rooftop as a public amenity is part and parcel of most of our District apartment projects. The skyline of Washington, more like that of Hemingway's Paris than of a contemporary skyscraper metropolis, is controlled by the Height of Buildings Act of 1910, which was legislated to preserve the dominance of the Capitol Dome and limits building heights to a maximum of 130 feet. The Height Act has both sustained the urbanism of the street and created a distinctive aerial landscape of apartment and office rooftops punctuated by the towers, spires, and domes of local and federal monuments, the spectacular views of which we have exploited by creating elaborate rooftop terraces (360° H Street, pages 58–59).

360° H Street,
Washington, D.C.

Rooftop terrace at
360° H Street.

L'Enfant Plan of
Washington, D.C.

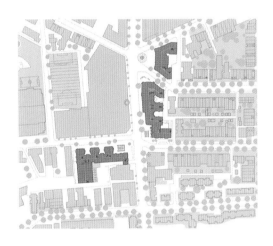

Three variations on
the courtyard *parti*,
Columbia Heights,
Washington, D.C.

L'ENFANT'S WASHINGTON

Many of our commissions in the District are designed to support and enhance the traditional urbanism of Pierre L'Enfant's original plan. Our primary goal is to insert new buildings in a way that integrates them with the broader neighborhood while also making a tangible contribution to the public realm. The signature building is resisted in favor of a powerful place, be it an extraordinary intersection (Columbia Heights, pages 44–51) or an ordinary residential street (Alban Towers, pages 72–75).

L'Enfant's complicated pattern of radial avenues and Cartesian street grid, absent a consistent block or lot geometry, often generates sites of widely varying shapes. This irregularity is exacerbated in infill conditions or in our many public/private commissions, which tend to be piecemeal lot acquisitions by the city. More often than not, we work to create integrating urban forms through the manipulation of a conventional sixty-five-foot deep, double-loaded corridor building. The curved façade of Park Place (pages 68–71), for instance, adjusts the corridor building type to celebrate the terminus of New Hampshire Avenue. The front- or rear-facing courtyard apartment building is a common District type, and we often utilize it to address deep sites and reconcile the dimensional difference between ground-floor retail and upper-level apartments. Highland Park (pages 44–51) and the Ellington (pages 52–55) both have this *parti*, and Park Van Ness (pages 76–79) uses it on both the street and the park faces, creating a building where some 80 percent of the units enjoy a park view.

The complicated geometry of the L'Enfant plan also often results in unresolved transitions between the District's two dominant housing types: the mid-rise apartment and the urban rowhouse. Many projects such as the Ellington (pages 52–55) derive their urban idea from the reconciliation of the two, adopting a Humpty Dumpty, put-the-pieces-back-together-again urban strategy. We are constantly engaging in an architectural tug-of-war between the fixed and unyielding cadence of repetitive housing units and very specific and highly idiosyncratic local conditions. Real estate viability, and professional fees, place a premium on the smallest number of unit types with the highest degree of repetition, while the unique gesture that locks a building form to its location—be it a special façade or a carefully sculpted massing detail—always argues for yet another unit type.

SUBURBAN REPAIR

Projects in the inner-ring suburbs present a very different set of challenges. Many of these suburbs around the District have become rapidly urbanized in response to housing pressures, much of the development stimulated by new transit and concentrated around Metrorail stops. The conditions of these sites vary, from those with fragments of an urban place to those without any distinctive context. In the case of the former, we look to contribute pieces to the puzzle in a process of addition that over time will create urbanity. Our two buildings at Lyon Place in Clarendon (pages 92–95), for instance, add to the remnants of a formerly vibrant 1940s commercial corridor, creating a critical mass of new building that reestablishes its Art Moderne spirit. Our Shirlington project (pages 80–81) performs a similar transformation, retrofitting a fledgling one-block open-air suburban mall with new infill development to create a multiblock urban district.

When we operate in automobile-dominated suburban sites without a context to connect to, our projects are the pioneers that begin the process of urbanization. We often start with the public realm, and look to establish a place scaled to the person and not the car. At Nannie Helen in the Deanwood neighborhood at the edge of the District (pages 96–97), for instance, we pulled our apartment building right up to the street wall. With public

ABOVE
Main Street in
Shirlington Village,
Arlington, Virginia.

BELOW
Gables Pike
District, Rockville,
Maryland.

uses on the ground floor, it creates a one-block patch of urban sidewalk along an otherwise automobile-dominated roadway, beginning the thoroughfare's transformation into an urban boulevard. At Gables Pike District (pages 86–87), we recast a structured parking garage as a generator of urban activity. Surrounding it with new buildings, linkages, and a modest set of public uses, we created a new node of public activity. These projects strive to establish place in the nondescript landscape of suburbia and have taught us a great deal about the fundamentals of urbanism, giving us greater insight into our urban infill projects.

SPECULATIVE APARTMENT DESIGN AND THE CITY

The design of ordinary housing is often a search for the innovations that satisfy lifestyle requirements and market demands while meeting the safety and health standards required by building codes. New housing types are often born out of that nexus and tend to impact the city in waves. A first project tests a new type that, if successful, is quickly imitated by others. While not an urban gesture per se, the collective impact of new residential types alters the character of urban life and the form of the city.

The District and its environs have recently been impacted by innovations in unit design, stimulated both by the extraordinary costs of urban real estate and by the increasingly appealing images of urban life. The loft unit, harkening back to refurbished units in warehouse districts such as SoHo, New York, is a new type that locates a recessed bedroom at the rear of the living space. Increased ceiling heights, sometimes sufficient for an upper-level mezzanine, together with free-flowing interior space and substantial window glazing permit a unit depth greatly exceeding that of a conventional unit. We utilized it in several of our early projects such as the Columbia Heights buildings (pages 44–51) and the Ellington (pages 52–55), where it found a fit with the edgier states of these just-emerging neighborhoods.

The buried-bedroom unit, which removes the bedroom from the exterior wall and opens it to other living spaces through large doors or sliding walls, and the micro-unit, an apartment that is as little as 200 to 300 square feet, are more recent innovations that are also making an impact on the District and its environs. The small size of micro-units reduces rents, making them affordable to young people living alone, even in high-rent markets. When matched with the amenities of the building and the broader neighborhood,

ABOVE
Loft unit in
Park Triangle,
Washington, D.C.

BELOW
Plan of corner
"mingles" unit.

they offer a rich urban lifestyle, harkening back to Hemingway's Paris. Prominent in the District because of recent changes to building codes, the buried-bedroom unit allows more flexibility in room arrangement, permitting living spaces to run the length of the façade, creating a "great room." Both unit types leverage the spatial qualities of conventional modernism—large expanses of glass, walls that float free of the ceiling, sliding walls or "barn doors," functional rooms condensed to a slick piece of furniture—to enlarge minimal spaces, impacting the image of Washington streets as they change from solid brick to shimmering glass.

Though these innovations impact the market and our work, they add to, rather than replace, existing types. The workhorse of apartment design, the conventional double-loaded corridor building, is a mainstay in our typological toolbox. Corridor buildings easily accommodate a range of demographics, such as "mingles"—two or more unrelated people living together—and families. We design units for the former with multiple suites of private rooms (bedrooms, walk-in closets, and bathrooms)

Park Place,
Washington, D.C.

and a central, common living space; for the latter, we maintain a bedroom hierarchy. We often place family units on the ground floor with individual unit entries or small private exterior spaces. And we often enlarge these types of rooms by adding sculptural features to the façade, especially balconies and bays. These features not only expand interior spaces but also engage the apartment interior with the outside world. Because the District's zoning codes do not count such projections into the street toward allowable building square footage, our clients are often prompted to include them in their projects. Devising architecture out of the limits of zoning regulations is an age-old part of residential design, influencing individual projects and at times the *genius loci* of an entire city or neighborhood, as is evident in the character of Capitol Hill townhouses with their distinguishing bays.

MAKING FAÇADES

Residential buildings are most typically the background buildings of the city, establishing the pattern of ordinary streets and blocks. Our façade designs

Notch 8,
Alexandria,
Virginia.

balance interior needs with this larger urban role, seeking to make the city legible through their pattern and cadence. The relationship between the building façade and the street, or on occasion the square, is an intimate one, and influences not so much a selection of style but a determination of character. The episodic nature of the Kenyon Square façade (pages 44–51), for instance, has everything to do with the jazzy, scenographic nature of 14th Street, while the restraint and regularity of Park Triangle (pages 44–51) relates to the formal urban plaza on which it sits.

As a firm comprised of many designers, we operate in a broad range of languages, from reinterpretations of historic styles to modern idioms supporting traditional urbanism. We explore them within the confines of speculative development, with its limited budgets and pressures on site yields and building costs. These constraints often force us to use basic construction systems with the greatest efficiency and lowest cost. When concrete construction wins, we enjoy the most liberty, availing ourselves of deep walls and more plastic building forms. Wood construction presents greater challenges, and we must search for the languages and expressions that will convey the permanence associated with urbanity, including façades of sufficient richness to sustain the public realm (Notch 8, pages 98–101). Wood construction and the District's height limit often require us to render large building programs as long, horizontal forms with lots and lots of street wall. In such cases, we frequently utilize a strategy of multiple façade types, gauged to what we call the "urban increment," subdividing a block-long building into sections of different character (360° H Street, pages 58–59) to establish a cadence of façades appropriate to the street.

CONCLUSION

When we completed City Vista, it was bereft of near neighbors. Surrounded by parking lots, it stood isolated, in a condition not dissimilar from the housing that initiated the development of New York's Upper West Side or Boston's Back Bay. Like those pioneering buildings, City Vista has been absorbed into the neighborhood that has since grown up around it, bringing new life to a previously vacant part of the city, reestablishing it as a place of residence, and resuscitating the mid-rise apartment building as an essential component of its urbanism.

The Dakota apartment building, New York, ca. 1890.

LEFT
Google aerial view of City Vista, Washington, D.C., ca. 2005.

Columbia Heights

WASHINGTON, D.C.

ABOVE
Figure ground,
before revitalization.

BELOW
Figure ground,
after revitalization.

OPPOSITE
Riots in downtown
Washington, D.C.,
April 1968.

Washington, D.C., like many cities across the U.S., suffered from the urban destruction wrought by the riots following the assassination of Martin Luther King Jr. in 1968. Four commercial corridors in the city were impacted: 14th Street in Columbia Heights; U Street downtown, the District's "Black Broadway"; 7th Street Northwest; and H Street Northeast. Though the residential neighborhoods abutting these corridors survived more or less intact, the commercial avenues—many of them the center of the public life of their communities—languished for decades. Few involved in the riots could have anticipated the duration of their impact. As community activist Stanley Mayes told CNN, "I had no idea it would take us thirty years to rebuild it. I thought my neighborhood would come back. This is a great neighborhood."

New life began some twenty years later, when a combination of social, political, economic, and demographic factors spurred redevelopment. Two of these were key: the opening in the 1990s of several of the District's Metrorail stops, which had been planned and platted decades earlier, and a city administration dedicated to rebuilding the corridors, stimulating development through a plethora of competitions, public/private partnerships, and other initiatives.

The rebirth of 14th Street in Columbia Heights is the flagship of revival. In the aftermath of the riots, the Green line running north from downtown was rerouted from 13th Street to 14th Street in a prescient decision to stimulate growth in the neighborhood's devastated commercial heart. In the late 1990s, in concert with the opening of the Columbia Heights Metrorail station, the city announced several competitions simultaneously, a largely successful effort aimed at rebuilding Columbia Heights' commercial center in one fell swoop. DC USA, the pioneer big-box development downtown, was the first to be completed. With a Target, a Marshall's, and hundreds of thousands of square feet of new retail, it provided the economic engine for the street's revitalization.

1940s

Commercial buildings along 14th Street.

April 1968

Aftermath of the riots, damaged commercial buildings.

ca. 2002

View of 14th Street.

ABOVE

Park Triangle,
Washington, D.C.

OPPOSITE

Kenyon Square
and the Columbia
Heights Civic
Plaza, Washington,
D.C.

We were fortunate to win two of the public competitions with our partner Donatelli Development, as well as a private commission with Park Triangle Development, and we created an ensemble of buildings surrounding the Metrorail stop. It consisted of four mixed-use buildings—Kenyon Square, Victory Heights, Highland Park, and Park Triangle—which brought new residential units and street-level retail to 14th Street. An important city goal was to provide housing options that would reinvigorate the neighborhood yet allow existing residents to remain, and the projects included market-rate, affordable, and senior units. Both enhancing and integrating seamlessly into the diversity of the surrounding community, the project was hailed by Harriet Tregoning, then the director of the Office of Planning, as "a great model for urban neighborhoods of the future."

Located well north of the limits of the L'Enfant Plan and its expansive street widths, 14th Street in Columbia Heights possessed a uniquely narrow right-of-way with a distinctive jog near the Metrorail stop. We decided to celebrate those differences and formed two of the buildings, Kenyon Square and Highland Park, around the Metrorail stop, creating a bow-tie plaza to provide spatial relief and a powerful place for one of the city's most active street scenes. Farther north, the Park Triangle building created a civic plaza that focused on the landmark Tivoli Theater, which was revitalized by Horning Brothers with new retail, office, and arts uses. The city subsequently formalized the plaza with distinctive paving and a popular fountain, and we developed an appropriately sober and restrained façade for Park Triangle to complement the formal square.

Though we designed the buildings as an ensemble, we chose different façade strategies for each. Kenyon Square, along 14th Street, was the longest building and contained the distinctive jog in the 14th Street frontage, which we

1997–2003

Community charrettes to plan the rebuilding.

2004

Rendering of Kenyon Square along 14th Street.

ca. 2008

View of Kenyon Square after completion.

Highland Park,
Washington, D.C.

chose to celebrate with a break in the façade language. We set Victory Heights, an affordable senior building, back behind the Metrorail stop and gave it a more traditional, Colonial-inspired language of arched openings and tall vertical bays. In contrast to Kenyon Square, Highland Park had a short façade on 14th Street and a long one on the narrow side street. We created a building mass to respond to this configuration, forming half of the bow-tie space around the Metrorail stop and alleviating the pressure of the narrow street frontage with multiple street-facing courtyards. We chose a uniform Art Deco–inspired façade language, which we felt maximized the pavilion nature of the massing and afforded wonderful long views from corner windows down the narrow side street. The vertical reconciliation required in both buildings, given their location above the Metrorail tunnels, was substantial, and we are proud of our greatest inspiration, the incorporation of a vertical subway exhaust shaft into the Art Deco–style tower on the 14th Street façade of Highland Park.

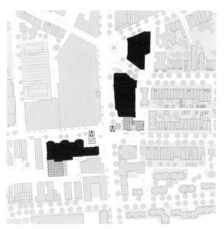

Retail plan.

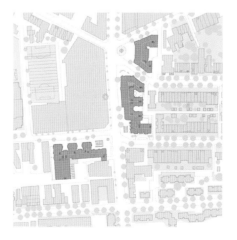

Typical residential plan.

OVERLEAF
Night view of 14th Street in Columbia Heights, looking south.

The Ellington

U STREET, WASHINGTON, D.C.

ABOVE
Figure ground.

RIGHT
View of the corner
of U and 13th
Streets NW.

Once the epicenter of African American culture, U Street was dubbed the District's "Black Broadway" by Pearl Bailey and was a haven for businesses, institutions, entertainment, and jazz venues owned, operated, and designed by African Americans. An eclectic mix of commercial and institutional structures, the street boasts several landmark structures such as the Whitelaw Hotel and the True Reformers Building. The abutting residential neighborhoods predate the street and are largely defined by Victorian rowhouses.

The opening of a Metrorail station in 1991 and several city-sponsored competitions initiated the development that began the street's resurgence. The Ellington, named to honor Duke Ellington's long association with the street, was one of the first large-scale projects and helped to jump-start revitalization. Located at the corner of 13th and U Streets, the site was at the nexus of the area's Victorian and Black Broadway identities. We decided to create a design that would pay tribute to both, stitching the city back together at the intersection. Working with our partner Donatelli Development, we created two connected but stylistically different sections. A red brick portion at the intersection, composed of loft units with ground-floor retail and a distinctive corner tower, paid tribute in scale and character to the Victorian rowhouses up 13th Street. We articulated the longer and taller building face along U Street with a series of courtyards that separated the frontage into several vertical pavilions, using an Art Deco language that evoked the

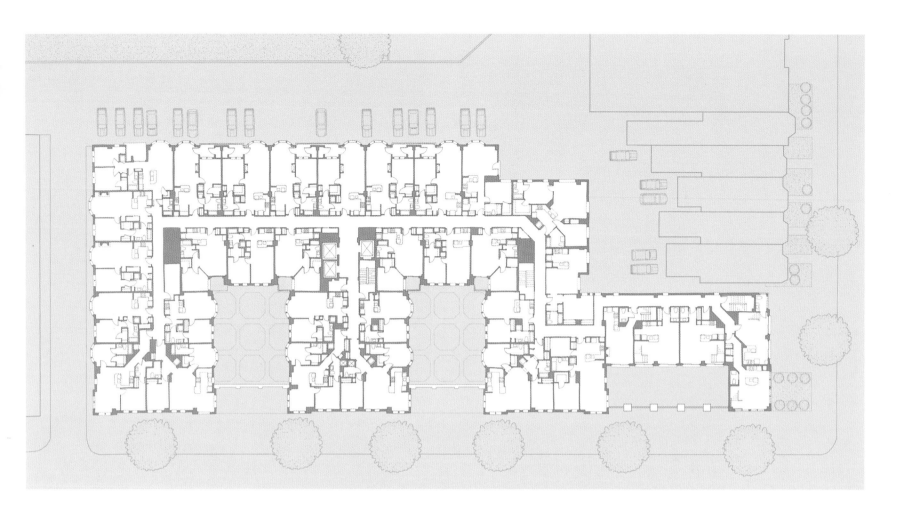

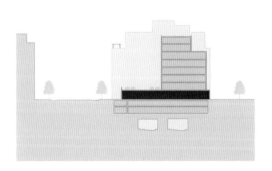

TOP
Typical residential
plan.

ABOVE
Building section.

RIGHT
Typical residential
plan in context.

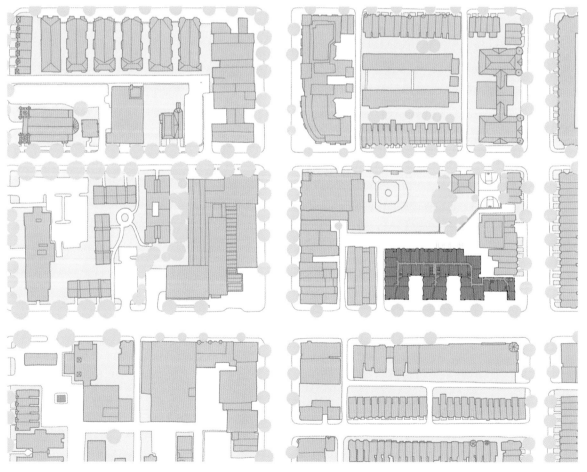

ABOVE
Rooftop terraces.

RIGHT
Façade at
the residential
entrance.

street's heyday, and we scaled back the building's height with a series of upper-level terraces. A new restaurant took advantage of the courtyard recess on the ground floor with a gated outdoor seating area, bringing new activity to the street.

THE ELLINGTON

The Bentley

WASHINGTON, D.C.

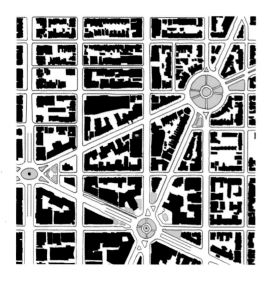

Figure ground.

More than a decade after completing Columbia Heights, we returned to the 14th Street corridor with the commission for the Bentley, a boutique apartment building at the street's intersection with Rhode Island Avenue. By this time, the corridor was bursting with new life and development, the latter increasingly pushing into the city's nooks and crannies. The Rhode Island Avenue end of 14th Street was historically home to a number of car dealerships, a fact that inspired both the building's name and our design. Our clients were two private developers, Richard Dubin and Irwin Edlavitch, who had been working in the region for more than fifty years and saw the project as an important part of their legacy. After early conversations, they became amenable to rethinking their conventional approach and exploring some of the latest trends in small units.

The project site was wedged between two-story commercial buildings on the avenue side and taller buildings along 14th Street. Complicated zoning and an emboldened local citizenry, concerned about maintaining the neighborhood's character, instigated lots of meetings with extensive discussions about the image of the building. Utilizing both deep lofts and micro-units, we created a U-shaped building with a courtyard open to Rhode Island Avenue. Rising three stories above the Rhode Island Avenue frontage, the building afforded long views from the loft units facing the avenue and street views from the micro-units along its other sides. The massing, stepped back at the uppermost level, reduced the building's scale to fit in with the context and created terraces with spectacular views. The character of many of the surviving car showrooms inspired the façade's big industrial frame, metal infill panels, and dropped cornice, which we wrapped around the three sides of the building exposed to view. The ground floor, ironically for a building whose themes revolved around the automobile, is now occupied by a furniture showroom, and we designed it with the pop-out storefronts typical of 14th Street.

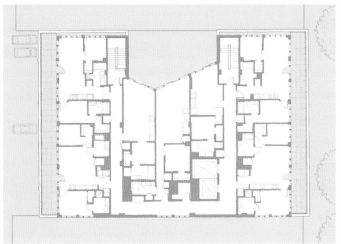

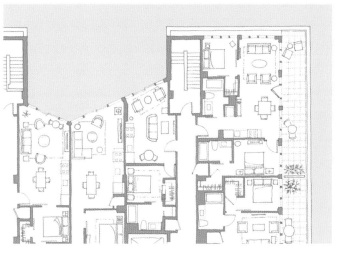

360° H Street

WASHINGTON, D.C.

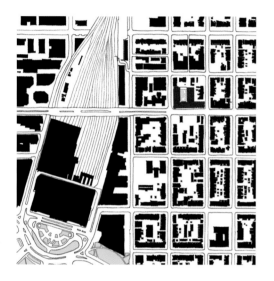

In the span of a single decade, H Street NE has experienced a tremendous rebirth. Before the riots, it was a bustling commercial artery whose vitality was surpassed only by the city's main shopping district downtown. By early 2000, it was in a state of disrepair, pockmarked along its mile-and-a-half length with vacant parcels and buildings. Over the next decade, new development spurred by myriad city initiatives, including street upgrades and, most significantly, a new streetcar line, led to its resurgence.

Our site, at 360° H Street NE, was within walking distance of Union Station, in the area known as the "Hub." Occupied by a defunct gas station, it was owned by the Steuart Investment Company, which, confident that the street's fortunes were improving, developed a mixed-use apartment program, negotiating the deal for the first supermarket built east of the Capitol in fifty years. The site was flanked on one side by the monumental, multi-level garage of Union Station and on the other by the rambling assemblage of small-scale commercial buildings and retrofitted rowhouses that characterized most of the street. We designed the building as a transition between the two, articulating it as two distinct structures. Placing the grocery store on the eastern, Hub, side, we embedded it in a six-story volume with a red brick, industrial-inspired language to establish an emphatic beginning to the street. The adjacent volume, clad in yellow brick, related to the smaller-scale H Street façades, picking up on one of their most distinctive features with a prominent set of metal-clad vertical bays. We subdivided the ground-level grocery store façade into multiple sections to read as individual shop-front windows. Proximity to downtown afforded great rooftop views of the Capitol and Library of Congress domes, which we maximized by creating an elaborate roof terrace with an extensive green roof.

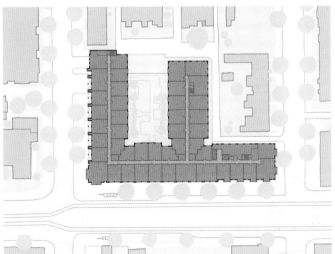

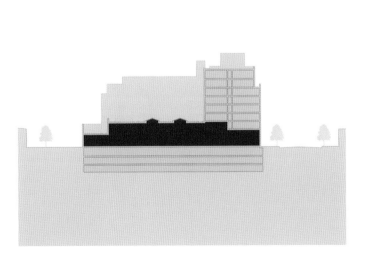

FAR LEFT
Typical residential
plan.

LEFT
Building section.

8th + H Street

WASHINGTON, D.C.

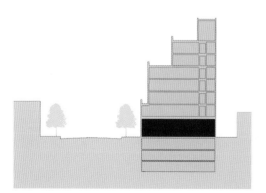

We returned to H Street several years after our 360° H Street project, this time in the section of the street known as the "Shops," formerly the home of some of the first department stores in the city. The physical destruction during the riots decimated the street's retail core, and in their aftermath, The Rappaport Companies developed the H Street Connection, a suburban-style strip center of neighborhood-serving convenience retail. City investments in the 1990s and ongoing development moving incrementally west from the Hub prompted Rappaport, in conjunction with his residential partner, WC Smith, to redevelop the Connection site, returning it to the mixed-use, main street character that had existed before the riots.

We were challenged by the length of the site, which extended two full city blocks between 8th and 10th Streets, and a development program with considerably greater bulk and density than the modest scale of the surrounding fabric. Utilizing flat loft and conventional units, we created a building of two distinct characters, with a variegated low-rise volume right at the street, and a taller eight-story mass rising above it and set back some fifteen or twenty feet. The lower façade was orchestrated as a series of buildings in the three- or four-bay widths typical of the street. The language of the recessed mass mimicked that of the lower level but with a more subdued vocabulary. Despite its role as a major retail street, H Street has very narrow sidewalks. At the 8th Street intersection, the more visible and highly trafficked of the two corners, we broke free of the street wall, marking the corner with a curved, predominantly glass building mass, creating a generous south-facing café zone at the street.

City Vista

WASHINGTON, D.C.

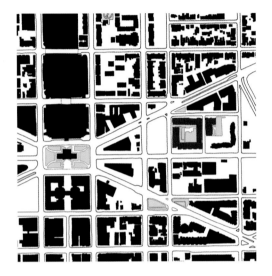

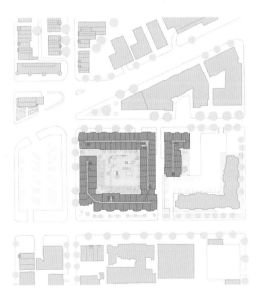

Located in the Mount Vernon Triangle area of downtown and in close proximity to Washington's new Convention Center, the site of our City Vista project had a rich history, having been the location of a market, a convention hall, and the National Historic Wax Museum. But at the time of our commission it was in the middle of thirty acres of underutilized land. A focus of attention since the adoption of the "Living Downtown" policy in 1984, the Triangle was viewed by the city administration as a prime location for a new inner-city, mixed-use neighborhood, and its development was initiated by a competition for the City Vista site, which we won with our development partner Lowe Enterprises.

The urban design plan for the Triangle identified the competition site, a full half block at the intersection of 5th and K Streets, as a major activity node to be enhanced with a public plaza at its corner, and 5th Street as the district's retail artery. We bookended our 5th Street frontage with the major activity generators—the grocery store entrance on the minor corner and restaurants around the plaza—connecting them along the 5th Street frontage with additional retail. The residential program included both rental units and condominiums, separated in discrete volumes. Their design was a collaborative effort with Marshall Moya Design, which was responsible for the rental building. Consisting of two L-shaped buildings on top of the grocery store, with a small wing across the mid-block alley, the residential complex formed a large, one-acre courtyard. The

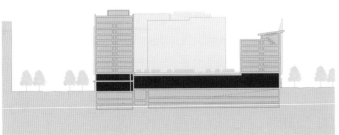

landscaping of this rooftop courtyard has since matured, creating a natural retreat in the middle of downtown that remains one of the largest green roofs in the city. Extensive discussions with the city revolved around the language of the building, which as the pioneer development would set the tone for the future neighborhood. We reached consensus for a decidedly modern look, with sleek glass-and-steel bays and vertical recesses.

OPPOSITE

View of 5th Street
NW, looking north.

BELOW

Typical residential
plan.

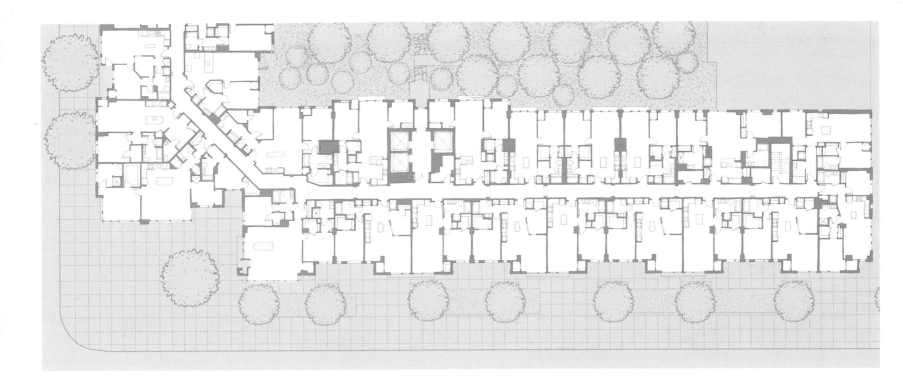

Urban
Buildings

Georgetown
Safeway

ABOVE
Figure ground.

BELOW
Grocery-level
plan.

RIGHT
View along
Wisconsin Avenue
NW, looking north.

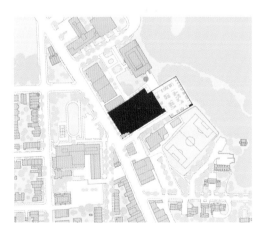

Locally known as the "Social" Safeway, one of several grocer-ies in the District with a nickname reflecting its broader role in the community, the Georgetown Safeway was constructed in the 1980s with a conventional suburban layout. Set well back from the street, the single-story store was fronted by a large, surface-level parking lot that ran the full length of the site's Wisconsin Avenue street frontage. Following the suc-cess of its City Vista project, Safeway decided to continue its investments in the District, developing an ongoing pro-gram to replace their suburban-style stores with more urban models.

Part of Safeway's desire in rebuilding their urban stores was to exchange the "brand" identity of their suburban build-ings for styles in keeping with the urban stores' respective neighborhoods. With this approach in mind, we created a scheme that would repair the Wisconsin Avenue street front and extend Georgetown's charming streetscape of retrofitted townhouses and small-scale commercial buildings. Placing the grocery store on the second floor, we ran a row of small-scale shops along the Wisconsin Avenue sidewalk, situating a structured parking garage that included all of the loading facilities behind them. Additional parking was located at the rear of the site in a single-story parking garage whose rooftop parking provided direct access to the store. Our inspiration for the façade was the urban market hall, which we expressed in a composition of repetitive bays with deep piers, extensive upper-level glazing, and sun-shading devices.

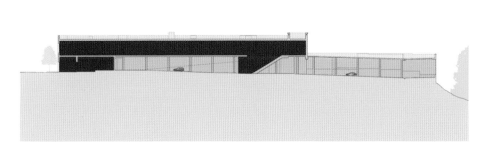

FAR LEFT
View of the former
Safeway.

LEFT
Building section.

Park Place, Petworth

Safeway, *and* the Swift

WASHINGTON, D.C.

ABOVE

Figure ground.

OPPOSITE

Petworth Safeway
and the Swift,
view along Georgia
Avenue NW,
looking south.

Although our two projects in the Petworth neighborhood were developed independently, they worked like part of a coordinated plan to revitalize the commercial heart of the neighborhood on Georgia Avenue. We won the first project, Park Place, with our partner Donatelli Development in a public competition for a mixed-use building above the neighborhood's Metrorail station. The block-long site was challenging; it was barely wide enough for a double-loaded corridor building and had a twenty-five-foot drop in grade. Yet it also possessed great assets, including the Metrorail stop and its frontage at the intersection of New Hampshire Avenue. Our strategy was to emphasize these features with gestures that would bring new life to Georgia Avenue and enhance the neighborhood's identity along the corridor. We organized a segment of the façade around a two-story arch above the Metrorail entrance, creating a motif and experience that celebrated coming to and going from the neighborhood. A curved deflection at the northern end of the building, accentuated by a bold frame and an abstract cornice, celebrated the New Hampshire Avenue intersection. Different color palettes, languages, and relationships to the site grade distinguished the two segments of the building, tying them to their specific local context. To complete the project, we built seven new townhouse units on a leg of the site that fronted the side street at its rear.

We returned several years after the completion of Park Place with a commission from Safeway to bring a new store to Petworth. Given the scale of development occurring in the neighborhood, we were convinced that a mixed-use building was viable and persuaded Safeway to add apartments to the program, creating the mixed-use building now known as the Swift. They subsequently brought on a residential partner, Duball, LLC. We decided that a restrained approach was the right urban strategy for the Georgia Avenue

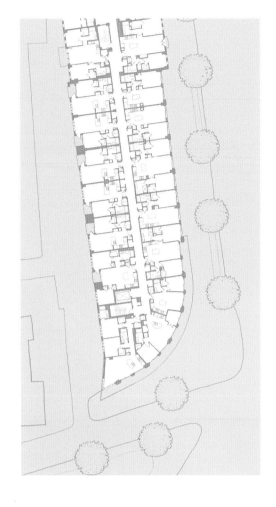

site, and we filled the block with a simple courtyard building distinguished by a rich façade of repetitive bays, which proved more of a challenge than at Park Place because of the project's wood construction. Our one big urban gesture was an embedded circular tower marking the grocery store entrance at the corner of the site. The project included a lavish set of common spaces, among them a rooftop terrace affording spectacular views of Washington National Cathedral.

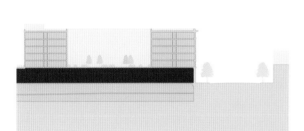
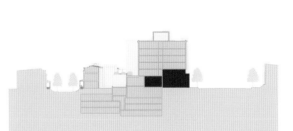

ABOVE

View along Georgia
Avenue NW,
looking south.

FAR LEFT

Building section of
Petworth Safeway
and the Swift.

LEFT

Building section of
Park Place.

Alban Towers *and* the Residences at Alban Row

WASHINGTON, D.C.

Figure ground.

Constructed in 1929, Alban Towers was once among the most fashionable apartment hotels in Washington, D.C. Located on Mount St. Albans, one the city's highest elevations and site of Washington National Cathedral, the building is a fine example of Gothic Revival architecture and listed on the National Register of Historic Places. Originally featuring round-the-clock maid service, a public dining room, a ballroom, and a bowling alley, it epitomized 1930s luxury apartment living. But the departure of local streetcar lines, changing urban demographics, and multiple ownership led to the building's gradual decline, leaving it in significant disrepair by the 1960s.

We were commissioned by the Charles E. Smith Company to update apartment layouts and provide additional building amenities, including off-street parking. We quickly realized that the commission was not only about the building but also about repairing the fragmented block surrounding it. On a vacant parcel at the rear of the site, we built eight new duplex units, siting them above a partially buried parking garage. The garage provided off-street parking for both the apartments and the duplexes; we devised a way to give the duplexes individual garages with internal house access. Borrowing an old D.C. builder trick—using one floor plan with multiple façade interpretations—we cast the duplexes in neo-Romanesque and Georgian styles, completing the street and matching the diversity of the existing townhouses on the other side. An elongated butterfly garden above the garage mediated between the apartment building and the new houses, adding a fine, semipublic space shared by the building's residents and the broader neighborhood. Johnson & Martinez oversaw the restoration of the apartment building's exterior to pristine condition, and Hartman Design Group returned the interior public rooms to their original glory.

Alban Towers, view of the Wisconsin Avenue entrance.

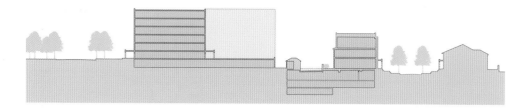

BELOW
Section of Alban
Towers and the
Residences.

RIGHT
Alban Towers,
view of the lobby.

OPPOSITE
View of the
Residences along
38th Street.

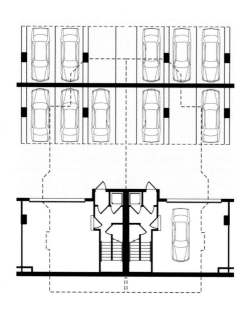
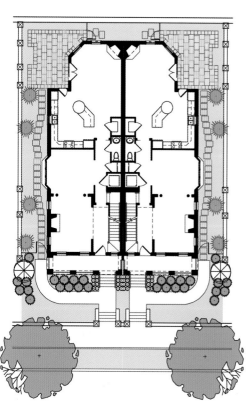
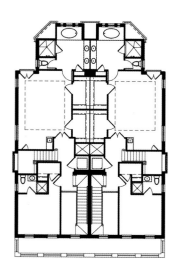
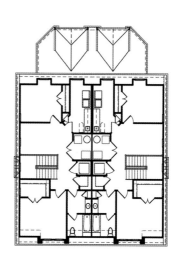

Floor plans of the
Residences.

Park Van Ness

WASHINGTON, D.C.

ABOVE
Figure ground.

BELOW
Decorative panel
with pre-cast
bas-relief.

RIGHT
View along
Connecticut
Avenue NW at
the archway.

Across from the campus of the University of the District of Columbia, Park Van Ness is at the center of one of the commercial nodes that dot Connecticut Avenue as it traverses the largely residential neighborhoods on the north side of the city. Connecticut Avenue has a distinctive pastoral identity, thanks to its proximity to Rock Creek Park, the city's largest park system, and a typology of mid-rise apartment buildings with landscaped, street-facing courtyards. The topography of the street varies considerably as it heads north from the largely flat terrain of downtown Washington, and at our Park Van Ness site, there is an enormous change in elevation—a drop of some five stories from the sidewalk to its rear frontage on Soapstone Valley Park, a finger of the Rock Creek Park system.

The stretch of Connecticut Avenue around the Van Ness commercial node at our site had no visual relationship with the park. Working with our client, the B. F. Saul Company, we developed a strategy to remedy that, linking our site to the park through a grand, two-story archway in the center of our building, on axis with Yuma Street, bringing the view of the park's majestic tree canopies, highly visible because of the drop in grade, right to the street. We embellished the relationship between the street and the park with courtyards on both the street and the park sides of the arch. The courtyard on the street side features a circular drive achieved through laborious negotiations with the city's Department of Transportation. The courtyards along the Connecticut

Analysis
diagrams by
Michael
Vergason.

TOP AND
BOTTOM RIGHT
Connecticut
Avenue analysis.

FAR RIGHT
Building *parti*
diagrams.

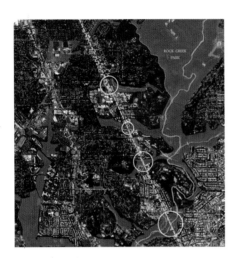

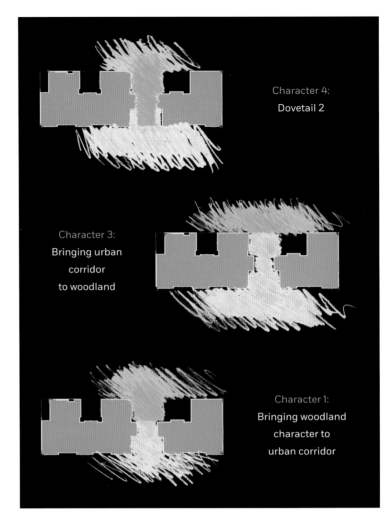

Character 4:
Dovetail 2

Character 3:
Bringing urban
corridor
to woodland

Character 1:
Bringing woodland
character to
urban corridor

Avenue frontage divided the building into a series of vertical pavilions, which
we articulated with an Art Deco language inspired both by the building that
had previously occupied the site and by the Kennedy-Warren, a landmark
1930s apartment building also owned by our client. We carried the Art Deco
vocabulary to the rear of the building but gave it a more porous façade with
extensive glazing, visually immersing the rear-facing units, which comprise
almost 80 percent of the total program and common spaces, in the park. With
its elongated, eleven-story piers, this façade appears to mingle, especially in
winter, with the park's towering trees.

Sketch *parti*
section.

FAR LEFT
Aerial view.

LEFT
Residential
entrance.

BELOW
View along
Connecticut
Avenue,
looking north.

Shirlington Village

ARLINGTON, VIRGINIA

Our commission for Shirlington Village was one of our first experiences working with Federal Realty Investment Trust, a development firm devoted to reviving retail in mixed-use, main street formats. The project involved the area around Shirlington Village in Arlington, Virginia, built in the 1940s and one of the first suburban shopping centers in metropolitan Washington. Its center, a single-use street of commercial buildings encircled by parking lots, is located in the arts and entertainment district of Arlington and was a successful place, widely visited and attracting substantial crowds on evenings and weekends.

With an eye to leveraging the reasonably urban character of the existing commercial street into a broader urbanism, we developed a suburban retrofit

ABOVE
Figure ground.

RIGHT
View of the loft
building along
Main Street.

strategy based on two key principles. The first was to create an identifiable public realm of streets, plazas, and open spaces. We began by linking the two most powerful public elements—the commercial street and a large county park to the north that has an extensive and well-used trail system. The connection we devised was an L-shaped street that created a place and a plaza at its crook for a new branch library and doubled the length of the existing commercial street. The second was to diversify the site's uses through substantial new residential development; additional retail space, including several restaurants and our first full-service grocery store; the library; and structured parking to support the new development and replace the existing surface lots. A mixture of lofts and conventional apartments, the new residential units were introduced in mixed-use buildings, many of which were narrow liner buildings inserted between existing structures to create a continuous building front along the new street and articulate the plaza at the library. A twelve-story high-rise terminated the new street on the park; paired with a hotel across the way, it served to establish a gateway. Federal Realty had particular expertise in crafting finely detailed streetscapes; working with them, we developed a variety of architectural styles to animate the street, including a modern language of cantilevered metal canopies and infill panels for the loft buildings and a more traditional language of bays and balconies.

ABOVE	BELOW LEFT	BELOW RIGHT
View of Main Street.	Retail plan.	Typical residential plan.

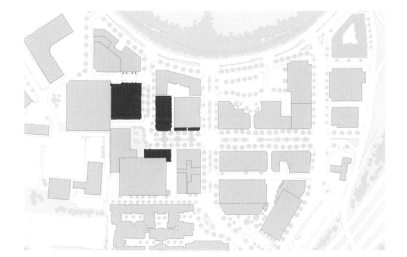

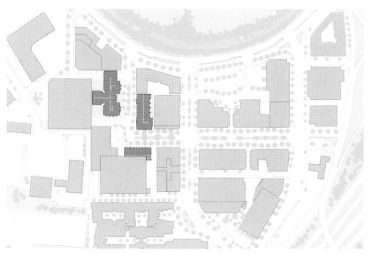

Suburban
Repair

Upstairs at
Bethesda Row

BETHESDA, MARYLAND

ABOVE
Figure ground.

BELOW
Building section.

RIGHT
View along
Bethesda Avenue,
looking east.

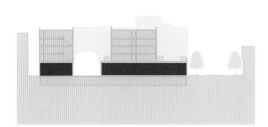

Our commission in Bethesda continued our work with Federal Realty, this time in the heart of the upscale municipality on the edge of the District. Federal Realty had been developing in Bethesda for some time, and their Bethesda Row project, a mixed-use site that we were commissioned to complete, was effectively shifting the downtown's center of gravity, known as "100 percent corner," to the prow end of their development. Until this commission, Shirlington Village had been our sole experience working with a retail developer, and we stepped into Bethesda's highly competitive retail environment with some trepidation. When we expressed our concerns to Steve Gutman, Federal Realty's client lead, his response was, "We will teach you the retail; you bring the housing and the urbanism," a pronouncement that proved correct, as the success of our Bethesda Row project and the multitude of mixed-use commissions that followed has demonstrated.

Our site, at the opposite end of the block from the "100 percent corner," had three street fronts and was adjacent to a county parking garage. Looking to respond to the vibrancy of the surrounding street scene and maximize the amount of retail frontage, we developed our scheme around an old inner-city retail type—the mews shopping street. We inserted this pedestrian street right through our site, more than doubling the street-level retail frontage. We lined its upper levels with a single-loaded wing

82

BUILDINGS

ABOVE LEFT
View of the mews street through the Bethesda Avenue archway.

ABOVE RIGHT
View of the mews street, looking north.

of lofts that screened the parking garage on one side and conventional apartments organized around west-facing courtyards on the other. The need for the residential units to be connected as one building gave us a rationale for introducing upper-level bridges above archways at either end, thereby heightening the spatial power of the mews. Inspired by the character of narrow Italian streets, and wanting to reinforce the spatial enclosure of the mews, we clad it in hard surfaces, including stone paving, and strung lights across it in Fellini-esque fashion. Lined on one side by café tables, the space operates both as an outdoor room and as an elegant pedestrian way. Movable urban amenities—a Christmas tree in winter, umbrellas and tables in summer—make and re-make the character of the space throughout the year.

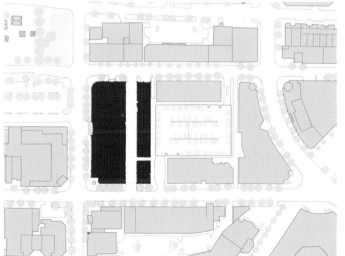

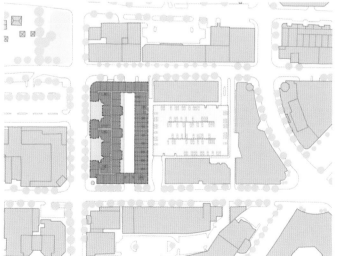

View of the mews
street, looking
south.

Retail plan.

Typical residential
plan.

Gables Pike District

MONTGOMERY COUNTY, MARYLAND

Figure ground.

There are some projects you work on for a long, long time, and Gables Pike District is one of them. A less than five-minute walk from the White Flint Metrorail station, the site is located two blocks from Rockville Pike in Montgomery County. It is part of a large, reassembled suburban block that includes a county park, an aquatic facility, and a huge surface parking lot. Rockville Pike, currently a major artery that is a sea of parking lots and stand-alone retail, has been re-envisioned through county planning efforts as an urban boulevard surrounded by mixed-use districts. Working with Gables Residential, we saw the retrofitting of their site, bringing a new urban order to its suburban character, as instrumental to the county's efforts.

At 4 acres, the site was some 650 feet long and sloped almost three full stories across its length. The site's location between two new mixed-use neighborhoods prompted us to think about the advantages of connectivity, so we introduced a pattern of new streets and pathways through the site, making it more porous to car and pedestrian traffic. We divided the residential program of almost 450 apartments into three distinct building masses and located them on the parcels established by the new grid, which also gave us a strategy to deal with the sloping street grade. Recognizing the potential of a parking garage to be an activity generator, we consolidated all the parking for the existing public facilities and the new apartments in a structured garage and located it entirely within Gables' site. Surrounding it with additional community and retail uses, we created a node of activity in the center of the site and improved the quality of the existing park by eliminating its surface lot. Uses on the ground floor of the three residential buildings evolved with the character of adjacent streets and included retail, amenity, and residential spaces. Opting for a modern, rationalist language for the entire ensemble, we developed a kit-of-parts façade strategy that unified the three buildings but allowed each to have a distinctive identity.

ABOVE
View from
Grand Park
Avenue,
looking west.

LEFT
View of a
mews street.

The Upton at Rockville Town Center

ROCKVILLE, MARYLAND

ABOVE
Figure ground.

RIGHT
View from the
judiciary buildings,
looking northeast.

Like many other cities, Rockville, Maryland, undertook an ambitious urban renewal program in the 1960s, demolishing most of its historic downtown and replacing it with a shopping mall and suburban, automobile-oriented development. After the mall's failure in the late 1990s, the city embarked on another ambitious plan, this time to rebuild its downtown. The first phase, now complete, is a multiblock, mixed-use town center built on the site of the failed mall. It is located north of the city's many judicial buildings, which are clustered around the original courthouse.

The last piece of the puzzle in putting the downtown back together again, our site was a vast 16-acre parking lot located between the new town center and the judicial buildings. Our client, Duball, LLC, envisioned complementing the town center's urban uses by adding a hotel, high-rise apartments, and new retail. We subdivided the site and development program into two sections divided by a central street, establishing a pedestrian-scale block structure. The city required us to provide parking for the new uses as well as replace the 1,000 spaces in the existing parking lot. Challenged to create urbanism with all that parking, we developed a wedding-cake massing strategy. The lower levels of the building were composed of single-loaded retail and residential uses wrapped around an above-grade parking garage, and the six levels above the garage were designed as a double-loaded corridor building, set back from the lower levels. We used a range of architectural languages to respond to the different characters of the surrounding context. Inspired by the bold modernism of the judicial buildings to the south, we chose a modernist language of projecting glass bays and asymmetrical window and balcony rhythms. Adjacent to the town center on the north, we decided on more traditional languages, including an Art Deco–inspired vocabulary of deep, elongated piers, horizontal striping, and a pronounced verticality.

View from Rockville
Town Center,
looking south.

Residential
entrance.

Building section.

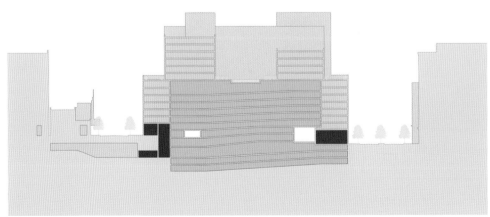

Detailed view of
the southeast
corner.

Lyon Place at
Clarendon Center

CLARENDON, VIRGINIA

ABOVE
Figure ground.

RIGHT
View from Clarendon
Boulevard, looking
south.

Located in the heart of Clarendon, the historic downtown of Arlington County, Lyon Place is a stone's throw from the Metrorail stop at Wilson and Clarendon Boulevards. Named by the American Planning Association as two of the Great Streets in America, the boulevards are the primary commercial corridors of the county. Their resurgence was spurred by the opening of an Orange line Metrorail station in the late 1970s, followed by intense transit-oriented development throughout the following decades.

We were commissioned by the B. F. Saul Company to design two blocks on the boulevards with a mixed program of rental apartments, speculative office space, and ground-floor retail, including several restaurants and a Trader Joe's grocery store. Both blocks contained existing small-scale commercial buildings in the Art Moderne style of the corridor's early development, one of which was the distinguished 1939 Underwood Building. The irregular route of the boulevards and their collision with the regular grid of the adjacent residential neighborhood created downtown blocks of irregular shape and acute angles, many of which were developed with the curved prows characteristic of the style. To strengthen the downtown's sense of place, we designed our buildings in compatible languages and developed two different urban gestures to address the acute site angles. By giving a subtle concave curve to the prow of the taller residential building, which we articulated with Art Deco–inspired elongated bays and piers, we created a small urban plaza in front of it. For the building on the other side of Clarendon Boulevard, we utilized the Art Moderne style of the Underwood Building, celebrating the prow with a sleek curved tower and exaggerated horizontal expression. On the boulevards we maintained a sleek ground-floor storefront style, while on the side streets adjacent to the Underwood Building we developed the pop-out storefronts seen on many of the older commercial buildings.

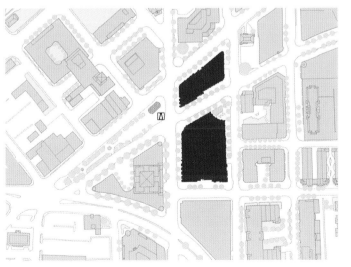

LYON PLACE AT CLARENDON CENTER

SUBURBAN REPAIR

View along Clarendon
Boulevard, looking
southwest.

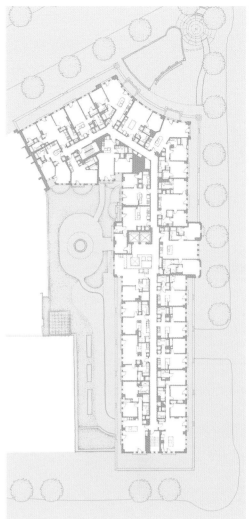

The Nannie Helen
at 4800

WASHINGTON, D.C.

ABOVE
Figure ground.

BELOW
View of the site,
before.

OPPOSITE TOP
View along Nannie
Helen Burroughs
Avenue NE.

Named for Nannie Helen Burroughs, a gifted teacher and educator who
founded a school for African American girls in 1901 on a site just east of the
project, the Nannie Helen at 4800 is part of the District's ambitious plan to
rebuild a nearby public-housing project. Part of the first phase of off-site development, designed to provide family housing in advance of the demolition of
existing public-housing units, the project was developed by several city agencies and A. Wash & Associates, the firm of a local businessman and developer
who was inspired to improve housing opportunities in his neighborhood.

Located in the Deanwood community, the site fronted the avenue named
for the gifted educator. Upgraded by the city as part of its Great Streets Initiative, a program designed to stimulate investment in emerging corridors, the
avenue was improved with new sidewalks, streetlights, landscaped median,
and sustainable features, beginning its transformation from suburban roadway to urban boulevard. Building on that shift in identity, we placed our five-
story building directly on the street's right-of-way and activated the sidewalk
with ground-floor uses, including corner retail and an adult enrichment center. Despite budget pressures, we were determined to design a building that
felt like part of the city, rather than an isolated development typical of low-
income housing. Utilizing two types of siding, we created a dignified façade
of deep piers, projecting bays, and a Mondrian-inspired grid of windows and
panels. Containing workforce and market-rate units, in addition to public
housing, the project was targeted toward small families, and we provided as
many amenities for family living as possible, including ground-floor patios,
a small play area, and extensive bike parking. The last we heard, the building had a long, long waiting list.

 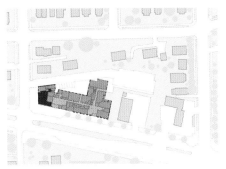 

LEFT TO RIGHT
Typical residential
plan; street-level
plan; typical
residential plan in
context.

THE NANNIE HELEN AT 4800

SUBURBAN REPAIR

Notch 8

ALEXANDRIA, VIRGINIA

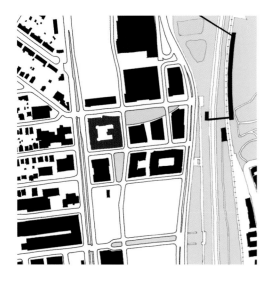

ABOVE
Figure ground.

BELOW
Residential entrance fronting the green on the south.

Sandwiched between the George Washington Parkway and U.S. Route 1, and a stone's throw from the main runway at Reagan National Airport, Potomac Yard is being developed on the site of a decommissioned rail yard, once one of the busiest on the Eastern Seaboard. The master plan, by Cooper Robertson & Partners, based on the time-honored urbanism of nearby Alexandria, Virginia, creates a distinct set of traditional neighborhoods, including a medium-density, mixed-use town center in the blocks around our Notch 8 site.

Located on Route 1 and within walking distance of both a planned infill Metrorail station and new Bus Rapid Transit (BRT) route, Notch 8 was developed by JBG and was the first of several buildings in the master plan designated to create the curved enclosure of a new public park. The conceptual design of the building was developed by SK+I, who maximized the impact of the curve with a bold façade design, composed of a panelized wall with a big grid/little grid motif. The remaining sides of the building were articulated with a red brick, industrial-inspired frame, evoking association with the out-buildings of the former rail yards. A new Giant grocery store is located on the ground floor. We began work on the project after the zoning-approval phase, further refining the façades, enlivening their color palette, and working to restore key features that had been lost in the budget-trimming process. We focused on the design of the interior courtyard, introducing a finger building that subdivided it into discrete areas for different outdoor activities. Because the neighborhood is bursting with new development, our client decided to include a rich set of building amenities, among them an indoor/outdoor bar, yoga studio, shared laptop worktable and docking station, and a hammock zone.

ABOVE
View of the
southwest corner.

BELOW
Building section.

RIGHT
Typical residential
plan.

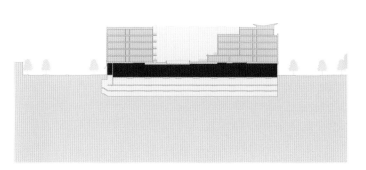

NOTCH 8

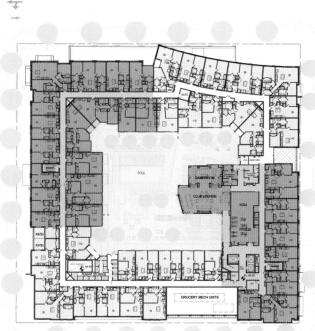

TOP LEFT
View of the
entry lobby.

BOTTOM LEFT
View of the
courtyard.

CENTER LEFT
View of the
game room.

View along U.S.
Route 1, looking
south.

The Bartlett

ARLINGTON, VIRGINIA

ABOVE
Figure ground.

RIGHT
View of the
residential
entrance.

Located in Pentagon City in eastern Arlington County, Metropolitan Park will complete the transformation of the area from an industrial suburb of Washington to a high-density, mixed-use district with its own identity. With a master plan by Robert A. M. Stern Architects, the development of the 16-acre site will create more than 3,000 new residential units, 100,000 square feet of ground-floor retail, and a new park, complementing the existing Pentagon City development, which is largely dominated by a regional mall.

Stern's master plan developed a fine-grained street grid, subdividing the 16 acres into six mixed-use blocks, all organized around a central green. We were commissioned by Vornado to design the project's fourth phase, which included a large building of almost 700 residential units. Eyeing the huge uptick in the residential population, we proposed a new grocery store in the building's ground floor to service the increase in residents. For the building, we developed a massing of fifteen-, seventeen-, and twenty-two-story volumes organized around a south-facing courtyard. We were joined in the building's design by Maurice Walters Architect, and together realized the building's exterior façade as a dignified composition of traditional classical components influenced by 1920s and 1930s urban high-rise apartment buildings, such as those facing Central Park in New York City. Despite the complications generated by the building's massing, we were successful in designing its floor plates for the optimal benefit of the residential units, resulting in unit plans that seemed the result of inside-out, rather than outside-in, thinking.

ABOVE
View along the park, looking east.

BELOW
View of the grocery entrance on 12th Street South.

RIGHT
View from the park, looking north.

Residences at
the Greene

BEAVERCREEK, OHIO

Located in a largely residential area outside of Dayton, Ohio, the Greene town center was designed to create a new downtown for the suburban community, bringing new office, retail, entertainment, and dining opportunities, as well as a vibrant set of public spaces. The 72-acre development, now ten years old, was developed by Steiner + Associates and Mall Properties.

The master plan, developed by DDG, organized the mixed-use development around a central green. We were commissioned to design one of the mixed-use buildings fronting the green, with ground-floor retail and three levels of residential units above. A key to our scheme was dignifying the residential entrance, located at the rear of the building, which we addressed by designing a paseo in the center of the building on axis with the green, creating a new street at the rear, and lining it with shallow townhouses. Composed of both open and closed courtyards, the building was articulated with three different façade types to break up its length and give it a scale appropriate to the adjacent street and green. The façade styles we chose, utilizing authentic traditional languages within the limitations of the project budget and the building's wood-frame construction, were inspired by the main street architecture of older Ohio towns. They included a formal red brick section topped by a central pediment on the green and a yellow section with a bold cornice and piers. Michael Vergason Landscape Architects designed the courtyards, including a winter courtyard with a gas fireplace and a summer one with a fountain, bringing vibrant life to the public spaces of the building year round.

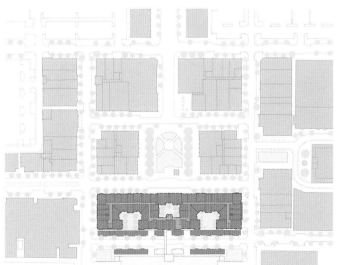

FAR LEFT

Retail plan.

LEFT

Typical residential

plan.

Suburban
Repair

4665 Steeles
Avenue

MARKHAM, CANADA

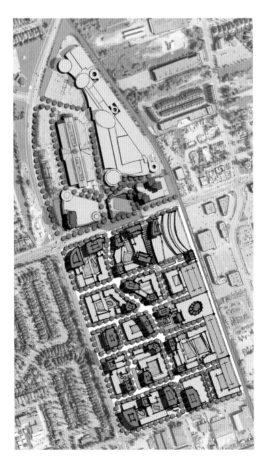

Sitting on the boundary between the northern limits of Toronto and the southern border of the rapidly growing town of Markham, the area of Steeles Avenue near the new Milliken Metrolinx Transit Station is ripe for development. Home to a large Chinese immigrant population, the area was originally largely zoned for industry. We developed a master plan that envisioned its transformation into a new downtown, complete with new housing, office, retail, and cultural amenities for the surrounding residents. Working with the Global Fortune real estate company and our strategic partner Michael Morrissey, we developed a gateway complex for the parcel at 4665 Steeles Avenue East, adjacent to an existing Chinese mall. Utilizing the slim, elongated high-rise style common to Vancouver and codified in Toronto's zoning laws, we created a new development of more than 1.6 million square feet that includes a retail galleria with more than 200,000 square feet of retail space, 600 apartments, and a new hotel. We gave the complex a sleek modernism of steel panels, glass curtain walls, curved towers, and ground-floor transparency punctuated by video screens and arresting signage, all to establish a powerful presence in the otherwise suburban environment.

TOP LEFT

Figure ground.

BOTTOM LEFT

Master plan.

RIGHT

View from Steeles
Avenue.

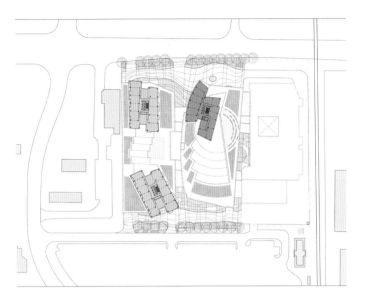

Tower, retail, and
garage-level plans.

RIGHT
View of a festival
street.

+ NEIGHBORHOODS

CHERYL A. O'NEILL

The Inextricable Link

"Where, after all, do universal human rights begin?
In small places, close to home—so close and so small
that they cannot be seen on any map of the world.
Yet they are the world of the individual person:
The neighborhood he lives in . . ."

ELEANOR ROOSEVELT

"I think that the point of being an architect
is to help raise the experience of everyday living,
even a little."

DAVID CHIPPERFIELD

For most people, the word *neighborhood* occupies a special place in their imagination. Whether it is the memory of the place where they grew up or a vacation spot in a foreign country where they spent an idyllic week, or even Dickens's description of life in the slums of Victorian London, the term has the capacity to evoke powerful associations. Usually composed of ordinary urban spaces and buildings, a neighborhood produces "something" that exceeds the everyday and becomes memorable. The creation of that "something" is the focus of the projects in this section.

OPPOSITE: View of the City West neighborhood, looking toward downtown Cincinnati.

Aerial view of Fort
Belvoir, Fairfax
County, Virginia.

Whether private commissions in greenfield sites or public/private ventures in inner-city areas or on military bases, these projects involve the design of hundreds if not thousands of housing units and their arrangement in blocks, streets, and larger neighborhood patterns. Combining city or town planning and housing design in a particular way, they are the result of our conscious efforts at place making. Inspiration has come from the rich repository of existing historic neighborhoods as well as from the challenges of solving unique design problems.

When designing neighborhoods, we must act both as planners—establishing the pattern of streets and open spaces, the size and geometry of blocks, and their subdivision into lots and housing parcels—and as architects, creating the dwellings that respond to the needs of everyday life and give character to public spaces. The relationship among all these elements is so intricate and so intertwined that we coined the term *the inextricable link* as a way to describe both the design challenges and our aspirations. It is our "something."

NEIGHBORHOODS

Mansion apartment buildings at Celebration, Orlando, Florida.

Our neighborhood projects began with several private commissions on greenfield sites in Florida, coming on the heels of the work of Duany Plater-Zyberk in the town of Seaside. Medium-density housing commissions that were the first rental communities in their respective towns, these projects stimulated our early search for a type of architecture that could replace conventional suburban types and support walkable urbanism. Our project at Celebration (pages 128–29) transformed two of those types, creating housing that was more fully grounded in the landscape of southern Florida. Clothing the breezeway apartment building, a banal suburban type, in the dress of a Neoclassical Southern mansion, we married it with townhouses dressed in a variety of expressions, including a Mission-style house in saturated colors.

These transformations were followed by other inventions, particularly middle-range types that created apartment densities without large footprints or the need for acres of surface parking. Four- or six-unit apartment buildings, duplex units, stacked flats, corner-turning units, and live/work units, many with integral garages, introduced both a richer architecture and, when mixed on a single block, walkable block dimensions. Using this diversity of types in both our Celebration and Baldwin Park projects enabled us to replace the acres of surface parking and unwieldy dimensions of the typical suburban multifamily "pod" with the framework of an urban neighborhood. We

NEIGHBORHOODS

Townhouses
at Celebration,
Orlando, Florida.

further diversified the architectural character of these neighborhoods by designing multiple variations of the different types, creating the idiosyncrasies of a neighborhood that has grown over time and merging the new neighborhoods with the larger idea of their respective towns.

We continued these investigations on subsequent projects, developing a canon of house types capable of articulating nuanced urban plans. The side-yard Charleston house was a particularly rich source of inspiration, yielding elegant stacked flats at King Farm in Rockville, Maryland (pages 260–63) or small-scale apartments integrated with single-family homes in the variegated streetscapes of College Park in Memphis (pages 168–71) or Belmont Heights in Tampa, Florida (page 172–75). In our mixed-income projects, these types proved essential in supporting the diversity of demographics and income levels we believe essential to a just urbanism.

An important part of these investigations was the calculating of street widths, block sizes, housing types, and unit yields that is a fundamental component of speculative development. Our housing types and urban design plans had parallel lives as products and yields, required to meet the demands of the marketplace and the developer's financial goals. The translation of a neighborhood site into blocks of housing of a specific type, with an associated sale or rental value, pressured us to produce the design with the most profitable financial equation. We quickly recognized that this benefited the neighborhood as a whole: the tightest urban design plan created the most powerful urbanism, while the assemblage of the housing types with the highest value left the most money on the table for the architecture. We developed an iterative process to achieve that goal, engaging in cycles of invention in which housing types, block types, and the project's financial results were arranged and rearranged until they were all at their optimum.

Though our neighborhood projects have been located in a variety of contexts, including urban infill conditions, most have not been in markets that could support underground parking. Consequently, the fixed dimensions of parking spaces and drive aisles impacted block sizes and larger urban design strategies. Pressures on site yields quickly familiarized us with the most efficient block geometries of different building types. The rowhouse, for instance, little changed from its medieval predecessors, operates most efficiently in narrow strips as minimal as 125 feet deep, while mixed-use buildings containing retail require blocks of greater dimension to accommodate their greater parking demands. Projects such as the town center at Baldwin Park (pages 130–33) attest to the warp and weave required to accommodate mixed-use programs. The insights into basic block types and dimensions that we have derived from our neighborhood projects have proved very useful in much of our town planning work (see the Places section).

MIXED-INCOME HOUSING

A substantial number of our neighborhood commissions have resulted from local and federal policies designed to address affordable-housing needs. The largest of these was the Department of Housing and Urban Development's (HUD) HOPE VI program, begun in the early 1990s and continuing throughout the years of the Clinton presidency. The program's goal was to replace the 100,000 most distressed public-housing units in the country with mixed-income, mixed-use neighborhoods. Awarding commissions through competitions, the program was influenced in its early years by the leaders of the New Urbanism, placing an emphasis on traditional neighborhood design.

The majority of our HOPE VI projects replaced public-housing communities that had been part of the urban-renewal projects of the 1950s and 1960s. We largely restored the traditional neighborhood character that they had had prior to those interventions. Above all, these projects impressed upon

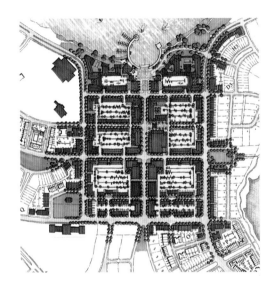

Master plan of the Baldwin Park town center, Orlando, Florida.

NEIGHBORHOODS

us the power of the street. We remember one early meeting at Lafayette Courts, later Pleasant View Gardens, our first HOPE VI project, when we were struggling over how to bring an isolated group of buildings at the edge of the site into relation with the rest of the neighborhood. A resident raised her hand and asked, with the intuitive understanding of a city dweller about what makes a house in the city part of the city, "Why don't we put a street in front of them?" That statement might serve as a motto for all of our HOPE VI projects. Put a street in front of them. Reconnect the grid. Create street addresses and housing that looks like everyone else's.

Replacing the monoculture of low-income public-housing neighborhoods with mixed-income programs, these projects typically contained three tiers of housing—low-income, workforce, and market-rate units—all with a wide range of family sizes and tenure types. They taught us the importance of diversity, especially with regard to income, which provides the economic glue that holds a neighborhood together and is the regulator that allows it to flourish under a range of economic conditions and pressures. Family units typically comprised a substantial portion of these programs, and we explored the housing types that would not only provide key amenities that dignify family living, such as separate entrances and access to outdoor space, but would also work in programs that either increased on-site densities or were significantly denser than their surroundings. Stacked flats inserted into a string of rowhouses (City West, pages 162–63) or small-scale apartments inserted between one-story bungalows (Belmont Heights, pages 172–75) are but two examples.

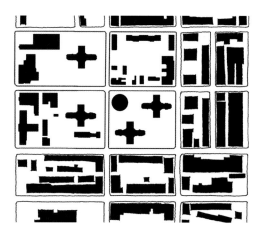

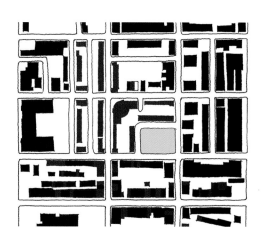

TOP
Martin Luther
King Plaza,
Philadelphia,
before.

ABOVE
Martin Luther
King Plaza,
after.

LEFT
Streetscape at
City West,
Cincinnati.

Investigations into streetscape design also led us to different expressions
for typological diversity and a rich repository of ideas about neighborhood
character. Often it was in this realm that we found a means to elevate the
architecture of what were typically very modest houses. We designed the
streets of College Park in Memphis (pages 168–71), for instance, as a delib-
erate assemblage of highly variegated and detached building forms, mirror-
ing that of the surrounding single-family neighborhood and expressing the
internal diversity of unit types and family sizes. For Martin Luther King Plaza
in Philadelphia (pages 158–61), in contrast, we suppressed typological diversity in favor of repetitive townhouse strings patterned on Philadelphia's regular rows. Such differentiation of the streetscape became for us a powerful
design tool in neighborhood formation, helping to articulate urban plans
and enhance the architecture of simple houses. We developed a technique
of three-dimensional paper "pop-up" models of neighborhoods with small-
scale unit elevations, which helped us to marry the idea of the street to that
of the architecture, and subsequently to decide on style, language, and building materials.

An important component of all of our HOPE VI and other affordable-
housing projects was their creation through an interactive process involving a
broad range of stakeholders, including our clients—typically a public/private
venture between a public-housing authority and a private developer—local

citizens, city agencies, and the existing public-housing residents. In most other projects, the needs of the end user were conveyed to us in marketing reports or through our developer-client. In these interactive sessions, we received feedback directly from the end user, impressing upon us the essential humanity of our endeavor, both to satisfy basic physical needs and to address important psychological desires for home and community.

MILITARY-FAMILY HOUSING

Commissions from the military privatization program, begun under the presidency of George W. Bush, were awarded, like those from the HOPE VI program, through intense competitions. The scale of these commissions, however, was considerably larger, at times numbering thousands of units. Competition submissions were comprehensive, requiring detailed architectural, urban design, and financial information, and allowing little wiggle room for changes after the project was awarded. If you were successful enough to make the shortlist, the evaluation process included a grueling multi-hour interview.

We began to refer to this early competition phase as a "chase." Importing the interactive process from our HOPE VI work, we developed our submissions in intense sessions with our client, Clark Realty, with whom we formed a strategic alliance for the majority of our military projects, and whose sister company, Clark Builder's Group, was responsible for their construction. Through these sessions we acquired some of our most meaningful and fruitful experiences in neighborhood formation, learning a great deal about the "something" between architecture and urbanism that creates distinguished neighborhoods.

Aerial view of San Diego Naval Facilities Command, looking toward the harbor.

The size of these projects presented a basic delivery challenge, both to us as architects and urbanists and to our client as developer and financier. Although the programs were less complicated than their HOPE VI counterparts, they had their own nuances, including housing types tightly orchestrated by military rank and often distributed geographically, which sometimes meant that a neighborhood of hundreds of units could be composed of only three or four types. Challenged to create diversity while keeping a project manageable, we developed the concept of the project "chassis," a basic building type with multiple variations for military rank and style, massing, materials, and color schemes. This approach streamlined construction, achieving budget and time efficiencies and leaving room for the details and façade variations that create neighborhood character. We adapted this strategy to many of our other neighborhood projects, utilizing the rowhouse, for instance, as the chassis for both Princeton Faculty & Staff housing (pages 138–39) and City West (pages 162–63).

Built on a massive scale, the military projects were largely the product of mass-production construction systems, which impacted both their architecture and their urbanism. Dependent on repetition, mass-production building limits unit diversity, eliminating the one-offs so often needed to solve unique site conditions. Our urban designers learned to operate largely without *poche*— the irregular unit plan that finesses the corner of a block or plugs a hole in a space—and tended to stick to simple variations on the grid, using special events such as a civic building, a linear green, or a pocket park to establish local neighborhood identities. We often worked hard to develop plans that kept existing landscape features, especially mature trees, valuing them for their environmental benefits and their ability to lend character to a neighborhood and instantly ground it in its environs.

Decades of suburban development, especially along the East Coast, have populated the world of manufactured parts with the details of Georgian, Colonial, Craftsman, and Italianate styles. The availability of the parts and pieces of these styles, as well as our recognition of the range of architectural expression that exists in neighborhoods, including everything from fine renditions of historical styles to their garden-variety interpretations and local vernaculars, informs our decisions about style and language. We make conscious choices based on project budgets and other factors about where on the "quality" spectrum we need to be. In our neighborhood work, we often shoot for the vernacular or low-style ranges, where language is carried by a few elements on the external façade. We spend a great deal of time honing those details, and in our military projects we used full-scale mock-ups to ensure quality for ourselves, assure budget conformance for our clients, and provide a valuable teaching tool for subcontractors who were involved in the construction of hundreds of units. There is a lot of trading in this style-and-budget realm—brick houses with less detail for siding houses with more, a simpler Colonial porch for a more complicated Italianate one—until we feel all the dollars are spent in the right place, for the right amount, for the biggest bang for the place.

CONCLUSION

A microcosm of the city, the neighborhood is a platform for social justice and equity and achieves something extraordinary when its architecture and urbanism are in perfect equilibrium. It transforms modest things into something more sublime—a place, the stuff of memory.

Neighborhood green at Fort Belvoir, Fairfax County, Virginia.

Arts and Crafts rowhouses, Princeton Faculty & Staff housing, Princeton, New Jersey.

The Garlands of Barrington

BARRINGTON, ILLINOIS

ABOVE
Figure ground.

OPPOSITE
View of the tower
entry from the
park.

Looking back, we feel that the stars were aligned for our project in Barrington, Illinois. A bucolic site, our client's aspiration to create a legacy project in their hometown, and our vision all combined to produce the Garlands, a continuous-care retirement community. Our client, Barrington Venture, was inspired to provide a community where older members of the town could move a few blocks and spend their later years in the same community that they had lived in and helped to build.

The existing site, located several blocks from the village center, was marked by numerous stands of majestic trees. From the beginning, the idea of a campus informed our approach, but the requirement that all of the apartment buildings be linked by internal walkways meant that the program would occupy a large footprint on the site. Determined to maintain the site's bucolic character, we organized the interconnected apartment buildings around two partially enclosed quadrangles, creating a variety of incident and picturesque views and negotiating around the tree stands. An extended wing containing all of the complex's public amenities fronted a small plaza on the most prominent street, creating a public activity node and connecting the community to the village. Influenced by English vernacular and Chicago North Shore estate architecture, we enhanced the building façades with balconies, vertical bays, dormers, and chimneys, developing a rich and varied architectural palette compatible with our vision of the site as a picturesque campus.

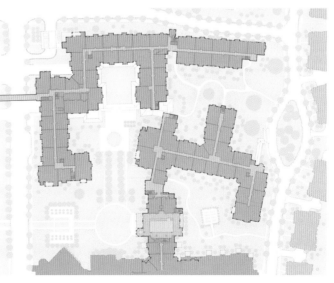

OPPOSITE
Barrington
townhouses.

ABOVE
Typical residential
plan.

FAR LEFT
Ground-level plan.

LEFT
Typical residential
plan.

View from the village green on the north.

Centergate at Celebration

ORLANDO, FLORIDA

ABOVE
Figure ground.

BELOW
Neighborhood
plan.

OPPOSITE
View of the new
apartments
and rowhouses
overlooking the
golf course.

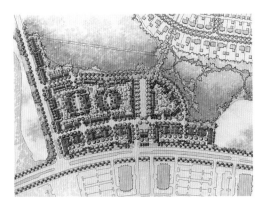

Located on 10,000 acres just outside of Orlando, Florida, Celebration followed on the heels of the resort town of Seaside. The project was developed by the Walt Disney Company under the eye of CEO Michael Eisner, who encouraged company executives to "make history" and create a town worthy of the Disney name. Planned by Cooper Robertson & Partners and Robert A. M. Stern, the town includes signature civic and commercial buildings by renowned architects. A pattern book governs the design of the town's residential architecture, providing guidelines for five regionally inspired building styles.

We were commissioned by Pritzker Residential to design the town's first rental-housing neighborhood. Inspired by the domestic architecture of the region, we created a set of five residential types, including multiple variations on two- and three-story rowhouses, a carriage house, courtyard apartments, and mansion apartment buildings. Those, in combination with the five styles of the pattern book, gave us a "Chinese menu" of residential forms and expressions that we used to diversify streetscapes, integrating the neighborhood with the rest of the town. Multiple corner-turning and integral garage units allowed us to subdivide the typical suburban multifamily "pod" into a set of walkable, small town blocks. Working with our color consultant, we developed a diverse palette grounded in the vernacular of southern Florida. Built with the parts, pieces, and at times ruthless speed of mass production, the project owes much of its quality to the watchful eye of Celebration's town architect, Geoffrey Mouen. Originally intended to provide rental housing for town staff and workers at nearby Disney World, the units were later sold as condominiums, testifying to their quality but unfortunately eliminating the social and economic diversity of the original commission.

Centergate at Baldwin Park *and* Baldwin Park Town Center

ORLANDO, FLORIDA

ABOVE
Figure ground.

OPPOSITE
View of the
Charleston-
inspired stacked
flats along the
entry road.

Our commission for Baldwin Park followed our work at Celebration. Located northeast of Disney World, the project was built on the site of the Orlando Naval Training Center, one of many decommissioned military facilities made available for private development by the Defense Department's Base Realignment and Closure Commission (BRAC). Pritzker Residential purchased the project from the original development team, inheriting the primary development agenda—to create an authentic town.

Including the design of a new neighborhood of rental housing and master plan of the town center, the project built on the success of the Celebration project, both as a real estate venture and as an architecture and urban assemblage. We utilized similar block strategies and residential types, developing architectural styles and expressions to respond to the new context and the pressures of a smaller development budget. The project's urbanism was enhanced by the planning regulations of the City of Orlando, which permitted reduced parking counts and street widths. Unique to the project was the "flex" building, a string of multistory, mixed-use units with flexible ground-floor plans that accommodated either small commercial spaces or residential studios. The type allowed commercial uses to evolve as the town matured, making mixed-use buildings viable in a greenfield project. We articulated these flex buildings, located on secondary streets adjacent to downtown, as grand London-style terrace houses with uniform façades and classical detailing. For the town center, we revised the master plan inherited from the first team, subdividing their superblocks into a walkable network and developing a nuanced set of urban spaces, including a farmers' market, lakefront promenade, and mixed-use Main Street.

OPPOSITE
View of a flex building with retail in the ground floor.

ABOVE
View of the neighborhood along the Cady Way trail.

FAR LEFT
Master plan of the town center.

LEFT
A townhouse in the Florida coastal style.

Masonvale

FAIRFAX, VIRGINIA

ABOVE
Figure ground.

OPPOSITE
Streetscape in the
Colonial hamlet.

Like many colleges and universities in high-priced real estate markets, George Mason University in Fairfax, Virginia, has had difficulty attracting and retaining faculty members because of housing costs and availability. As a result, the university became an advocate for affordable housing in their local community, and with the Masonvale project undertook development in a public/private venture for the first time. The project comprises 155 transitional housing units that provide ongoing affordability and accommodate the full demographic range of the university's faculty and staff, including young singles, families, and empty nesters.

The site was an underutilized fragment of land just east of the main campus, crossed by several streams and stands of mature trees. We leveraged these natural features as powerful place-defining elements in the neighborhood's design, creating a large, V-shaped nature preserve around them. We arranged the housing in two small hamlets nestled against the edges of the preserve. Streets were laid out to exploit views into and along the green space and link the site to the residential neighborhood on the east and the campus on the west. Arguing against the dorm format originally proposed by the university, we advocated for stacked flats and rowhouses, both for their ability to convey the urbanism of a traditional neighborhood and for the better quality of life they offered. Each hamlet has a different architectural style, breaking up the neighborhood into smaller-scale elements and heightening the experience of moving from one to the other and across the preserve. The western hamlet was designed in a Colonial language that responded to the conservative style of the main campus; the eastern, in a Craftsman language of heavy overhangs and bracketed cornices. Diversity in housing types, massing, and materials provided variety in the otherwise stylistically integrated hamlets.

Neighborhood
green in the
Colonial hamlet.

ABOVE
View along the
nature preserve in
the Colonial hamlet.

BELOW
Colonial- and
Craftsman-style
building details.

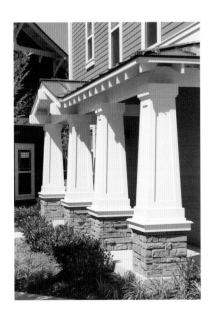

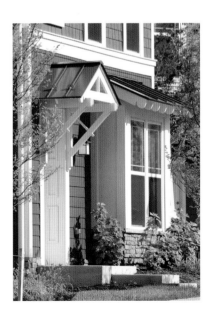

Merwick Stanworth

PRINCETON, NEW JERSEY

OPPOSITE TOP
View looking south
toward downtown
Princeton.

OPPOSITE
BOTTOM LEFT
View from the
forest preserve.

OPPOSITE
BOTTOM RIGHT
View of the
neighborhood
from the southern
green.

Just north of the Princeton University campus, on the site of the former Merwick Hospital, we designed a new "town-and-gown" affordable-housing neighborhood. Locally referred to as "Green Hill," the site was prized for its bucolic character and development potential, and seen by community members as one of the keys to Princeton's future. It was also a significant component of the university's ongoing Housing Master Plan, which, in light of Princeton's high-priced real estate market, called for the augmentation of housing programs for faculty and staff. The site was programmed with affordable-housing units available to university faculty, staff, and the broader community and developed in a public/private venture between the university and American Campus Communities.

Preserving the natural assets of Green Hill, including the many stands of mature trees, was a top priority of our design. For inspiration, we drew on the early twentieth-century communities of Clarence Stein and Henry Wright such as Chatham Village in Pittsburgh. Forming a set of rambling blocks that meander in and around existing trees, we shaped the townhouse strings into idiosyncratic assemblages of English Arts and Crafts– and Tudor-style housing units, using their roof forms and irregular, asymmetrical compositions to embellish the architecture of what were very modest houses. We integrated small-scale apartment buildings with the more prevalent rowhouse strings, providing accessible units and achieving necessary site yields. Extensive grading and tree removal were avoided both through adjustments to building placement on the Merwick site and by retaining the roadbeds and foundations of the former barracks housing and Stanworth graduate and faculty housing, which we re-used in the northern portion of the site. In coordination with the university architect, a single color scheme was chosen for the entire project, strengthening its campus feel and association with the university.

Ormanada

ZEKERIYAKOY, TURKEY

Ormanada is a new mixed-use community north of the Istanbul metropolitan area in Zekeriyakoy. Like Istanbul itself, the site is characterized by steeply sloping topography, which offers spectacular views of the surrounding hills, valleys, and the Black Sea in the distance. The project takes its name from two sources: the season of the year that is favorable to the poppy flower, which is the region's symbol, and a small spring in a cleft in the site. We won the project commission through an invited competition sponsored by the Eczacibasi Group, and were responsible for both the community's master plan and the conceptual design of its architecture.

Comprising several small neighborhoods with a strong overall community identity, our site plan was crafted to maximize the site's spectacular views. The individual neighborhoods were assembled around open spaces linked by pathways and streets whose curved geometries were established by the site's topography and formed a strong public realm. A central square at the site's summit contains retail and restaurants, as well as a social club and pool, creating a vibrant node of public activity. Extensive greenery and a vocabulary of L-shaped courtyard homes maximized privacy and interaction between interior space and private courtyards. Individually terraced into the hillside, the houses were designed in a mid-century modern and contemporary architectural language. Expansive glass, projecting bays, and other features optimized the interaction between the indoor living spaces and the courtyards, engaging family life with the surrounding natural features.

TOP LEFT
Figure ground.

CENTER LEFT
Roof plans.

BOTTOM LEFT
Master plan.

OPPOSITE TOP
View of a house
and private yard.

OPPOSITE
BOTTOM LEFT
View of houses
along the street.

OPPOSITE
BOTTOM RIGHT
View of an interior
living space.

Kemer Country

ISTANBUL, TURKEY

The site for Kemer Country in Istanbul, Turkey, lay in the shadow of a sixteenth-century aqueduct constructed by the Turkish Renaissance architect Koca Mimar Sinan. Our client for the project, Esat Edin, was inspired by Turkey's rich urban and architectural tradition to create a neighborhood born of it but responding to contemporary life. We were hired after the completion of the development's town center, designed by Duany Plater-Zyberk, and were commissioned to design two residential neighborhoods.

With two principals and a host of employees from Turkey, we have had a long familiarity with the country, and welcomed the opportunity to work on a modern-day project incorporating its urban and architectural traditions. The city of Safranbolu was our primary inspiration for the neighborhood's urban design, and we modeled our plan on its medieval arrangement of winding streets, pedestrian paths, and focused, picturesque views. The design of the houses drew on the distinctive features of the traditional Turkish *yali*, a type of waterside housing first developed along the Bosphorus strait. These features—heavy bracketed cornices, overhanging bays, and covered porches—all address the local climate and engage with the water, and we incorporated

Master plan.

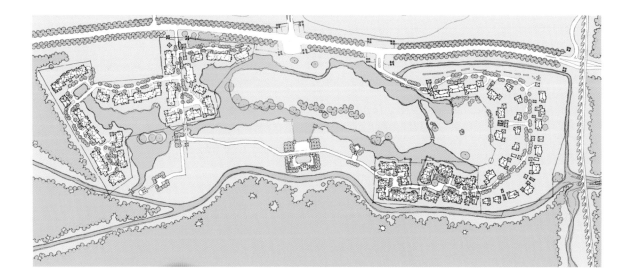

View of the apartments from the street.

them into our plans for small-scale apartment buildings and attached villas. We also variegated rooflines and pavilionized massing to mitigate the scale of the buildings and give them a varied expression. Red tile roofs and the saturated colors of the region, echoing the deep reds and ochres of the country's spices, completed the ensemble. This was the first neighborhood we designed that combined small apartment houses and attached villas in the same building. The diversity in massing and scale helped create a place reminiscent of traditional Turkish villages.

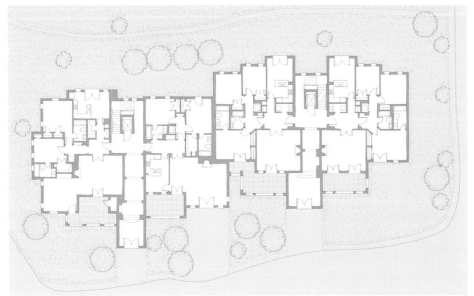

LEFT

Floor plan of the apartments.

ABOVE

Rendering of the neighborhood from a pedestrian pathway.

BELOW

Elevation of an apartment building.

LEFT
Rendering of the
water view.

ABOVE
View of the
apartments and
villas along the
water.

Arabian Canal Courtyard Neighborhood

DUBAI, UNITED ARAB EMIRATES

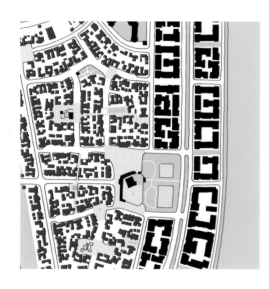

ABOVE
Figure ground.

OPPOSITE
Renderings of the courtyard houses from the street.

In the desert landscape of Dubai, few things are valued above water. Located twenty-five kilometers from the Arabian Gulf in Dubai, a new city envisioned by our client, Saeed Saeed, with a master plan by Calthorpe Associates, was given water—and therefore life—with the construction of a seventy-five-kilometer canal that begins and ends at the Gulf. Arabian Canal City, comprising multiple town centers and neighborhoods, was formed around and by the canal. We were commissioned to provide conceptual designs for the westernmost town center and the first residential neighborhood.

The original statement of our commission was to design a neighborhood of prototypical Western townhouses. We replaced that approach with one founded on the cultural traditions, climatic conditions, and house types of the region. Inspired by the Pearl Diver neighborhoods and the Al Bastakiya quarter along Dubai Creek, some of the few remaining historical areas of Dubai, we developed a set of courtyard houses, arranging them in the incremental and fragmented pattern of a desert city. We created curvilinear streets and blocks in a variety of shapes, reinforcing the idiosyncrasy of the architecture and respecting the enclosed views of an internal world. Winding streets, shaded pathways, and small plazas ventilated the large blocks, providing privacy and shade. We designed eight distinct courtyard house types with strict separations between public and private areas, articulating them with a language of thick walls, decorative privacy screening, and picturesque massing inspired by traditional Islamic architecture, all of which resulted in the same site yield as the original townhouse concept.

Rendering of a
courtyard house.

Neighborhood
plan.

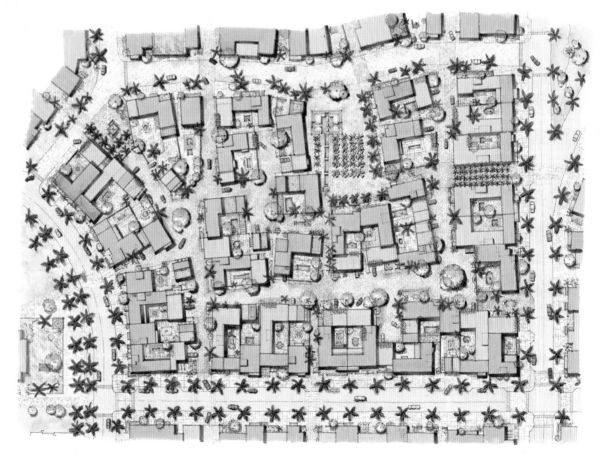

TOP LEFT
Arabian Canal
City Master Plan,
by Calthorpe
Associates.

**CENTER AND
BOTTOM LEFT**
Illustrative
plans of canal
neighborhoods.

TOP RIGHT
First-floor plan of a
courtyard house.

BOTTOM RIGHT
Second-floor plan
of a courtyard
house.

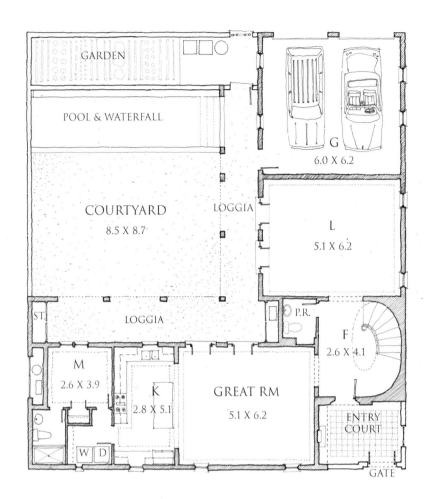

GARDEN

POOL & WATERFALL

G
6.0 X 6.2

COURTYARD
8.5 X 8.7

LOGGIA

L
5.1 X 6.2

ST.

LOGGIA

P.R.

F
2.6 X 4.1

M
2.6 X 3.9

K
2.8 X 5.1

GREAT RM
5.1 X 6.2

ENTRY
COURT

W D

GATE

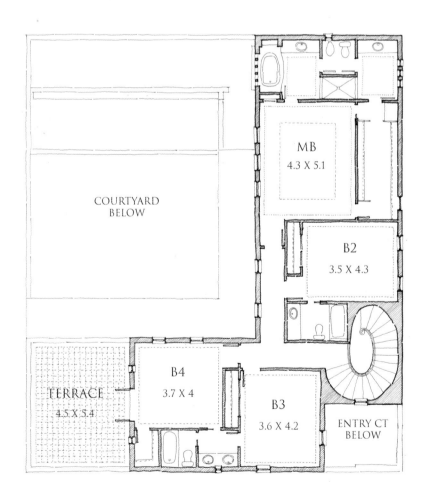

COURTYARD
BELOW

MB
4.3 X 5.1

B2
3.5 X 4.3

TERRACE
4.5 X 5.4

B4
3.7 X 4

B3
3.6 X 4.2

ENTRY CT
BELOW

Devanhalli

BENGALURU, INDIA

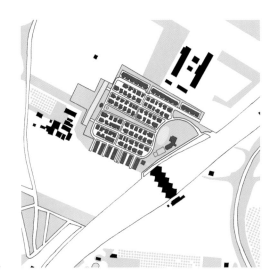

Figure ground.

Known as both the "Garden City" and the "Silicon Valley of India," Bengaluru is rapidly expanding with new residential neighborhoods. We were hired by the Tata Housing Development Company, one of the most prominent residential developers in the Indian market, to devise a master plan and provide conceptual architectural design for a new middle-class neighborhood. Strategically located on the outskirts of the city along its burgeoning northern growth corridor, the site was a former industrial area, in close proximity to several IT parks and infrastructure projects, including the new Bengaluru International Airport.

The density of most Indian cities places a cultural premium on open space. One of our first notions in designing the neighborhood was to include powerful green spaces, elevating the neighborhood's character and providing a strong sense of place. We created a signature park with a curvilinear geometry and relaxed pathway system at the site entrance, connecting it to a long linear green that threads the open space through the small neighborhood. After numerous conversations, our client committed to a high level of sustainability on the brownfield site and pursued a LEED Gold rating, very uncommon in India.

We designed a new clubhouse, which houses a variety of recreation and community uses, in a high Neoclassical style, siting it in the middle of the park, on axis with the linear green. The new housing units—a combination of freestanding villas and attached houses—were distributed along the several residential blocks that subdivided the neighborhood. Working in a consistent

Neoclassical style, in part inspired by British colonial architecture, we developed a system of porches, overhangs, and upper-level walkways that covered the front-loaded carports, suppressing their impact and creating strong, pedestrian-friendly streetscapes. The interior layout of the units incorporated the traditional Hindu principle of *vastu*, or "science of architecture," a system of placement and orientation that works on a nine-square grid, which, together with the project's Neoclassical look, reflected the hybrid nature of contemporary Indian culture.

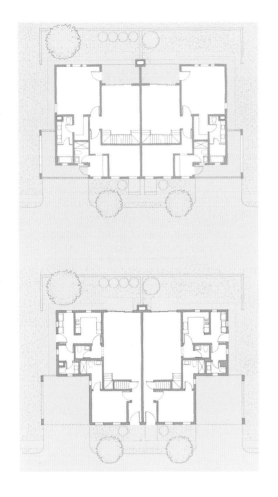

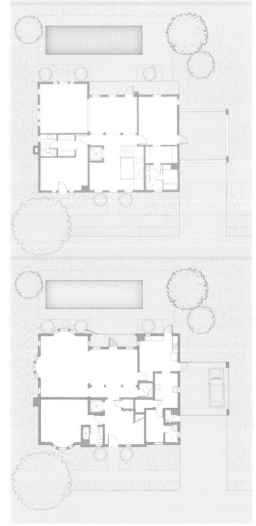

ABOVE LEFT
Semi-detached villa, first- and second-floor plans.

ABOVE RIGHT
View of a detached villa.

BELOW
View of a detached villa.

RIGHT
Typical villa, first- and second-floor plans.

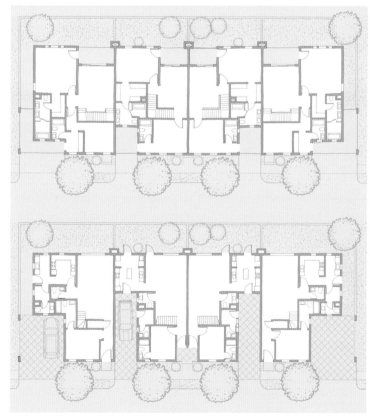

ABOVE

View of rowhouses
along the street.

RIGHT

Rowhouses, first-
and second-floor
plans.

Community Centers

VARIOUS LOCATIONS

Many of our neighborhood commissions have included community centers as an important civic component. Typically composed of meeting rooms, communal spaces, and specialized programs such as computer labs, day-care facilities, or exercise rooms, they have also often included large outdoor spaces, such as playgrounds, terraces, and swimming pools.

A significant aspect of our approach to community centers is to establish the building's engagement with the broader neighborhood. We developed several site strategies, including locating the building on a significant open space or placing it in a more visible location such as an active perimeter street or a highly visible site edge. Strong inside/outside spatial relationships extend the interior communal life of the building to that of the broader neighborhood; to achieve this outreach, we often utilize large front porches, loggias, or extensive terraces, such as the front porch at MacDill Air Force Base or the grand terrace at Woodlawn.

The design of these buildings allows us to exchange our typical background housing forms for that of signature structures. We often use expressive massing—singular roof profiles or iconic features such as towers, rotundas, or belvederes—to project a civic identity, such as the Community Center at the San Diego Naval Training Center. Our choice of style has varied; at times, such as at Addison Terrace or Capper/Carrollsburg, where the

building was in a prominent public location, we utilized a modernist language that contrasted with that of the neighborhood, whereas in other instances, such as the Community Center at Miramar, where the building was immersed in the center of the neighborhood, we felt that a sympathetic language was more appropriate. In several instances we have been inspired by the civic sobriety of Frank Lloyd Wright's Unity Temple, such as the centers at the Plaza at Centennial Hill and Woodlawn Terrace.

ABOVE
Woodlawn
Community Center,
Fort Belvoir, Fairfax
County, Virginia.

LEFT
Barry Farm
Recreation Center,
Washington, D.C.

Addison Terrace Community Center, Pittsburgh.

Capper/Carrollsburg Community Center, Washington, D.C.

Miramar Community Center, San Diego.

San Diego Naval Training Center Community Building.

MacDill Air Force Base Community Center, Tampa.

Centennial Hill Community Center, Montgomery, Alabama.

Martin Luther King Plaza

PHILADELPHIA, PENNSYLVANIA

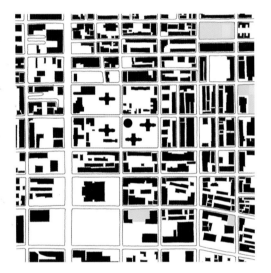

Figure ground, before.

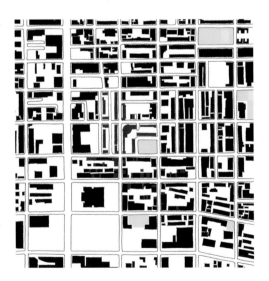

Figure ground, after.

Like many of our neighborhood revitalization projects, Martin Luther King Plaza, located in the Hawthorne neighborhood of South Philadelphia, underwent remarkable change in a little over fifty years, being transformed from a traditional rowhouse community into a public-housing high-rise development and back again in that short time frame.

Our involvement with the community began in the mid-1990s, when we worked with the public-housing residents then living in the high-rise development and the Philadelphia Housing Authority to determine the neighborhood's future. By then, the high-rise towers were almost half vacant and the community was plagued by innumerable social, economic, and physical ills. We were subsequently part of a development team comprised of Pennrose, a Philadelphia-based housing developer, and Universal Companies, a local non-profit development organization founded by Kenneth Gamble, a South Philadelphia native and famous "Sound of Philadelphia" R & B producer. The team was charged with obtaining the funding and implementing the neighborhood vision through HUD's competitive HOPE VI program.

Unique to our approach was an emphasis on the public-housing site and the surrounding Hawthorne neighborhood. A third of the new rowhouse units were located in Hawthorne, the rest on the site of the demolished towers. We replaced the tower superblocks with a new fine-grained pattern of streets based on Philadelphia's unique major/minor street rhythm. Low-rise unit plans, including rowhouses, live/work units, and small apartment buildings, were designed on a traditional 16-foot, or one-rod, house width, allowing similar types to be used on- and off-site. Heavy cornices, façades arranged in pairs or in long terraces, a sprinkling of the distinctive Philadelphia bay, and saturated brick colors achieved local patterns with a minimal development budget.

FAR LEFT

View of the
former public-
housing towers.

LEFT

On-site
community
meeting.

ABOVE

View of the new
rowhouses and
Hawthorne Park.

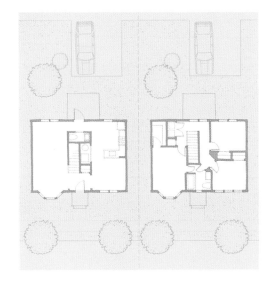

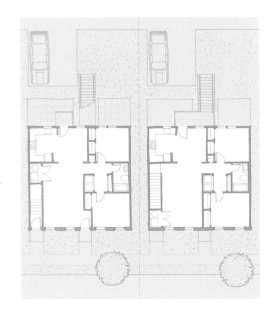

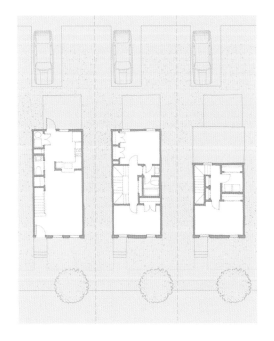

LEFT

Floor plans of typical units.

ABOVE

View of the new rowhouses.

Before revitalization, ongoing private housing investment had stopped at South Street, some seven or eight blocks north of the project site. Martin Luther King Plaza's revitalization changed that pattern. Fueled by the tremendous public investment and the neighborhood's reintegration, both programmatically and physically, into the fabric of the city, the private market took off, repairing derelict structures and infilling vacant lots in the intervening blocks. From time to time, Peter Piven, FAIA, a Philadelphia architect, calls the office as he drives through the neighborhood and says thank you for a job well done.

The best part of the neighborhood's transformation occurred after we left the project. A key part of our plan was the creation of a small park located at the edge of the public-housing site, in the center of Hawthorne. There were no funds left to realize it when the housing portion of the project was complete. A remarkable group of neighborhood champions rallied around the park, mobilizing public attention and requesting the funds (which ultimately came from a consortium of city, state, and charitable sources) needed for its implementation. With an elegant landscape design by Ground Reconsidered, the park is now alive with the sounds of children playing, soccer practice, and summer jazz concerts dedicated to keeping the "Sound of Philadelphia" alive.

Summer jazz
concert in
Hawthorne Park.

City West

CINCINNATI, OHIO

ABOVE
Figure ground.

BELOW
Neighborhood plan.

OPPOSITE
View of the new
rowhouses along
the western edge.

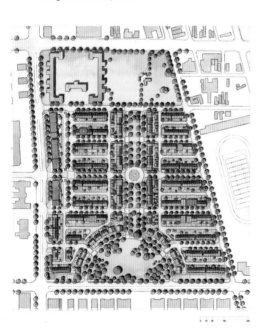

Unlike other public-housing sites we've worked on, Laurel and Lincoln Homes in Cincinnati, Ohio, the site of our City West project, was built in the 1920s and 1930s by the Public Works Administration (PWA). Housing more than 2,000 families, the development was in a state of disintegration and disrepair by the mid-1980s, prompting an agile resident leadership to have it placed on the Historic Register to protect it from wholesale demolition and the relocation of the existing residents. They subsequently successfully lobbied the Cincinnati Metropolitan Housing Authority (CMHA) for revitalization through HUD's HOPE VI program, and we were hired as part of the development team, led by the Community Builders, to revitalize the neighborhood.

The scale of the revitalization effort, including more than 1,000 mixed-income units, created a place for everybody who wanted to return and leveraged the funds for a high-quality development. To develop a plan for the new community, we held several on-site charrettes, working closely with the resident leadership and CMHA. Our site plan introduced an urban street grid, creating walkable residential blocks and restoring connections to downtown, which had been severed both by highway construction and the PWA site layout. An enormous, poorly maintained, and undersupervised city-owned park that at the time of our charrettes was encircled on the public-housing side by an eight-foot-high chain-link fence, was recast as the center of the neighborhood, with a manageable scale and unique semicircular shape inspired by the pattern of existing trees. The building block of our plan was the rowhouse, which we developed in a variety of styles, including a neo-Italianate inspired by the nearby Dayton historic district. Glaserworks, a local architecture firm, was an integral part of the design team and responsible for project detailing. Their efforts, the developer's high ambitions, and the funds leveraged by the project's size produced a housing stock and neighborhood of fine quality.

Salishan

TACOMA, WASHINGTON

ABOVE
Salishan, before.

OPPOSITE
Aerial view of
new homes and a
bioswale, looking
toward the harbor.

When we started to plan our charrette for the design of Salishan, a 188-acre public-housing development in Tacoma, Washington, we were told that we should expect to do our presentations with the assistance of language translators, four of which were required. A rich blend of Ukrainian, Cambodian, Vietnamese, Hispanic, and American families, the community was housed in dilapidated buildings constructed during World War II as temporary housing for shipyard workers. The residents referred to their community as "My Salishan," signaling their attachment to the neighborhood despite its abysmal physical condition. Certainly one of our aspirations was to create a new neighborhood whose physical form reflected the power and grace of its inhabitants.

The project was located in the watershed of Commencement Bay, around a defunct salmon stream. Armed with state grants to support a highly sustainable approach, the Tacoma Housing Authority set a high bar that resulted in ninety-one LEED platinum houses and a system of bio-infiltration swales that restored the stream as a salmon spawning ground and helped improve water quality in the bay.

Our site plan incorporated a sustainable approach, creating residentially scaled blocks and a town center all organized around a linear, 30-acre nature preserve that flanked the stream, which was linked to the bio-infiltration swales that ran through the blocks. A diverse set of housing types responded to the community's varied demographics, some arranged in a regionally inspired courtyard configuration. The Craftsman style's powerful historical association with the Pacific Northwest and its great variety of exterior details, including bold roof forms with brackets and deep eaves, prompted us to design the entire neighborhood in that style.

Lorig Associates was responsible for bringing the neighborhood to life. The combined leadership of the design team, the development and construction team, and the Tacoma Housing Authority ensured that the neighborhood was built with tender care for this truly great community.

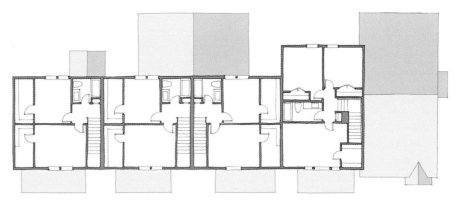

ABOVE
Multilingual
public charrette.

BELOW
Master plan.

TOP RIGHT
Townhouses,
second-floor plan.

BOTTOM RIGHT
Townhouses, first-
floor plan.

OPPOSITE
View of the new
Craftsman-style
townhouses.

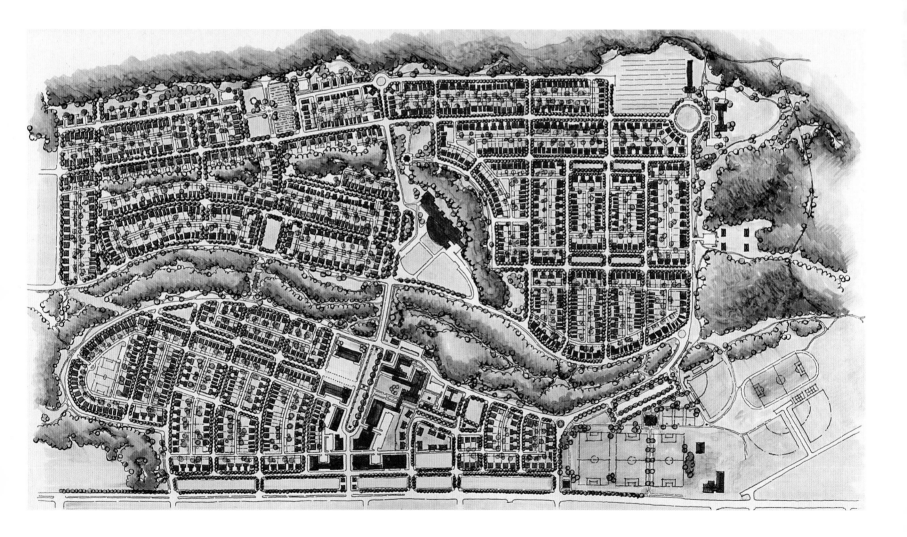

Mixed-Income
Housing

College Park

MEMPHIS, TENNESSEE

ABOVE
Figure ground.

RIGHT
Streetscape with
new housing and
heritage trees.

We inherited the College Park project, formerly the LeMoyne Gardens public-housing community, from another team who, together with the Memphis Housing Authority (MHA), had sufficiently advanced the project to relocate the existing residents, demolish the garden apartments they had inhabited, and develop a master plan for their replacement in a new mixed-income neighborhood.

Located across the street from LeMoyne-Owen College, a private institution founded in the nineteenth century that has historically served African American students, the 36-acre site was bordered by a cemetery, a working railroad line, and a small neighborhood of bungalows and modest single-family houses. What struck us on our first site visit was the power of the many stands of mature trees that had survived demolition, especially those bordering the vacated streets, and how alien in character the townhouse-based former master plan was to the surrounding neighborhood. We committed to addressing both, and developed a site plan that incorporated the existing streets and created open spaces, especially a number of linear greens, around the trees. Parallel projects in Norfolk and Richmond, Virginia, made us aware of a distinctly Southern neighborhood type that inspired our unit design for College Park. Composed of a range of detached volumes, including both houses and small-scale apartment buildings, communities like Ghent in Norfolk delivered a density equivalent to the rowhouse but with a distinctly Southern feel and

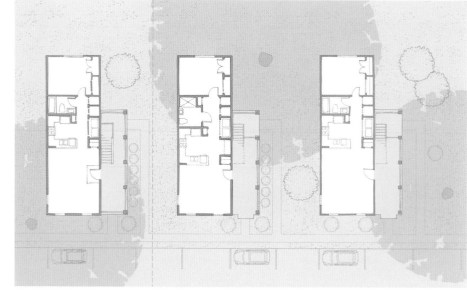

ABOVE LEFT
Streetscape with
new housing.

ABOVE RIGHT
Floor plans of the
stacked flats.

BELOW LEFT
First-floor plan of a
camelback house.

BELOW RIGHT
View of a duplex
unit and a camel-
back house.

OPPOSITE
Neighborhood
plan.

charm. We developed a range of units, including regionally inspired camelback houses and an interpretation of the side-yard Charleston house as small-
scale apartment buildings, that delivered not only the density required for
the program but also the spatial character and, we thought, improved livability of the context. A new senior building with a big, double-story porch
faced the historic college across the street, matching its scale and restrained
neo-Georgian architecture. Developed in a public/private venture between
MHA and a private development team comprised of Urban Atlantic, the
Integral Group, and a national homebuilder, the project's execution was an
early experiment in the possibilities of creating an authentic architecture at a
vinyl price, pushing the details of mass-production housing as far as possible.

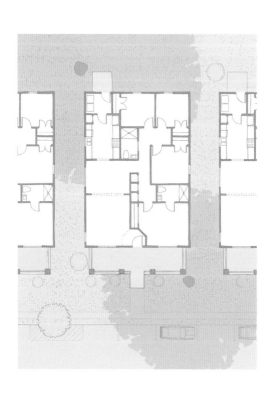

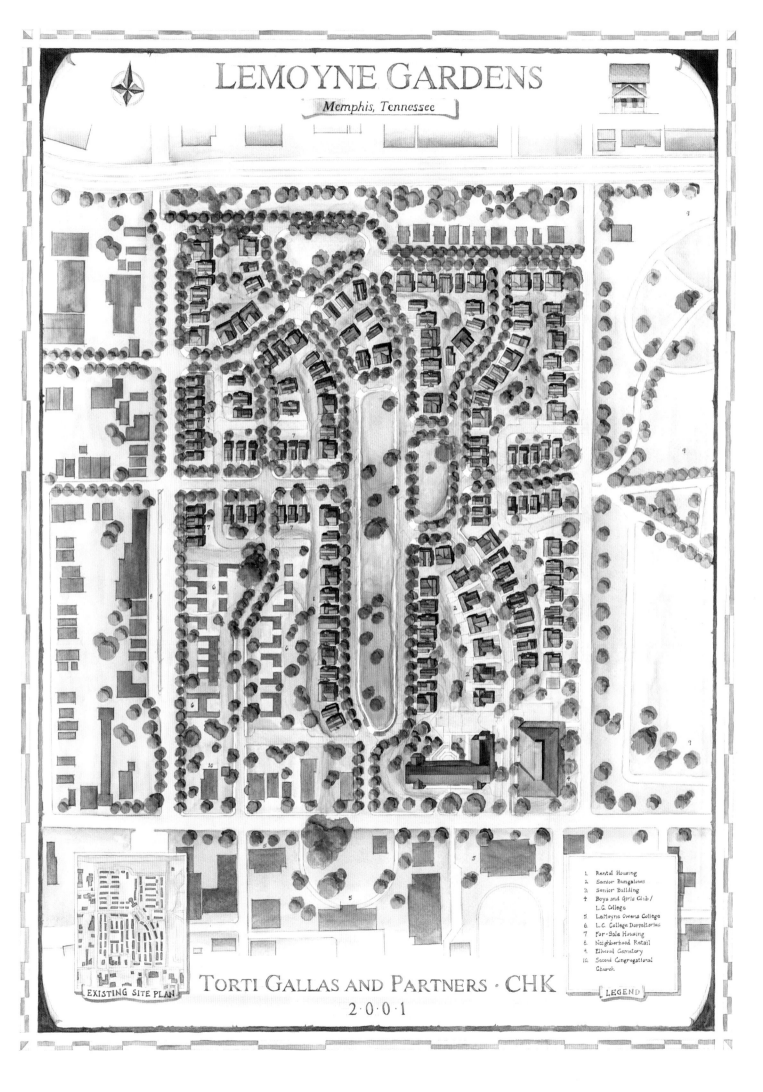

LEMOYNE GARDENS

Memphis, Tennessee

TORTI GALLAS AND PARTNERS · CHK

2·0·0·1

EXISTING SITE PLAN

LEGEND

1. Rental Housing
2. Senior Bungalows
3. Senior Building
4. Boys and Girls Club / L.C. College
5. LeMoyne Owens College
6. L.C. College Dormitories
7. For-Sale Housing
8. Neighborhood Retail
9. Elwood Cemetery
10. Second Congregational Church

Belmont Heights

TAMPA, FLORIDA

Belmont Heights was another public-housing project we inherited from a plan begun by others. The Michaels Development Company, our client, originally hired us to develop the architecture for the new mixed-income community on the outskirts of the city, which replaced a public-housing development of more than 1,000 units. Due diligence in the early phases led us to the discovery of a city ordinance protecting grand trees, which were scattered throughout the site, prompting our redesign of the existing master plan.

Our revised site design was born not only out of conformance to the grand tree ordinance but also from a real desire to ground the new neighborhood in the existing landscape. We developed three distinct strategies for preserving the trees, all of which drove the plan: locating them in green spaces, in particular a large green at the center of the site; setting units back from them; and utilizing the camelback house type developed in the Memphis project to tuck houses beneath their immense canopies.

Tampa at that time was governed by suburban ordinances prohibiting basic urban features such as on-street parking; we often had to come up with inventive interpretations, such as calling a street with parallel parking a parking lot, to achieve the normative urban design features of a traditional neighborhood. The unit types were similar to those of our Memphis project, including the camelback house and Charleston apartment buildings, but we clothed them in the plantation style indigenous to southern Florida. When we returned to the site several years after the project had been completed, we were very gratified that our taxi driver refused to believe, after we told him we were there for a meeting with public-housing residents, that we had given him the correct address.

Figure ground, before.

Figure ground, after.

ABOVE
View from the
central green.

LEFT
Views of the
surrounding
neighborhood.

View of the camel-
back units beneath
the existing tree
canopy.

Master plan.

View of the senior
bungalows along
a pathway.

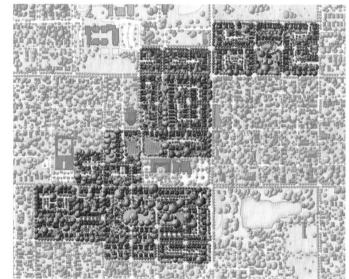

First- and second-
floor plans of the
duplex units.

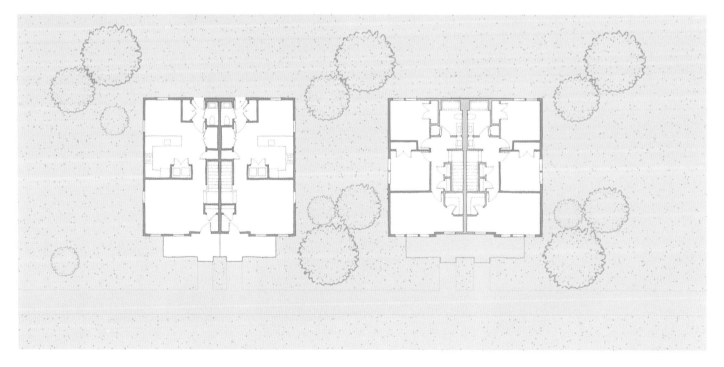

Westlawn

MILWAUKEE, WISCONSIN

ABOVE
Figure ground.

BELOW
Typical floor plan
of an apartment
building.

RIGHT
View of a new
apartment
building.

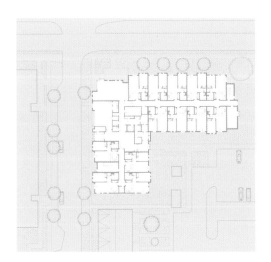

Originally containing more than 700 public housing units on a sprawling 74-acre site seven miles from downtown Milwaukee, Westlawn had reached the end of its lifetime by early 2000. The deteriorating condition of the large development prompted the Housing Authority of the City of Milwaukee (HACM) to make the bold decision to update the site in its entirety. With a successful track record transforming their communities into mixed-income neighborhoods, HACM leveraged the funds for Westlawn's redevelopment through state tax credits, for which they received the largest award in state history. Their revitalization vision had three goals for the residents: community, sustainability, and healthy living. The latter goal was an acknowledgment of the high incidence of lung ailments in the community, a consequence in part of Milwaukee's tough winters and poor indoor air quality.

The project site, surrounded by vacant lots and a suburban strip mall, lacked a powerful context. With the prompting of the executive director of HACM, we responded with a broad spectrum of languages, including a modernist vocabulary for the apartment buildings on the site's major street, which we thought would help to create a sense of place. We designed the low-rise buildings in a range of traditional styles, including a Midwestern barn-influenced language of minimalist aesthetics, vertical banding, and front-facing gables. Prioritizing sustainability and sensitivity to healthy living throughout our planning and implementation of the project

helped it to receive, upon its completion, the highest rating of any LEED Neighborhood Development project in the country. Car-charging stations, a community garden where local teens started a small business growing and selling fresh produce, and units with good insulation and ventilation were all part of the mix.

ABOVE
View of a new
duplex unit.

LEFT
View of the former
public-housing
units.

View of the new
rowhouses.

FAR LEFT
Neighborhood
children in front of
the new homes.

LEFT
Training at the new
mobile library.

BELOW
View of the
new apartment
buildings
along the entry
boulevard.

San Diego Naval Facilities Command

SAN DIEGO, CALIFORNIA

Figure ground.

We won our military-housing project in San Diego after four failed attempts at the intense competitions involved in obtaining the sizable commissions. Together with Clark Realty, with whom we developed a strategic alliance for this and the majority of our military-housing projects, we decided that we needed to go pedal to the medal and deliver a powerful vision. We developed a master plan for a traditional neighborhood that was antithetical to the suburban vision of the competition and broke almost every one of its rules. Although this approach came as a surprise to some at our grueling eight-hour interview, it was the right decision, not only delivering the award for the project to us but also shifting the military's perspective to embrace the benefits and attributes of traditional neighborhoods.

The San Diego Naval Facilities Command provided living quarters for military personnel and their families, from both the Navy and the Marines. Developed in four phases, the project included more than 4,000 new and renovated homes and several community centers. Military rank established the criteria for the units, including square footage and amenities, as well as neighborhood composition, which often meant as many as two hundred homes in a single section with only four different unit types. We developed a variety of strategies to eliminate the deadening monotony this uniformity might produce, using string composition, especially powerful with townhouse types, and multiple architectural styles and color schemes to develop a repertoire of sufficient variety to articulate our urban design and create diversified streetscapes. To achieve this variety, we employed a technique that we have used often: the creation of pop-up models of the neighborhood with small-scale versions of the houses, which we moved around until we matched the idea of the street with the arrangement of the units. A key part of our repertoire was deciding where to repeat and where to differentiate. We were inspired

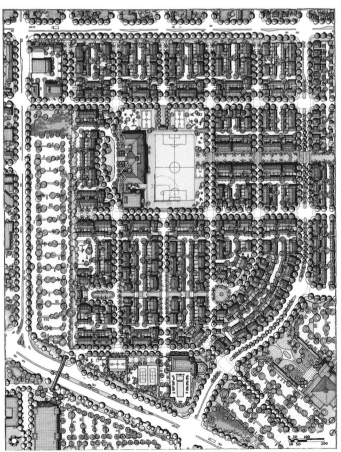

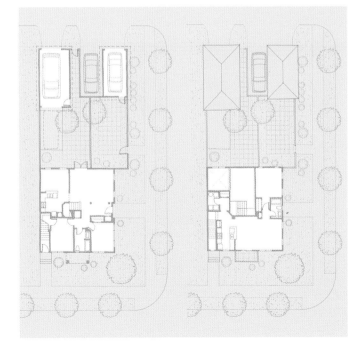

ABOVE
View of a pocket park and the new townhouses.

FAR LEFT
Neighborhood plan.

LEFT
First- and second-floor plans of the stacked flats.

181

by the rich tradition of Mission-style architecture in San Diego, with its vocabulary of deep, ochre-colored stucco walls and red tiled roofs, and used it in a classical format on major streets, assembled in long terraces with continuous arcades along a prominent linear green, and in a more casual, picturesque assemblage of duplex and single-family houses along minor streets and incidental spaces. We designed these houses in variegated two- and three-story masses with asymmetrical roof compositions, curvilinear façade profiles, and arcaded front porches.

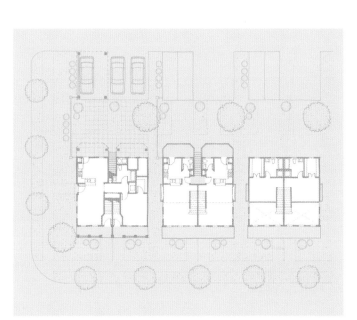

Fort Belvoir

FAIRFAX COUNTY, VIRGINIA

ABOVE
Figure ground,
before.

BELOW
Figure ground,
after.

An army base located just south of Washington, D.C., in Virginia, Fort Belvoir was one of our largest military-housing commissions. Involving the demolition of all the existing housing on the base except for the historic homes, the project created 1,600 new units in ten neighborhoods, including a mixed-use town center, the first of its kind on a military base. Influenced by its proximity to D.C. and the watchful eyes of the Pentagon, it was developed after the terrorist attacks of September 11, requiring us to meet new security and force-protection guidelines.

Located on a peninsula jutting into the Potomac River, the site was characterized by rolling terrain and many stands of mature trees, some clustered around streams flowing into the river. A mature landscape is a powerful tool in the creation of good neighborhoods, so we developed a site plan maintaining the existing suburban road system, avoiding the grading that would have disturbed the tree stands, and overlaid it with a fine-grained grid of streets that defined individual neighborhoods, each with a special moment—a linear green, a new community center—creating spatial focus and neighborhood identity. We came to think of the layout as a string of pearls on a necklace. It seemed to us that the existing non-residential buildings at the base's center on 12th Street had the potential of being transformed into a real downtown, and we designed the area as a new town center with ground-level retail and apartments above. Though lobbying for it was initially a hard sell, it proved to be a huge success, clearly responding to the need for public life and place absent from the previously suburban campus.

The architecture included three unit types, which we developed in two styles—an Italianate and a Colonial Revival—and we used urban design strategies and color to create diversity across the campus. The volume of housing production, combined with high aspirations for the architecture, inspired our client to invest in full-scale mock-ups of key details. These were an invaluable tool in our negotiations for the design, helping us to get the best details for

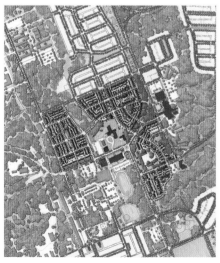

Clark Realty's budgets, and we spent days horse-trading with them on minute details. We had assumed that the mock-ups would be taken down after we had agreed on their details, but Clark found them such a powerful teaching tool for subcontractors that they left them up for the duration of the project.

Illustration of
neighborhood
façades.

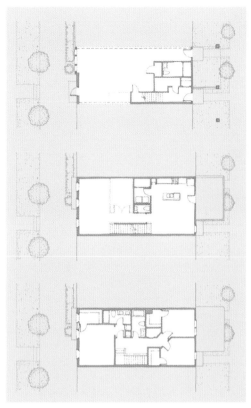

BELOW
Sidewalk activity
in the new town
center.

ABOVE LEFT
View of the new
townhouses near
the town center.

ABOVE RIGHT
AND BELOW
Floor plans of live/
work units and new
homes.

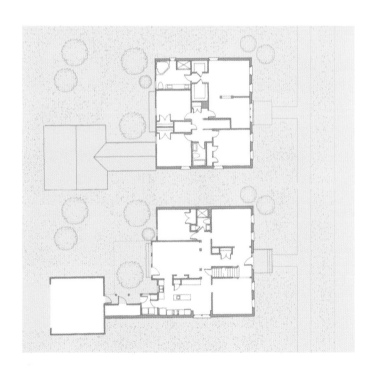

MacDill Air Force Base

TAMPA, FLORIDA

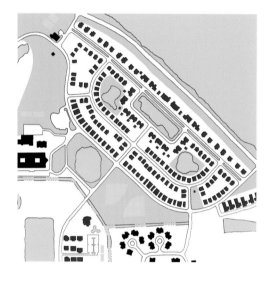

BELOW

Portico of the
house of a four-
star general.

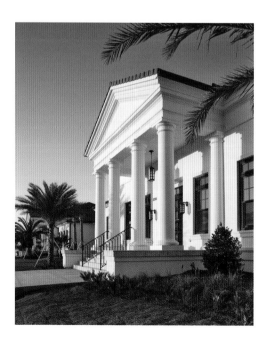

Located on Hillsborough Bay in Tampa, Florida, MacDill Air Force Base is home to both the enlisted ranks of the Air Force and higher-ranking officers, including the two-, three-, and four-star generals of the military's Special Operations and Central Command units. Developed after Hurricane Katrina, the project responded to new FEMA regulations and was one of our first to incorporate resiliency as an important part of our design approach.

Housing on the base was geographically coordinated by rank, with distinct neighborhoods for the officers and the enlisted ranks. Located on a bluff overlooking the bay, the officers' neighborhood incorporated resilient features in an otherwise traditional neighborhood with a strong sense of place. The heart of the neighborhood, which included a park and a parade ground surrounded by the homes of the ranks of highest distinction, was located at the topographical high point of the site, allowing the houses to sit on the ground in a conventional fashion. For the surrounding blocks, at an elevation below the floodplain, we adopted a "beach town" approach, elevating the houses on piers, with their habitable spaces above the flood level. Parking was located at the street level but accessed from rear alleys and screened by trellises, creating pedestrian-friendly streets with porches and sidewalks lined with trees. We developed the duplex units in a Craftsman style, with deep brackets and panelized siding, incorporating the prominent entry stairs into the vocabulary. Care was taken in the distribution of the housing of different ranks to separate them across alleys, rather than streets, eliminating the need for officers of different ranks to salute each other every time they left their house. For the generals we designed large single-family houses overlooking the bay in high Neoclassical style with elaborate public spaces reflecting their occupants' stature.

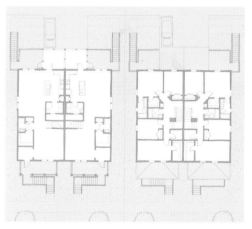

Fort Irwin

MOJAVE DESERT, CALIFORNIA

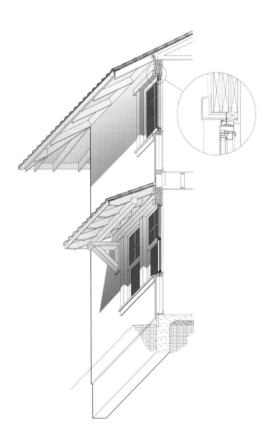

For Fort Irwin, located in the Mojave Desert, we focused our sustainable strategy on addressing the harsh effects of the arid climate. Home to many of the troops training for deployment overseas, the army base includes both family and dormitory units. Our commission involved multiple neighborhoods of both new and renovated units and, after our experience at Fort Belvoir, a new town center.

We concentrated our efforts on lessening the impact of the sun on both internal and external spaces, creating temperate outdoor conditions that would permit public and semipublic activities and also reduce energy costs. Our unit designs included several variations on courtyard houses, featuring usable exterior spaces with sufficient shade. Inspired by regional styles, we designed the buildings in a simple Mission style with stucco walls and concrete tile roofs, and we developed a range of external screening devices that could be adapted to different building orientation. Where possible, we developed neighborhood plans without rigid orthogonal grids to avoid wind and sun exposure and minimize the size and scale of exterior spaces. For the landscaping, we specified the use of irrigation-free xeriscaping throughout.

We located the town center on one of the most trafficked streets, transforming it from an arterial road into a mixed-use main street. Several mixed-use buildings, in a more exuberant Mission style with ground-floor arcades, provided new retail with dormitories above. A new community clubhouse organized around a central courtyard contained a distinctive cooling tower that created a temperate climate in the space.

TOP LEFT

Figure ground.

BOTTOM LEFT

Details of the
shading devices.

ABOVE

View of the new houses.

BELOW

Façade adaptations for solar orientation.

ABOVE
View of the cooling tower in the courtyard of the community clubhouse.

RIGHT
Floor plans of the community clubhouse.

FAR RIGHT
Floor plan of a single-family house, above, and duplex units, below.

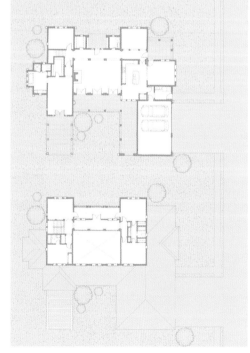

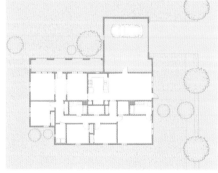

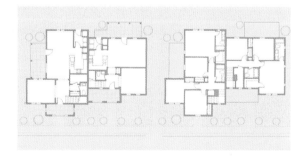

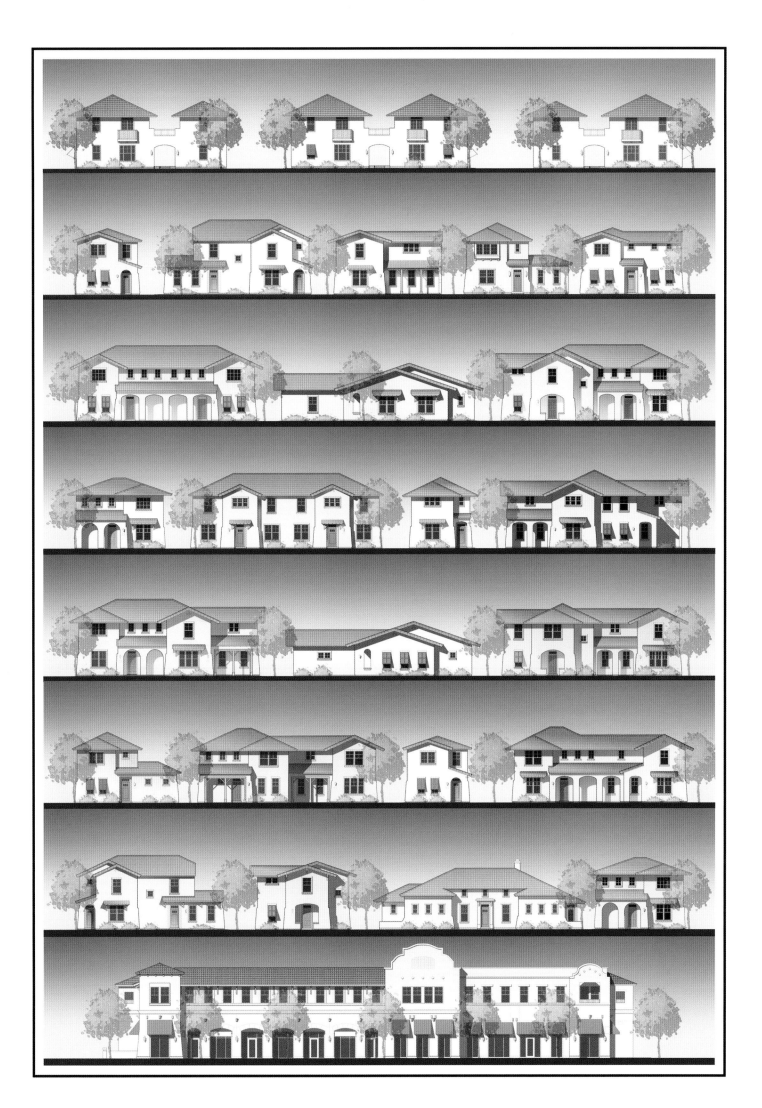

Illustration of neighborhood façades.

+ PLACES

"Our purpose in founding the city was not to make
any one class in it surpassingly happy, but to make the
city as a whole as happy as possible."

The projects in this section shift the scale of our endeavors from buildings
to towns and cities, including downtowns (Santa Monica, pages 250–51),
towns (King Farm, pages 260–63), corridors (Coast Highway, pages 244–
45), and counties (Albemarle, pages 258–59). Though they are aligned with
the principles and philosophies of the preceding sections, they differ in the
type of problems they address and the medium of our response. Instead
of focusing on the implementation documents of architecture and neighborhood, they communicate intentions through large-scale master plans
and codes, both of which guide rather than prescribe built form. A mix of
private and public commissions, they are about the creation of new places
and about fulfilling the policy objectives that will transform existing ones.
Rather than the here and now of today, tomorrow, or this decade, their time
frame is the distant future of the next fifty or one hundred years.

OPPOSITE: Rendering of a new neighborhood in Bahçeşehir, Istanbul.

NEAL I. PAYTON

Transit-Oriented Development

━━━━━━━━

Over the past two decades, a very public conversation has been taking place about the connection between the health of cities, the economy, and the environment. Study after study demonstrates that the "greenest" cities tend to be the densest, most walkable, and most functionally diverse, suggesting that these characteristics are in fact synergistic.

━━━━━━━━

Farmers' market in the Columbia Heights Civic Plaza, Washington, D.C.

As demands on highway infrastructure, coupled with concerns about global warming, have increased, the development of robust transit networks has become an increasingly significant priority for cities. Embracing a policy of "Transit-Oriented Development" (TOD) as a means for growth, metropolitan areas have been planning for transit not only as a means of getting from place to place but also as a tool to catalyze the development that promotes walking and biking and encourages economic activity.

TOD is characterized by equal parts Density, Diversity, Design, and Destination (the "four Ds"), and we at Torti Gallas embrace it, not as an end in itself but as a means to a set of ends. The obvious objective is to bring people and businesses close enough to transportation to make it vital. When TOD includes a healthy mix of workforce and affordable housing, it also provides equitable access to the benefits of a local economy and creates value at the transit stations themselves.

Given that reality, we approach the planning and design of TODs as an effort in catalyzing urbanism at its most intimate locations. The permanence of a fixed transit system like rail or Bus Rapid Transit (BRT) makes intensive real estate investment possible, to build or encourage great public streets and spaces framed by pedestrian-friendly buildings that sustain public life. Through TOD, we are not merely planning to mitigate traffic; we are increasing access to the social and economic benefits of a region and planning for the creation of wealth in an entire community.

Though the benefits of TOD are clear, the challenges of realizing its goals are significant. Going beyond the drawing board requires overcoming what may seem like insurmountable forces related to one or more of the four Ds. Existing zoning regulations, bureaucratic inertia, and well-organized groups of nearby residents may thwart any proposed increase in density. Conversely, local transit agencies may assume unrealistically high land values or density expectations, making it difficult for TOD developers to pencil in anything without large public subsidies. To that end, we have found that focusing on each of the four Ds provides significant lift in overcoming these challenges.

THE FIRST D: DENSITY

In an ideal world, sites for TOD would be "pre-entitled" for the appropriate levels of density even before development proposals are put forward. Transit authorities and public agencies would have a realistic view of market conditions and be flexible about short- and long-term development prospects.

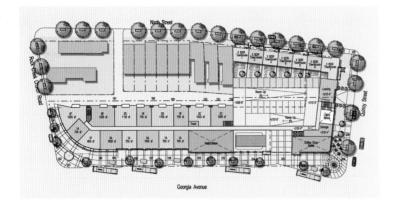

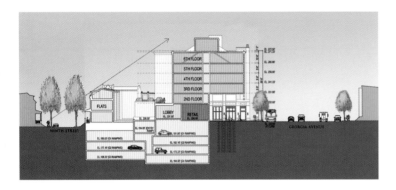

Typically, however, this is not the case. Public authorities who own or manage real estate assets close to transit often desire greater densities in order to: 1—maximize ridership by getting the highest number of transit riders living, working, shopping, or going to school near the stations; and 2—maximize land values to provide a steady stream of income through ground rents. As a result, TOD proposals can be buffeted by opposing forces, particularly those from nearby residents who often oppose significant increases in density, fearing that new development will overwhelm their neighborhood.

To overcome these objections, we look for creative density solutions that are site specific and support a pedestrian-friendly environment. A fine-grained mix of uses and building types supports vibrant neighborhoods. At the scale of the block, buildings can be conceived with both high and low densities, providing the blended forms that fulfill development objectives without looking monolithic. When we compose buildings, we take into account an entire block, recognizing the hierarchy of streets along the perimeter as well as the scale of adjacent buildings. Such mixed-density and mixed compositional strategies are not simple, but very often add both intrinsic and economic value. When faced with overly ambitious density expectations, we sometimes suggest a program of graduated densities, allowing lower-density, less-expensive building types (such as townhouses or duplex units) that are located farther from transit stations to be constructed first, thereby preserving land closer to the stations for later development, when market conditions may be more supportive.

THE SECOND D: DIVERSITY

Across a region, TODs should strive for a balance of households, employment, retail, and leisure opportunities within a walkable area. Diverse development provides a round-the-clock set of experiences, disperses traffic, and uses resources more efficiently, while allowing people to live, work, shop, and play within the walkable area. However, the ratios at any given station are not fixed and will vary according to the intended characteristics of the Destination as a whole. At the scale of the neighborhood, we design and code TODs to ensure that some buildings, blocks, or streets are dedicated to multiple uses and that the entire ensemble contains a robust mix of uses and price points.

To achieve this result, we sometimes find it necessary to encourage local governments to adopt more flexible zoning rules to permit diversity and be vigilant about not allowing the formation of "monocultures"—neighborhoods containing only one land use or housing type under the guise of "market forces." This may also require a developer who focuses only on one use or building type to partner with others to create a diverse program. Any development program should also take into account the existing pattern of uses in the area and augment them. Diversity comes from a cross section of the entire geographic area, regardless of who owns the land or how or when it is developed. Not every building needs to be mixed use for the diversity of uses to emerge.

Though ground-floor retail serving local needs around transit stations is an important amenity, we have observed that it is not realistic to expect the transit station to create retail demand substantially over and above the demand that new housing and employment density would naturally bring. To create a substantial retail-focused ground-floor experience, TOD site areas need to be visible and accessible from adjacent thoroughfares, and parking must be adequately sized and well positioned (screened from view but easy enough to find).

When planning for diversity, we are also mindful of the distance from a transit station to any given site; as the distance increases, the site value decreases, but not at an equal rate for all land uses. For example, research suggests that people will walk farther from their homes to a transit station than they will from a transit station to their workplace. That doesn't mean that, given market support, transit stations should be surrounded by offices, but it does mean that we pay careful attention to the nuances of programming and location that are unique to TOD.

THE THIRD D: DESIGN

TOD planning is urban design, that is, the crafting of the spatial experience of the street and sidewalk as constituent elements of the public realm. Our goal is not merely to design a project that supports transit but to provide

the envelope within which a community may flourish. In this domain, we ensure that adequate space is given to the sidewalk, gently embraced by buildings and landscapes that are pleasant and welcoming. We plan for lining the street/sidewalk ensemble with buildings that are deferential to their neighbors—buildings that may not be iconic in themselves but are part of the fabric that frames great streets and enables iconic spaces.

By Design, we are also referring to the concept of "urban transparency," which ensures that a pedestrian is not looking at blank walls or parking garages but is continuously stimulated by views into storefronts and courtyards or through landscapes to spaces beyond or between buildings. The spaces where people walk (sidewalks, lanes, and public open spaces) need to be appropriately shaded and scaled. As for the buildings themselves, we suggest design that supports pedestrian activity through detail that is best experienced at the speed of three miles per hour, and we favor those buildings that have enough activity at the ground-floor level to create "friction" within the pedestrian realm.

TOP
Wilshire Boulevard, Santa Monica, from 3rd Street, looking west, before.

ABOVE
Same view with proposed improvements to the sidewalk space.

THE FOURTH D: DESTINATION

Development atop and around transit stations should be calibrated to the scale, density, and aspirations of the surrounding community. The uniqueness of each TOD is derived not only from the surrounding physical environment but also from nearby social and economic characteristics. One-size-fits-all transit design, in which every station area along the line has the same elements as every other, is like using a blunt instrument for a detailed job. Good TOD planning necessitates developing singular design approaches that creatively address the issues of Density, Diversity, and Design on a station-by-station, area-by-area, corridor-by-corridor basis.

The concept that each station area represents a unique Destination requires incorporating a degree of flexibility and nuance into the design process, so that over time a larger vision for urban form, structure, and movement, all tailored to the specific place, can be accomplished. The TOD's unique "identity" will ultimately bear the indigenous characteristics of the surrounding neighborhoods—their locations, site conditions, development features and potential, histories, and community and natural resources. The urban

design, transportation, and development program, and even branding strategies should build upon these characteristics, enhancing and strengthening them to establish a powerful sense of place. This is essential to attracting and making viable TODs.

New civic plaza and park, downtown Westminster, Colorado.

BRINGING THE FOUR Ds TOGETHER

Transit-Oriented Development requires what might be thought of as creating a complex quartet in which the scores of the four instruments—Density, Diversity, Design, and Destination—must be interpreted individually and then sensitively conducted together to achieve harmony. Our efforts at composing TODs by addressing each of the four Ds results in projects that have overcome regulatory, political, and transactional challenges to transform station environments and neighborhoods. Our proactive attention to each of the four Ds is a significant factor in the success of these efforts.

ERIK J. AULESTIA

The DNA of Place

Form-Based Codes as Urban Design Vision

Great places, such as the boulevards of Paris, the residential green of a New England town, or the Mall in Washington, D.C., are easily recognized, capture the imagination, and are beloved by residents and visitors alike. Formed out of the marriage between buildings, streets, open spaces, and the natural environment, they are enlivened by the activities they sponsor.

Rendering of the Station Plaza, Wyandanch, Babylon, New York.

The creation of great places is one of our primary goals as urban designers. Realized by various professionals and owners across changing economies and over extended time frames, they require unique tools for their realization, one of the most effective of which is the form-based code.

THE DNA OF PLACE

In 1953 it was discovered that the vast complexity of all living organisms is contained in a small and simple set of instructions—DNA. Like an animal species, our favorite places are defined by a set of traits that establish their character; they have unique DNA. If we want to reproduce these places without designing every building, every street, and every public space, we can extract their DNA into a code of words and simple diagrams, and then use that code to create a new place that shares those characteristics. Just as DNA determines an animal form at conception, a form-based code can determine the physical form of a human settlement. A form-based code identifies a set of common "rules" for the formal components of the built environment. These may include building and open-space patterns, street types and their arrangement, building heights, spacing between buildings, building-to-street relationships, sidewalks, and open spaces, all codified at a scale that ranges from the individual block to the city.

THE PAST AND PRESENT OF FORM-BASED CODES

Form-based codes are not a new phenomenon. During Spain's colonization of the Americas, for instance, King Phillip II decreed that a regulation for the creation of colonies should be written, which became known as the Laws of the Indies. One of the most complete examples of a form-based code, the Laws realized innumerable towns and cities, including Quito, Ecuador (the first Unesco World Heritage site), where I was born. A set of formal instructions created to ensure that settlements on foreign lands were developed with a specific physical form that fulfilled their colonizing purpose, the Laws were unique in their specificity with regard to urban form. A sophisticated code, the Laws provided strict rules while also recognizing the need for variation to respond to climate and geography. Building setbacks, for instance, could be adjusted to provide more sunlight in cold climates or more shade in hot climates.

BELOW AND
BOTTOM
Before and after
site overviews
of Wyandanch,
Babylon, New York.

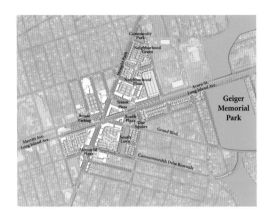

Open-space
diagram,
Wyandanch,
Babylon,
New York.

The rebirth of the use of form-based codes has come with the resurgence of interest in urban environments and the recognition that their DNA is profoundly different from that of the suburban landscapes that dominated development throughout most of the twentieth century. The principles of conventional suburban development have also become so ingrained in education, existing codes, and development circles that as a society we have had to re-learn the principles of sound urbanism and place making. Form-based codes have proven to be far superior to Euclidean zoning or less stringent design guidelines in providing a predictable and precise formal outcome. Jurisdictions recognize this fact and are scrambling to incorporate or create new form-based codes that will not only permit but also require urbane places. Developers, too, are interested in creating urbane neighborhoods, and, recognizing that they must respond to the realities of changing markets, they look to form-based codes as the regulating documents that both ensure implementation of the vision and provide for flexibility.

Excerpts from the
Wyandanch Form-
Based Code

RIGHT
Regulating Plan.

FAR RIGHT
Illustrative Plan.

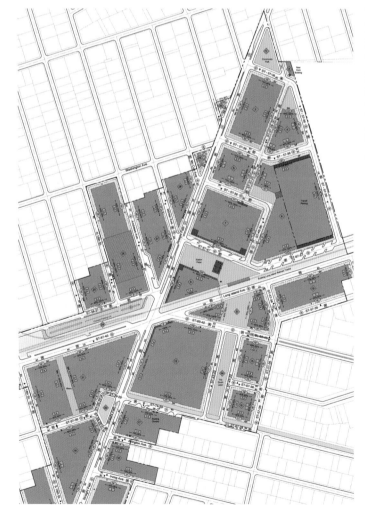

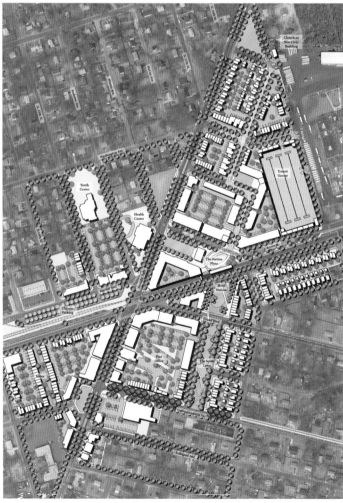

WHAT MAKES A GOOD FORM-BASED CODE?

Form-based codes are an integral part of our planning practice and have been at the core of many successful projects for both public municipalities and private developers. Built (or in process) projects realized through form-based codes include Downtown Wyandanch (pages 246–49) and King Farm (pages 260–63). Though there are common elements to all codes, it is critical to understand the unique parameters presented by clients, locations, politics, economics, density, duration, character, and vision. Codes must be tailored to the particulars of each project and fashioned to ensure implementation of the vision.

There are many technical and nuanced factors that go into a good form-based code, but common to all are four key factors:

- A specific and compelling vision

- An urban design *parti*

- A balance between sufficient specificity and flexibility

- An effective administration methodology

THE CHALLENGES FOR FORM-BASED CODES IN THE FUTURE

Over the past thirty-five years, many seminal neighborhoods have been created with the use of form-based codes, producing a much higher caliber of place. Municipalities, private developers, and urban designers have all become more sophisticated in applying them. Cities are seeking to create and adopt new form-based districts or entirely new form-based zoning ordinances, and developers are recognizing their value to facilitate entitlement approvals, as well as to ensure implementation over time. It is clear that form-based codes are here to stay, and it is precisely their growing acceptance and adoption that present challenges for the future.

The first challenge is one of ever-increasing geographic scale. Smaller sites have more predictable development types and shorter implementation time frames. As the size of an area to be coded increases, greater flexibility is needed to respond to different economic cycles, changing trends in building types, and changes in ownership. A regulating plan with rigid locational requirements for all streets, for instance, may become an impediment to

Master plan of
King Farm.

Rendering of the
new main street
in Wyandanch,
Babylon, New York.

development because it doesn't include provisions for changing building types and sizes. To avoid this inflexibility, we have had to come up with innovative tools. For example, we have developed a "provisional street" concept that, coupled with block standards, allows flexibility in the location of secondary streets while still maintaining the connectivity mandated in the regulating plan.

The second challenge is the need to incorporate existing neighborhoods into a form-based district. An individual jurisdiction may desire to create an entirely new zoning ordinance, but the political will, cost, time, and adoption risk typically make it unfeasible, and developing a new form-based district for every new neighborhood can be equally expensive and time consuming. As a result, we have come up with innovative processes to make incorporation of areas into form-based districts relatively easy and efficient, while ensuring a cohesive vision. For example, we recently developed a process that addresses this issue by linking comprehensive planning and owner/developer–initiated plans in a manner that allows incremental incorporation of neighborhoods and eventually the entire city into a form-based district, thereby replacing existing zoning ordinances over time.

The third challenge is juggling the complex interrelationships specific to the development of a given market and community: local development and construction economics, politics, administration expertise, and implementation time frame. We often have to walk a fine line between sufficient specificity to ensure implementation of the vision and sufficient flexibility to meet local conditions and changing needs. How we achieve that balance varies from place to place and project to project, and it can be effectively addressed only with a thorough understanding of the local parameters, interrelationships, and priorities.

CONCLUSION

The making of great places that will endure for generations and bring joy to people's lives is one of our central missions as urban designers. Walkable, environmentally sustainable, healthy, and beautiful places likewise help to

alleviate pressures on global resources that are the result of rapid urbanization. At Torti Gallas, we recognize and use form-based codes as the most
effective and predictable method of regulation that can deliver on the prom-
ise of a better world.

View of a
neighborhood
park in King
Farm, Rockville,
Maryland.

SIVA VENKATARAMANI

TransNational Urbanism

In the late 1990s we began to undertake commissions outside of the United States, first in Istanbul, Turkey, and subsequently in India, China, and the Middle East. These projects presented us with a new set of urban design and architectural challenges. Chief among them was the impact of rapid urbanization, which has taken hold in second- and third-tier cities such as Jaipur, India, and will soon be affecting large lower-income populations

Rendering of a courtyard house for Arabian Canal City, Dubai, United Arab Emirates.

whose lives are still closely tied to the daily rituals of traditional culture. We began a series of in-house conversations to define our approach to these challenges. In a seemingly counterintuitive move, we looked inward and formed a study group of people from our own diverse workforce, which includes representatives of more than twenty different countries. The members of the study group began with an almost academic analysis of the built environment in their native countries, identifying salient characteristics that could provide the foundation for our future work.

An early realization was the complexity of urban identity, reflecting the extremes in governance and cultural influence, as well as the long time frame, that have impacted urban form. The group distilled their findings into three dominant categories of urban forms: 1—a "traditional" landscape of indigenous, vernacular development often closely tied to religious beliefs and practices; 2—a "colonial" landscape of imported urban and architectural patterns

Neighborhood plan, Arabian Canal City, Dubai, United Arab Emirates.

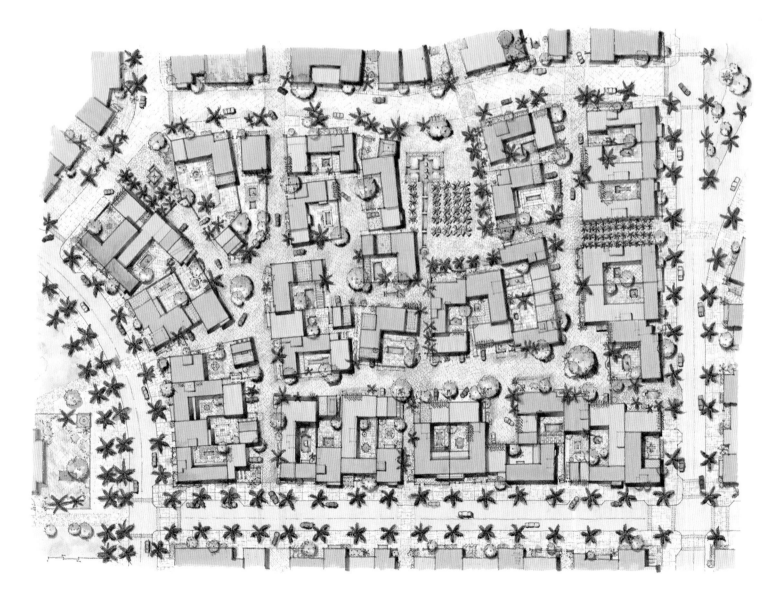

THE TNU TREE

REGIONAL TRANSECTS

COMPARISONS: SIMILARITIES/DIFFERENCES

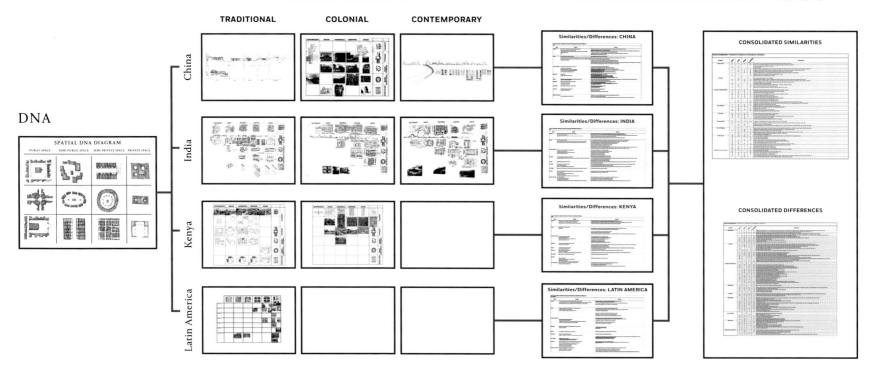

DNA

ABOVE

TransNational
Urbanism
Diagram.

RIGHT

Traditional
Transect: India.

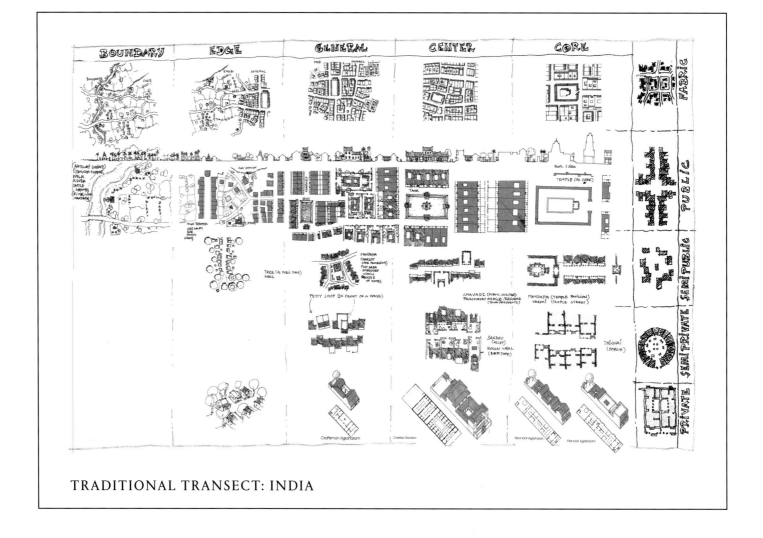

TRADITIONAL TRANSECT: INDIA

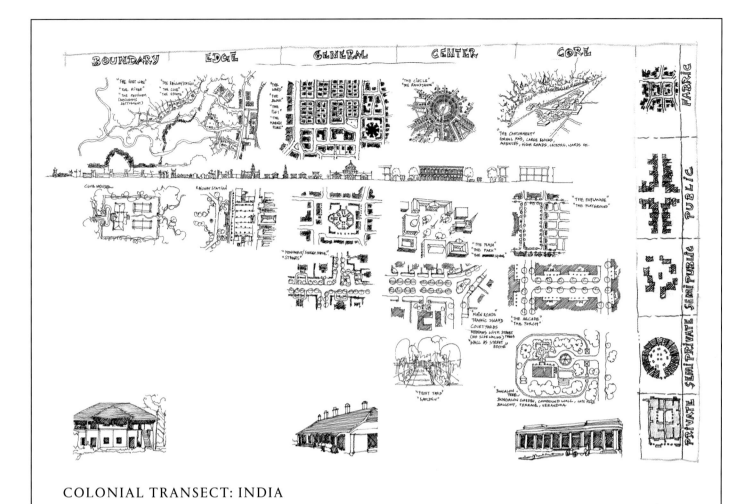

COLONIAL TRANSECT: INDIA

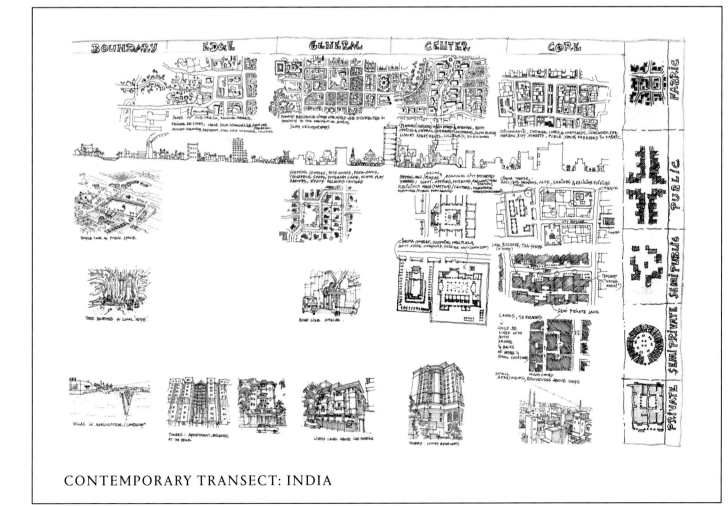

CONTEMPORARY TRANSECT: INDIA

View of the new
neighborhood,
Bahçeşehir,
Istanbul.

created by dominating foreign powers; and 3—a "contemporary" landscape of predominately Western development patterns. We tested these categories in the form of matrices that charted public and private components of the built environment, looking at their characteristics in settings from low-density rural areas to high-density urban centers. What these matrices revealed was the hybrid nature of urban form, suggesting an approach to identify specific characteristics of housing and urban patterns, the replication of which could extend and reinforce cultural identity.

We termed this approach TransNational Urbanism, meaning urbanism "beyond borders." It entails an analytical process to identify the core principles that comprise regional ideas of urban form, housing patterns, and place making. Housing, perhaps more than any other component of the built environment, is closely tied to the rituals of daily life and is thus both the repository and the perpetuator of culture. Through the use of Trans-National Urbanism, our goal is to prevent the dilution of culture, which is so often the result of rapid urbanization, replacing it with new developments that perpetuate and enhance cultural norms.

We have applied this approach to our growing body of international work. Our first project, for Bahçeşehir, Turkey (pages 268–71), was inspired by traditional Turkish housing and a key aspect of its urbanism—the way in which street and housing patterns are formed by the region's steep topography and the geography of the Bosphorus. Our many projects in the Mideast, such as the Arabian Canal City neighborhood (pages 146–49), Aflaj Al Foah (pages 278–81), and Umm Al Quwain (pages 282–85), were influenced by traditions of Islamic life, including strict notions of privacy, the separation of the male and family spheres, and the importance of the neighborhood unit. Their "cracked mud" pattern of organic-shaped blocks arranged in superblock configurations creates the limited internal street views and semi-public realm that reinforces the neighborhood unit. Courtyard houses provide strict spatial separation between public and private, and male and family spheres, as well as the closed internal views that reinforce a sense of privacy and the integrity of the family unit. In the burgeoning city of Bengaluru,

India, our Devanhalli project (pages 150–53) provides new middle-income housing in villas, inspired in part by British Colonial types, that are laid out according to the traditional Hindu planning principle known as *vastu*, a system of placement and orientation that works on a nine-square grid. Drawing on local and regional traditions, these projects are our first attempts to marry contemporary development with the architecture and urbanism that supports cultural norms.

CONCLUSION

As the demand for new housing increases all over the world, the pressures of cultural homogenization are also increasing. Our aim, using TransNational Urbanism, is to explore ways in which contemporary delivery systems can simultaneously support and enhance cultural identity through housing types and urban patterns that incorporate but do not mimic the cultural DNA, preserving identity.

Capper/Carrollsburg

WASHINGTON, D.C.

A former public-housing development that accommodated 707 families in barracks-style garden apartments, Capper/Carrollsburg is located in Southeast D.C., blocks away from the western banks of the Anacostia River. Long known as Washington's "second river" in relation to the better-known Potomac, the Anacostia—initially the commercial lifeline of the city—has been compromised by decades of manufacturing and shipbuilding at the Navy Yard, fill operations along its banks, and regional highway programs. Many of the adjacent neighborhoods such as Capper/Carrollsburg were the primary targets of 1960s-era urban-renewal actions, resulting in a concentration of public housing along the river and a legacy of social disruption that lives on to this day.

By the year 2000, the river was heavily polluted, its banks lined with federally controlled military bases, chronically underfunded and underdeveloped parklands, and struggling neighborhoods. It divided the District, both

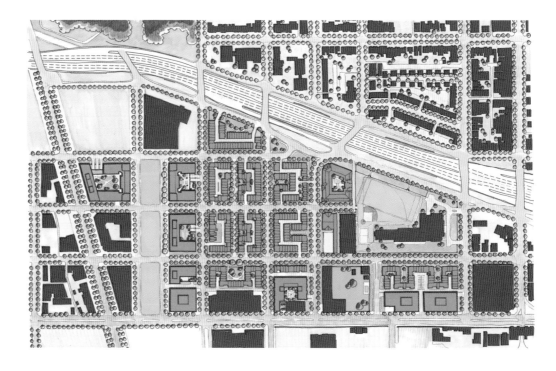

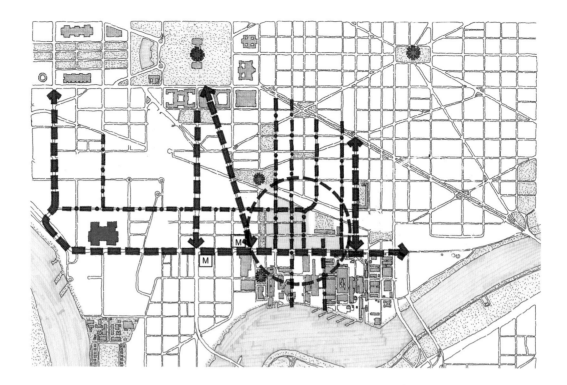

Urban design diagram.

View of 3rd Street SE, looking north.

literally and symbolically, between the more prosperous and largely white neighborhoods on the west and the predominately African American communities on the east, some of which, like Capper/Carrollsburg, were among the poorest in the city. When Anthony Williams was elected mayor in the early 2000s, he made revitalizing the river and its abutting neighborhoods a central part of his agenda. He saw its revitalization as a way to unite the city. "I wanted to use the river to broaden the view of what the city is, with a strategy that brings everybody together," Williams explained.

The Mayor's initiative turned a spotlight on Capper/Carrollsburg, and the District of Columbia Housing Authority (DCHA) followed suit, beginning the outreach and planning processes that launched the neighborhood's revitalization and immediately placing it on the list of projects to pursue for HUD's HOPE VI funding. We were hired as part of the revitalization team, which was led by a joint venture between Urban Atlantic, a local developer, and Forest City Enterprises, to pursue the HOPE VI grant and rebuild the neighborhood. We began by conducting a charrette for both the site and several other DCHA communities in the vicinity. Despite its state of disrepair, Capper/Carrollsburg had tremendous advantages: walking distance from Capitol Hill and its amenities, a recently opened Metrorail station, proximity to the river, and, like many public-housing communities, a long-time resident population with a powerful and interconnected web of relationships. The residents formed a potent and capable leadership team who successfully advocated for a one-for-one replacement of public-housing units as a condition of revitalization, a precedent-setting first in the city.

Part of L'Enfant's original grid of streets, the neighborhood possessed one of the "reservations," or large open spaces, that L'Enfant had designed for public and communal uses. At the time of our charrette, this space was a sea of pavement being used as a temporary parking lot for school buses. The L'Enfant plan gave the site two of its greatest neighborhood-making features: street continuity and a regionally scaled open space. The primary focus of our master plan was to realize their potential. We replaced the garden apartment superblocks with the finer block dimensions, narrow lotting, and continuous street frontage of rowhouses, accommodating the family portion of the mixed-income program in a variety of low-rise types and integrating our streetscapes with those of Capitol Hill. Developed by EYA, a local housing developer, the low-rise blocks had both the tightest urbanism and the most cheek-by-jowl mix of workforce, public-housing, and market-rate units we had ever achieved. A new community center provided a neighborhood focus and new amenities. Before the revitalization, the edge of Near Southeast Washington ended at the elevated highway that separated Capper/Carrollsburg from Capitol Hill to the north. The street and sidewalk continuity that the revitalization created moved the quadrant's edge to its proper location—the banks of the Anacostia River—and in so doing, reconnected the city with the river.

View of 3rd Street
SE, looking south.

Winter in Canal
Park, Washington,
D.C.

View of the Yards Park along the Anacostia River.

View of a weekend festival at the Yards Park.

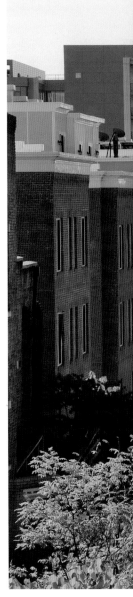

Our master plan envisioned the L'Enfant reservation as a new park, providing benefits for neighborhood residents and the broader Southeast community. We specified framing the park with high and mid-rise apartment buildings that would match the scale of adjacent structures along the park and M Street, including the new headquarters of the Department of Transportation, designed by Michael Graves. This new housing will not only enclose the park but also provide a great diversity of low, moderate, and market-rate units. A local developer, WC Smith, perceived the park's importance and formed a non-profit that, along with other city funds, sponsored a competition for the park's design. Named Canal Park, it was designed by David Rubin of OLIN Studios and evokes the canal that was once located on the site through a series of water features, including an ice-skating rink and a linear rain garden, all supported by an underground system that recycles 95 percent of the area's storm water. The sight of skaters on the rink summons up images of skaters on the canal in the nineteenth century, reconnecting the park with the past and creating a new image for the future.

An integral part of the Anacostia revitalization, Capper/Carrollsburg was a linchpin, galvanizing the area's rebirth, contributing to the health of the Anacostia, and restoring the city's connection to the river. Recently rebranded the Capitol Riverfront, the area is now a thriving community of almost 5,000 residents, the workplace of 32,000 daytime employees, the location of a new ballpark and three new public parks, and an exploding restaurant scene, all amounting to, in the words of Andrew Altman, a former director of the District's Office of Planning, "one of the most remarkable urban transformations in the United States."

View of 4th Street
SE, looking
south toward the
Anacostia River.

Camana Bay

GRAND CAYMAN ISLAND

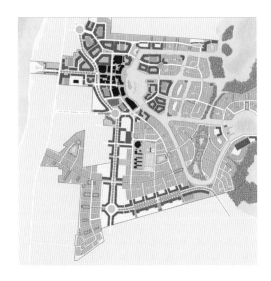

TOP

Master plan,
by Duany Plater-
Zyberk.

ABOVE

Plan of the canal
neighborhood.

A new downtown is emerging on Grand Cayman Island. The vision of Ken Dart, owner of Dart Realty, it stretches from the Caribbean Sea to West Bay. Though the port of historic Georgetown is the lifeblood of the island, and tourism reigns supreme, the visitors who disembark from the many cruise ships at anchor paralyze downtown and make it difficult for the financial service industry and the legal industry to function. Camana Bay was envisioned to provide an alternative, balanced lifestyle for Caymanians, a place where they can live, work, shop, play, learn, and recreate.

Moore Ruble Yudell and OLIN Studios developed the master plan for the harbor; subsequently, Duany Plater-Zyberk developed a master plan for the 650-acre site. These initial phases are characterized by lush landscapes and courtyards on a par with the best in the world. We were more recently engaged to create a new town center master plan for the remaining 80 percent of the downtown area that doubles the planned density and seeks to create a jobs/housing balance while retaining the special character that has come to define Camana Bay. A set of principles has been developed to ensure that future growth is consistent with the character of Camana Bay, including courtyard and street horizontal-to-vertical proportion rules, massing and tall building placement rules, building coverage rules, open-space ratios, and so forth. In a radical departure from the original plan, an elevated deck/plane is proposed that will span across Esterly Tibbetts Highway and West Bay Road, creating a continuous elevated passage linking the existing harbor to Seven Mile Beach along the western side of the island. This will allow pedestrians and cars to reach the beach without having to contend with crossing the island's two main north–south roads. One of the main features is a new green space that extends from the beach midway to the harbor, thereby bringing a sense of the beach into the heart of the town center.

We were subsequently commissioned to design two buildings in the original town center: a mixed-use office building and a condominium building.

ABOVE

Rendering of the promenade and neighborhood green along the canal.

RIGHT

Aerial view of the town center and resort village.

BELOW

Section from Seven Mile Beach (left) to the harbor (right).

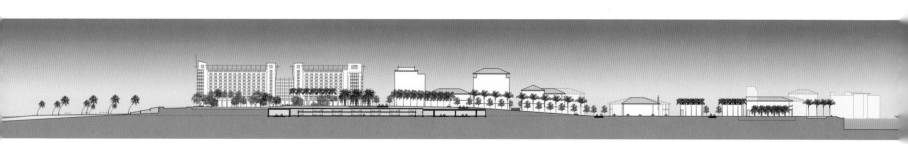

ALTERNATIVE CONCEPT DIAGRAM

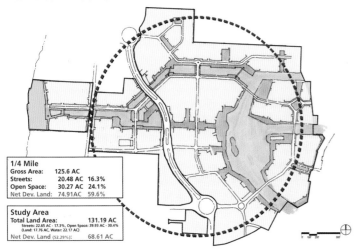

1/4 Mile	
Gross Area:	125.6 AC
Streets:	20.48 AC 16.3%
Open Space:	30.27 AC 24.1%
Net Dev. Land:	74.91AC 59.6%

Study Area	
Total Land Area:	131.19 AC
Streets: 22.65 AC - 17.3%, Open Space: 39.93 AC - 30.4%	
(Land: 17.76 AC, Water: 22.17 AC)	
Net Dev. Land (52.29%):	68.61 AC

TOP
Rendering of the
new housing along
the canal.

ABOVE
Downtown master
plan diagram.

BELOW
Elevation of the
condominium
buildings.

OPPOSITE
Renderings of
the diverse house
types in the canal
neighborhood.

TOP ROW LEFT
Brown Design
Studio

TOP ROW RIGHT
Moser Design
Group

SECOND ROW LEFT
Martinez & Alvarez
Architects

SECOND ROW RIGHT
Starr Sanford
Design

THIRD ROW LEFT
Starr Sanford
Design

THIRD ROW RIGHT
Torti Gallas +
Partners

BOTTOM ROW LEFT
Torti Gallas +
Partners

BOTTOM ROW RIGHT
Martinez & Alvarez
Architects

The office building anchors the north end of the harbor and the Promenade, which is the town center's gathering place. The defining features of this building are a distinctive tower that punctuates the corner and unique façade strategies for each face, tailored to the specific sun loads. They include a large aluminum brise-soleil facing south and a large coffered grid with deep inset windows facing east. The 156-unit condominium building is situated on a navigable canal and acts as a transition between office buildings and the adjacent residential neighborhood. One of the key design strategies was to divide the building into three-, four-, and five-story portions that act as transitions in scale and form a picturesque, human-scaled composition. The other key strategy was to identify and use Grand Cayman and Caribbean vernacular architectural features that also respond to the unique climate. Deep overhangs offer shade and protection from rain, punched windows provide shaded interiors, light colors reflect heat, and projecting balconies and terraces create outdoor living space.

We were also responsible for the design of the first residential neighborhood situated along a navigable canal. Teamed with Michael Watkins, the project's town architect, we created a neighborhood master plan with a public boardwalk along the canal that links to the town center, and a series of green spaces perpendicular to the canal that maximize visibility of and public access to the water. Once the plan was completed, we were tasked with leading an architectural design charrette for the single-family, courtyard, townhouse, and duplex homes. In addition to us, the designers of the homes included Starr Sanford Design Associates, Martinez & Alvarez Architects, Brown Design Studio, and Moser Design Group. All of the houses have been designed, and the power of the team's diversity is evident in the designs.

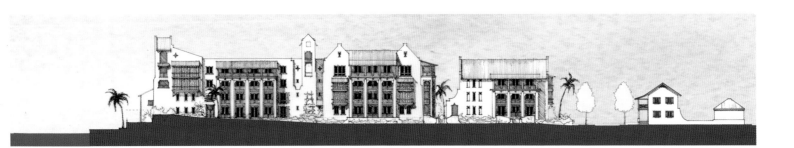

The Parks
at Walter Reed

WASHINGTON, D.C.

As the U.S. Army's hospital from 1909 to 2011, Walter Reed played a unique role in United States history and has a special place in people's hearts and minds, for both the medical care received and the physical character of the campus. Following the closure of the campus, the District developed the Small Area Plan and subsequently issued a Request for Proposals for a master developer. As part of the developer's team, Torti Gallas + Partners is the master planner/urban designer for the newly named Parks at Walter Reed and the architect for the first mixed-use building and the town center.

The Parks at Walter Reed is conceived as a healthy, mixed-use, sustainable community. Program elements include office and retail space; a hotel; a grocery; a brewery; a genomics research center; a living science center; facilities for pharmacological research, technological research, and clinical care; a conference center; a charter school; a museum; an arts district; for-sale residential, rental residential, senior, affordable, veterans, and artist housing; a hostel; historic trails; and a community pool. Our urban design began with answering the question, "What is the cohesive design philosophy that not only allows for the preservation and adaptive re-use of historic buildings but also accommodates new buildings and new uses in a harmonious manner that respects the history, character, and traditions of the site?" The character-defining elements included: the Great Lawn, historic landscapes, the topography, Building 1, Delano Hall, a unified campus, an architectural heritage of Georgian and Classical Revival buildings, key axes and vistas, and campus organizing principles. To derive campus-wide patterns and design principles, we first carefully analyzed the development of the campus, the existing site and landscape, the building styles, and existing building massing. These historic patterns and principles formed the foundation of our guidelines for new buildings and landscapes that will honor the significance

of Walter Reed, preserve the campus character, integrate the campus with the surrounding neighborhoods, and preserve and celebrate historically significant buildings. These guidelines will ensure the design of new buildings that are sensitive to historic buildings, a public realm sensitive to the historic landscape, and a healthy and highly sustainable community that is net positive/carbon neutral by 2040.

Rendering of a new park fronting a historic building.

ABOVE

Rendering of the
Arts Park.

RIGHT

Rendering of the
townhouses along
the northern edge
of the site.

BELOW LEFT

Master plan.

BELOW RIGHT

Landscape plan, by
Michael Vergason.

ABOVE

Rendering of the
town center.

OVERLEAF

Aerial rendering,
looking southwest.

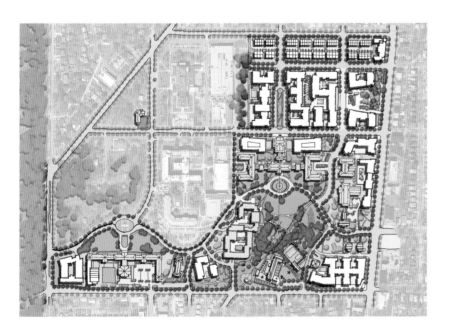

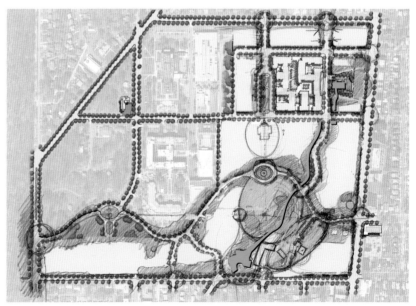

National Cathedral Close Master Plan

WASHINGTON, D.C.

Situated on a 59-acre site atop Mount St. Albans, one of the plateaus that surround the Potomac River basin and the monumental core of Washington, D.C., the National Cathedral Close was originally laid out by Frederick Law Olmsted Jr. Home to the Protestant Episcopal Cathedral Foundation and Washington National Cathedral, it is also the site of a number of related institutions, including three schools. Olmsted's master plan incorporated traditional aspects of a cathedral close, primarily a picturesque assemblage of Gothic buildings and a pastoral setting formed from the site's natural features.

Pressures for growth and concerns over maintaining the character of the close prompted the foundation to launch a master planning effort. Teamed with Michael Vergason Landscape Architects, we worked to develop the plan with representatives of the close's institutions, beginning with an analysis of Olmsted's plan, which provided inspiration throughout. Key features of the master plan included:

- Maintaining the pastoral character of the close and common identity of the foundation community

- Facilitating the growth and ongoing health of all close institutions through new programs and placing a limit on new construction as established by the Olmsted plan

- Conceiving new construction as extensions of the formal concepts of Olmsted's plan

- Strengthening the image of the close as a walking environment by establishing a sacred precinct around the cathedral

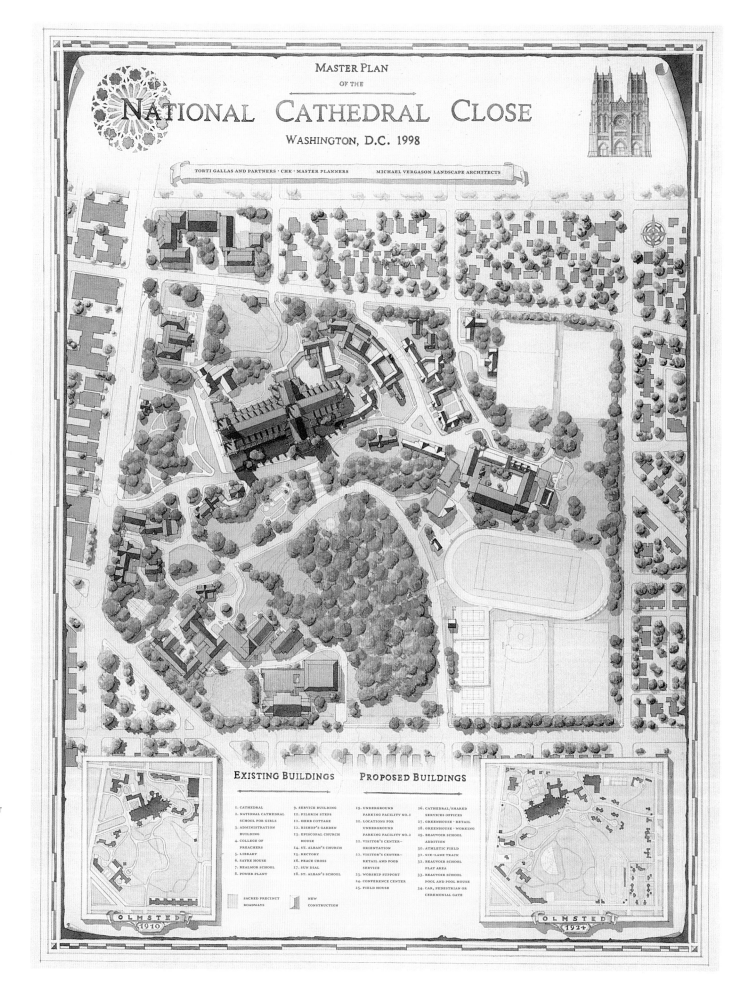

MASTER PLAN
OF THE
NATIONAL CATHEDRAL CLOSE
WASHINGTON, D.C. 1998

TORTI GALLAS AND PARTNERS · CHK · MASTER PLANNERS   MICHAEL VERGASON LANDSCAPE ARCHITECTS

EXISTING BUILDINGS   PROPOSED BUILDINGS

1. CATHEDRAL
2. NATIONAL CATHEDRAL
   SCHOOL FOR GIRLS
3. ADMINISTRATION
   BUILDING
4. COLLEGE OF
   PREACHERS
5. LIBRARY
6. SAYRE HOUSE
7. BEALMOR SCHOOL
8. POWER PLANT

9. SERVICE BUILDING
10. PILGRIM STEPS
11. HERB COTTAGE
12. BISHOP'S GARDEN
13. EPISCOPAL CHURCH
    HOUSE
14. ST. ALBAN'S CHURCH
15. RECTORY
16. PEACE CROSS
17. SUN DIAL
18. ST. ALBAN'S SCHOOL

19. UNDERGROUND
    PARKING FACILITY NO.1
20. LOCATIONS FOR
    UNDERGROUND
    PARKING FACILITY NO.2
21. VISITOR'S CENTER—
    ORIENTATION
22. VISITOR'S CENTER—
    RETAIL AND FOOD
    SERVICE
23. WORSHIP SUPPORT
24. CONFERENCE CENTER
25. FIELD HOUSE

26. CATHEDRAL/SHARED
    SERVICES OFFICES
27. GREENHOUSE · RETAIL
28. GREENHOUSE · WORKING
29. BEAUVOIR SCHOOL
    ADDITION
30. ATHLETIC FIELD
31. SIX-LANE TRACK
32. BEAUVOIR SCHOOL
    PLAY AREA
33. BEAUVOIR SCHOOL
    POOL AND POOL HOUSE
34. CAR, PEDESTRIAN OR
    CEREMONIAL GATE

SACRED PRECINCT
ROADWAYS

NEW
CONSTRUCTION

OLMSTED 1910

OLMSTED 1924

OPPOSITE TOP LEFT
View of the new
athletic fields with
the underground
field house on the
left.

OPPOSITE TOP RIGHT
View of the above-
grade portions
of the new field
house.

OPPOSITE BOTTOM
Rendering of the
apse end of the
cathedral.

- Addressing issues of bus and car circulation, as well as parking, through roadway and drop-off improvements and new underground parking garages

- Preserving key natural features, including the Olmsted Woods and making the close a model of ecological health

Since the adoption of the master plan in 1998, the majority of the building programs proposed in the plan, including a field house, reconfigured athletic fields, and an underground parking garage, have all been completed as envisioned in the plan.

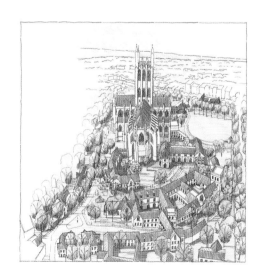

Monroe Street Market

WASHINGTON, D.C.

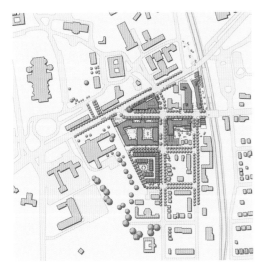

TOP
Neighborhood
retail plan.

ABOVE
Neighborhood
residential plan.

In an unusual strategy in the early 2000s, the Catholic University of America decided to improve their campus by shrinking its footprint, demolishing several dormitories built outside its traditional boundary on Michigan Avenue, and concentrating all residence halls on the main campus. The university leveraged the vacated land as a new campus asset and financial resource, soliciting ideas, future revenues, and a private development partner through a competition, which our team won.

We saw the site, located at the intersection of Michigan Avenue and Monroe Street and a short walk from a Metrorail stop, as ideally positioned for the creation of a new mixed-use neighborhood that could serve both the university and the surrounding Brookland community. We anchored the new "town-and-gown" district on Monroe Street, which we recast as a mixed-use main street, lining its three-block length with continuous ground-floor retail. A checkerboard massing of varied building heights and open-air courtyards above street level diversified the streetscape and residential program, which included units for students, young professionals, and empty nesters. All of the Monroe Street buildings were cast in a single, Forest Hills–inspired picturesque style, referencing but not imitating the Romanesque and Gothic structures of the campus. Picking up cues from campus features, we developed the frontage along Michigan Avenue with two towers and an urban plaza.

The portion of the site nearest the Metrorail was designed by Maurice Walters Architect as an art district in response to the burgeoning arts community inhabiting the small-scale industrial buildings along the Metrorail tracks. Two facing buildings of residential units above ground-floor artist studios formed a pedestrian street, or Arts Walk, culminating in an urban plaza that connected it to the Metrorail stop. The buildings' articulation as industrial warehouses inspired John Torti to suggest painting the Metro-facing façade with a giant Brookland sign, which has since become a neighborhood icon.

ABOVE
View from the
Metrorail station.

RIGHT
View along
Michigan Avenue
NE, looking west.

FAR RIGHT
View along Monroe
Street NE, looking
west.

Crystal City
Master Plan

Catalysts for
Transformation

ARLINGTON, VIRGINIA

ABOVE LEFT
Figure ground,
before.

ABOVE RIGHT
Figure ground,
after.

RIGHT
Rendering of the
master plan vision
of Crystal City at
buildout.

Initially developed in the early 1970s, the 260-acre portion of Arlington County known as Crystal City is characterized by superblocks, an automobile-oriented street network, tower-in–the-park building placement, and pedestrian activity relegated to an underground retail mall. Though the area has grown to include 25 million square feet of high-rise, mixed-use development, it reflects the anti-urbanist mindset of the modernist era, which failed to appreciate the value of an active street life and focused primarily on the convenience of automobile movement. The resulting placelessness is palpable.

The loss of 4 million square feet of office-space leases, resulting from decisions made by the Commission on Base Realignment and Closure (BRAC), prompted the county to initiate the area's transformation with the goal of reinvigorating it and simultaneously correcting the mistakes of the past. As it was already heavily built out, this presented a unique challenge.

Building on the existing mix of uses, the relative density, and the extensive transportation systems already in place, the plan we developed with the county and in an extensive outreach process involving key public agencies, private landowners, and county residents focuses future development on creating great streets and open spaces, and a true sense of place with an active public realm. It proposes realignment of streets to improve the scale of blocks, a substantial increase in street-front retail to activate the pedestrian experience, and the reconfiguration of an elevated, six-lane, limited-access arterial highway into an urban boulevard flanked by pedestrian-friendly sidewalks fronted with buildings. The network of well-defined public open spaces are

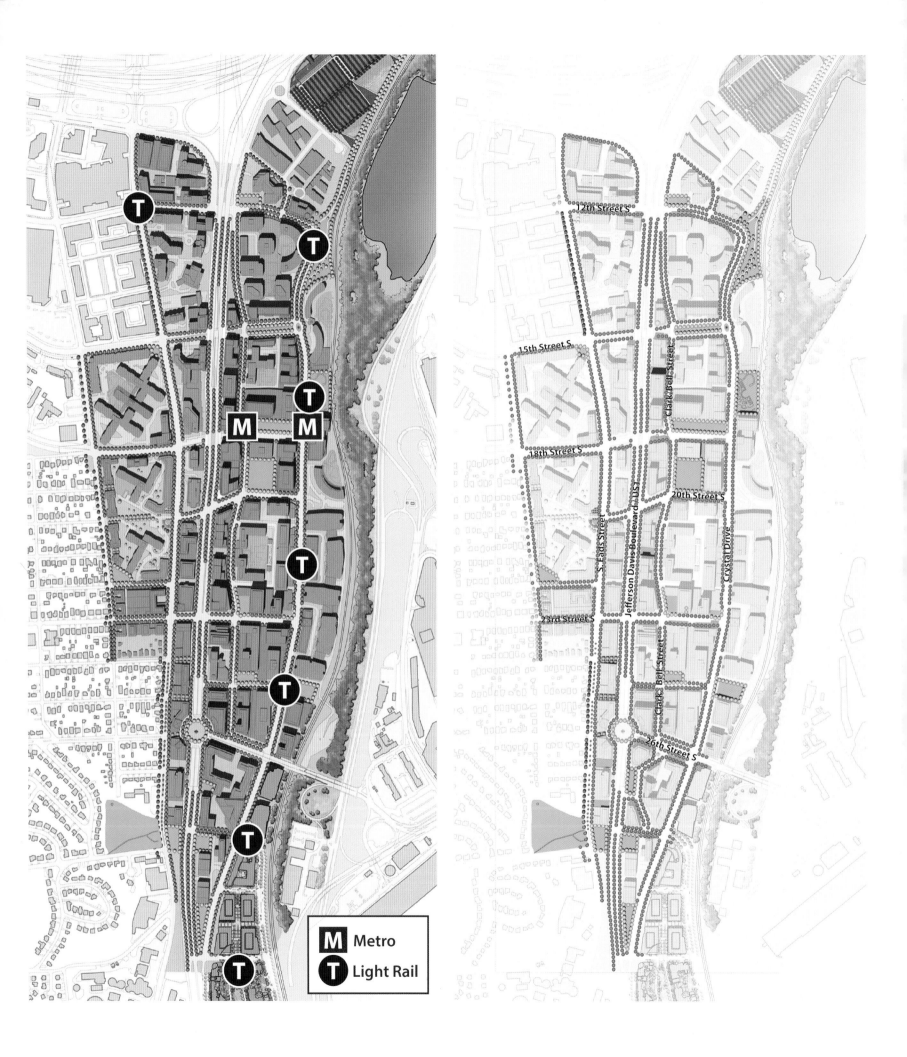

	Metro
M	
T	Light Rail

12th Street S

15th Street S

Clark Bell Street

18th Street S

20th Street S

S. Eads Street

Jefferson Davis Boulevard/US1

Crystal Drive

23rd Street S

Clark Bell Street

26th Street S

now partially framed by existing buildings. The plan envisions new buildings designed to fill in the gaps. Form-based building standards will ensure not only that each of these spaces will enjoy ample sunlight but also that that the ground plane along the street will support and encourage pedestrian activity.

OPPOSITE LEFT
Illustrative plan.

OPPOSITE RIGHT
Open-space
diagram.

ABOVE
Rendering of the
transformation
of Route 1 into a
boulevard.

MacArthur Park Apartments

LOS ANGELES, CALIFORNIA

BELOW
View of Phase 1
from the Metro
plaza (future site
of Phase 2).

Located in one of the densest neighborhoods in Los Angeles, this mixed-use project sits on adjoining blocks above an existing Metro station and tunnel, which are within a mere nine feet of the surface. The program requirements for the project included two seemingly conflicting demands: 1—to achieve a level of density appropriate to high-quality transit (at least 60 dwelling units per acre); and 2—to ensure that every family has the sense of "ownership" that comes from having one's own front door. We were able to meet both demands by marrying a mix of three-story townhomes and various types of walk-up units with the California Courtyard building type and by placing that arrangement above the parking podium.

This two-phased ensemble of buildings provides for a pedestrian sequence that begins from the moment one emerges from the Metro, facing iconic, much-loved MacArthur Park with its central lake. Configured to frame the Metro portal, Phase 2 is an arrival plaza lined with retail and community spaces and affording open views of the park. Extending east from this plaza is a pedestrian promenade directly on axis with the base of a grand staircase that leads to the residential courtyards of Phase 1. Though the courtyards are raised to accommodate the requirement to provide parking above the Metro, they create a communal space similar in character to that of Southern California Courtyard housing types. Each of the ninety affordable apartment units in Phase 1 has a direct connection to one of the courtyards, which facilitate natural breezes that contribute to the units' livability during the summer months.

More than just a circulation device, the grand staircase continues the pedestrian sequence that began at the Metro portal. A mirador, or lookout, at the top offers a sweeping view of that sequence and the park and lake beyond.

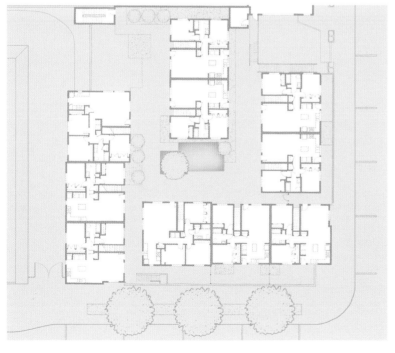

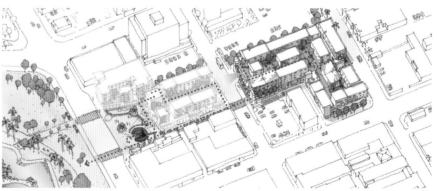

<table>
<tr><td>LEFT</td><td>TOP</td><td>ABOVE</td></tr>
<tr><td>Typical residential floor plan.</td><td>View from MacArthur Park.</td><td>Diagram of the pedestrian sequence.</td></tr>
</table>

Coast Highway Vision Plan

OCEANSIDE, CALIFORNIA

Rendering
of the area's
transformation.

Bathed in Southern California sunshine, the city of Oceanside has the makings of a great seaside destination but suffers from an ailing backbone—Coast Highway, the city's primary corridor. This three-mile thoroughfare has been plagued by lower property values than those in nearby communities and a ho-hum tourist infrastructure, so the city decided to revive it and take charge of its economic future, transforming a 485-acre area of the city in the process.

Reconfiguring an auto-oriented, underperforming thoroughfare into a lushly landscaped street with a series of distinct neighborhood centers, our plan envisions new transportation choices, a slimmed-down roadway, revitalized stream valleys, public art, reformulated urban design standards, and thoughtfully crafted policy initiatives and economic incentives, all with the aim of:

- Redefining the corridor as a place rather than a pass-through

- Reconfiguring the roadway as a shared space for all users, not only cars

- Incentivizing economic activity through a set of catalytic policy initiatives to attract private investment in key areas

- Maintaining regulatory flexibility to accommodate the community's emerging needs and safeguard the future prosperity of the reinvented corridor

- Capitalizing on proximity to water, including the Pacific Ocean, San Luis Rey River, Oceanside Harbor, and Loma Alta Creek to make great public spaces

- Linking high-quality urban design to synergistic land uses with realistic policy action items and an easy-to-read, aesthetically pleasing, and community-friendly Design Guide

The plan offers the city a step-by-step implementation strategy that translates all these concepts into feasible action items. It encourages the private sector to partner with the city by offering a set of regulatory and economic incentives that includes: programs for a robust mix of uses at five catalytic sites, reformed parking regulations, expedited permitting for development in key areas, and transferable development rights for idiosyncratic streetscapes.

ABOVE
View from Oceanside Harbor.

BELOW
Portion of the master plan.

Downtown Wyandanch
Master Plan

TOWN OF BABYLON, NEW YORK

The Downtown Wyandanch Master Plan acts as a catalyst to transform one of the poorest communities on Long Island into a mixed-use, transit-oriented development that is destined to become the new heart and gathering place for the community. Wyandanch's redevelopment has been a thirteen-year endeavor initiated by a dedicated public servant, Supervisor Steve Bellone, and countless other professionals. Having laid the groundwork for the revitalization, the Town of Babylon engaged us to lead a team of landscape architects, economists, civil engineers, cost estimators, a zoning attorney, public outreach specialists, and transportation planners. We were tasked with incorporating the vision of everyone on the team into a realizable plan that could easily be implemented by the private development community. We developed a new form-based district and code, including an architecture design code, to ensure realization of the vision, and we are currently overseeing its implementation in our capacity as town architect.

The fundamental element of the plan is a fixed framework of streets and open spaces that creates flexible blocks that can be "loaded" with structured parking or without and can accommodate various building types with the continuous building frontage that defines the public realm. The framework

Proposed streetscape
revisions.

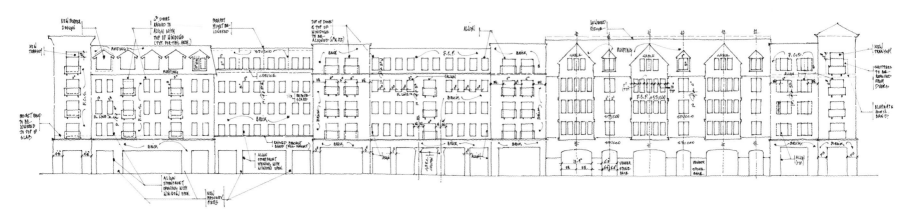

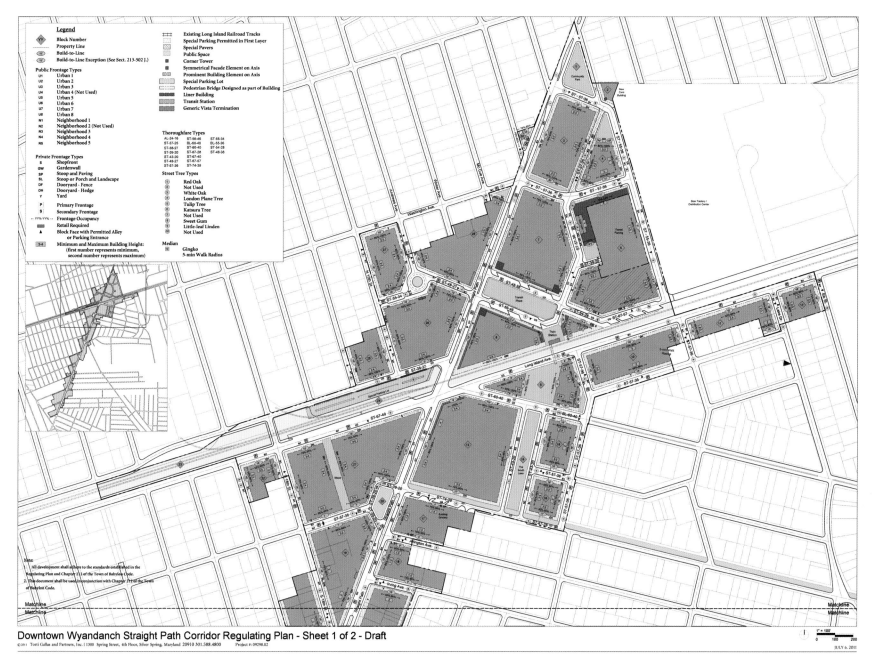

Downtown Wyandanch Straight Path Corridor Regulating Plan - Sheet 1 of 2 - Draft

© 2011 Torti Gallas and Partners, Inc. | 1300 Spring Street, 4th Floor, Silver Spring, Maryland 20910 301.588.4800   Project #: 09298.02

JULY 6, 2011

TOWN OF BABYLON, NY
TORTI GALLAS AND PARTNERS, INC.

WYANDANCH TRANSIT ORIENTED DEVELOPMENT

ABOVE	BELOW
Regulating plan from the form-based code.	Initial streetscape design, by BHC Architects.

TOP LEFT
Site overview,
before.

ABOVE LEFT
Site overview,
after.

ABOVE RIGHT
Rendering of the
Station Plaza.

RIGHT
Rendering of the
Station Plaza in
the winter.

has the train station at its center, from which emanates a series of public open spaces, including a new transit plaza with an outdoor performance space at the station, a linear residential green to the south of the tracks, and a skating rink to the west. To the north, a sequence leads to a new transit garage and square and culminates, via a cobbled residential street, in a civic building and a park. Along this corridor, a series of mixed-use nodes are planned, and new policies have been implemented that limit commercial uses to the nodes, thereby creating healthier and more vibrant retail destinations.

Rendering of the Station Plaza in the summer.

Santa Monica Downtown Community Plan

CITY OF SANTA MONICA, CALIFORNIA

ABOVE
Rendering
illustrating
the "signature
sidewalk" concept
for Wilshire
Boulevard.

RIGHT
TIM® rendering
of the Downtown
Plan with full
buildout.

Anticipating the arrival of the Exposition Line, which will provide a rail connection from downtown Los Angeles to the Pacific Ocean for the first time since 1953, the Downtown Plan will guide the next phase of the pedestrian-oriented evolution of this beachfront city. The plan encompasses roughly forty city blocks, six of which front the iconic Third Street Promenade, the vitality and pedestrian scale of which will be extended to the east and west.

Recognizing that no matter how one arrives in the downtown area, sooner or later everyone becomes a pedestrian, the plan lavishes attention on the public realm through streetscape improvements and roadway reconfigurations to prioritize pedestrian comfort, utility, and safety, as well as multimodal accessibility. Both by planning for a range of public spaces of varying scale and by treating the street network as the downtown's greatest public space, the plan offers an immersive pedestrian experience. "Signature sidewalks" are strategically incorporated throughout the plan area, created by enhanced building setbacks or by narrowing roadways, depending on the opportunities presented. Using Town Information Modeling, we tested various land use and development alternatives to arrive at design standards that are both predictable and flexible enough to promote creative and elegant buildings and public spaces. The standards we came up with focus on the design of the sidewalks and adjacent building façades to ensure human-scale, attractive, and inviting frontages. Although focused on the pedestrian, the plan provides strategic parking enhancements, aimed primarily at using existing parking assets more efficiently, and also proposes short- and long-term actions to increase the overall capacity of the circulation network, including an enhanced bicycle network and new street connections over the freeway. Incentives for desperately needed affordable housing and a greater range of cultural and arts amenities also feature prominently in the plan.

View of Lincoln Boulevard, existing conditions.

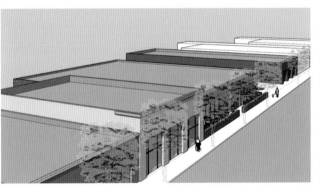

Typical existing sidewalk condition along Lincoln Boulevard.

Photomontage of Lincoln Boulevard, with expanded sidewalk after redevelopment.

Proposed expanded sidewalk after redevelopment.

Downtown Westminster

WESTMINSTER, COLORADO

The location of our downtown Westminster project is the 105-acre site of the former Westminster Mall, a once bustling, enclosed shopping center that until the early 2000s served as the social heart of the suburban municipality, situated midway between Denver and Boulder, Colorado. With the mall's decline and eventual demolition, save for two anchor stores, the city's political leadership re-envisioned the site as an authentic urban center, capitalizing on its proximity to a future commuter rail station and one of the busiest BRT stations in the region.

We designed our Downtown Westminster Specific Plan to embody that vision and create a vibrant downtown to replace the surface parking lots that once surrounded the mall. Developing a new street and block network, we aimed to reconnect the site physically and, by extension, socially and culturally to the surrounding community and the larger regional landscape. Our design tactics included:

- Extending Westminster Boulevard through the site as a new "main street" to a terminus at the future rail station

- Creating a new street grid oriented toward iconic views of Longs Peak to the northwest and Mount Evans to the southwest

- Repurposing an existing irrigation channel as the centerpiece of a new linear park

Master plan.

Rendering of the
new main street.

- Repairing connections at the perimeter to create a larger street network, influencing areas beyond the site and connecting to regional transportation corridors, including bike trails, BRT, and the future rail station

- Creating a public realm with a variety of open spaces for public interaction, spontaneous gathering, community-wide events, and locations for future civic buildings, to realize the site as a center for public life and cultural activity, one of the most important attributes of an authentic downtown

ABOVE

Aerial rendering of the new downtown, looking west toward the Front Range.

RIGHT

Rendering of a new mixed-use street.

Aerial rendering of
the new civic plaza
and park.

New Wyvernwood
Master Plan

LOS ANGELES, CALIFORNIA

Rendering of the
new central park,
with an arroyo for
bioretention.

Rendering of a new
mixed-use street.

Originally designed in the idiom of the Garden City movement, the 1930s-era Wyvernwood apartment complex consisted of 120 two-story buildings, housing a total of 1,270 units loosely arranged around a set of open spaces on six superblocks. Both the public space and the street network were virtually disconnected from the surrounding neighborhood, resulting in unintended consequences, including:

- Inhibiting access through the site's interior by emergency personnel and residents alike

- Limiting view corridors through blocks

- Making buildings difficult to identify and locate for visitors, deliveries, and policing

- Creating many small, narrow open spaces that are perceived as neither public nor private and hence underutilized or neglected

- Creating unsafe conditions due to a lack of "eyes" on public space

In response, the design of the New Wyvernwood begins with the physical repair of the urban grid and the creation of pedestrian-friendly streets and public spaces to ensure the seamless integration of the site with the surrounding urban fabric. The plan includes 4,000 new units, including 600 affordable units (ensuring that existing tenants have a guaranteed opportunity to return), and the addition of 300,000 square feet of office and retail space and 25,000 square feet of civic space, providing residents with access to goods and services, as well as the economic opportunities of greater Los Angeles.

Aerial view of the
New Wyvernwood
with downtown
Los Angeles in the
background.

Small parks are situated next to existing neighborhoods to the north, and linear parks along the new perpendicular streets help people find the park at the heart of the site. Framed by appropriately scaled buildings and by many of the site's heritage trees, this park consists of an expansive open lawn area and includes a linear "Arroyo Walk" for storm-water management and a civic plaza. Perpendicular to this park is the primary retail street, offering public gathering opportunities and a place for a variety of events.

The Neighborhood Model

ALBEMARLE COUNTY, VIRGINIA

Blessed with a beautiful setting along the eastern edge of the Blue Ridge Mountains in central Virginia, and enveloping the City of Charlottesville, home to the University of Virginia, Albemarle County was growing rapidly, and projections into the future saw this trend continuing, if not accelerating. Elected officials knew that they needed to take a fresh and comprehensive look at plans for growth that had been made a decade earlier. Over the next two years, in collaboration with a 23-person steering committee, we led the process to formulate a strategy—rather than a specific plan—for a better way to grow. Basically, the strategy called for the rural areas of the county to remain intact and for specified development areas to be transformed into walkable, livable, environmentally sustainable communities.

Working with Dodson Associates and the Center for Watershed Protection, we led a process to articulate the principles and guidelines that would define the character of each of the county's development areas. After establishing community development preferences through a series of community workshops and determining the adequacy of existing growth-area boundaries through build-out analysis, we came up with guidelines and developed a number of models for neighborhood plans. We then assessed the community and environmental impact of each alternative, and measured the extent to which each supported the county's growth-management goals. After finalizing and illustrating the alternatives to be included in the Neighborhood Model, we assembled them into an easily interpretable manual to guide their application in a master planning process for each of the development areas that would enable continued growth in an environmentally sustainable manner.

Rural area: existing conditions.

Rural area: with suburban growth.

Rural Area: growth with the Neighborhood Model.

Developed area: existing conditions.

Developed area: with suburban growth.

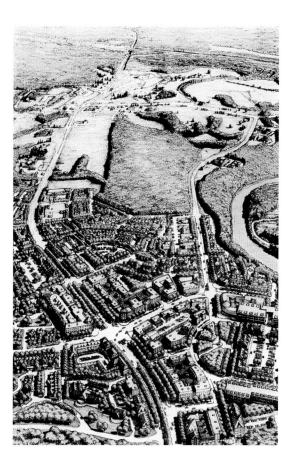

Developed area: growth with the Neighborhood Model.

King Farm

ROCKVILLE, MARYLAND

King Farm, a 440-acre site that remained in family hands longer than the surrounding areas, is located just outside of Washington, D.C., in the city of Rockville, Maryland. Encircled by 1950s-era suburban neighborhoods, the site is at the transfer point between the end of one of the District's Metro-rail lines and a proposed light rail line.

We were commissioned by the Penrose Group and Pritzker Residential to develop a master plan for the site, as well as the architecture for several of the higher-density residential neighborhoods. Our site plan envisioned a self-sufficient town of five distinct, walkable neighborhoods, inspired in part by the gridlike system of blocks and central green squares of traditional Mid-Atlantic towns. We organized the neighborhoods with a *cardo* and *decumanus* system of intersecting primary streets. King Farm Boulevard was conceived as the town's main street, leveraging the impact of the future light rail line, which will run along its central median. The primary east–west street was spatially terminated on either end by ceremonial open spaces—a circular park reminiscent of one in Bath, England, on the west, and a large, 4-acre park on the east. We located the town square at the intersection of the two roadways in the center of the site and situated the town's grocery store and mixed-use buildings with ground-floor retail there.

Largely constructed by production homebuilders, the project was an early test of their capacity to realize the architecture that could support traditional urbanism. Its success owes much to the perseverance of the town architects: Matthew Bell, Ralph Bennett, and Larry Frank. Completed over a decade ago, the town's landscape and community have since matured. Ironically, the loudest opposition to the new light rail, which is now in its implementation phase, is being voiced by the community.

View of the new
homes from a
neighborhood
park.

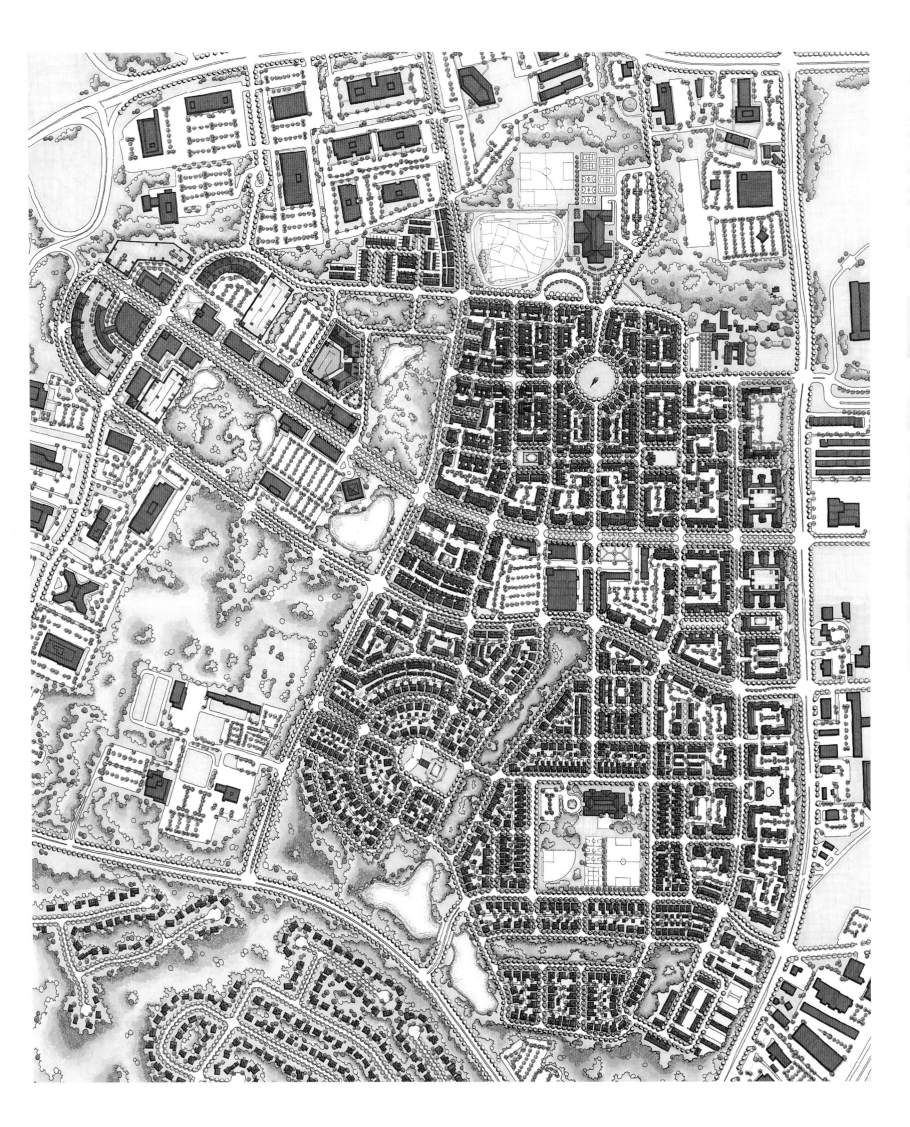

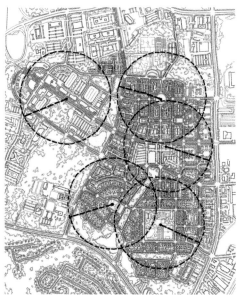

OPPOSITE
Master plan.

ABOVE
View of the new
houses facing the
school park.

FAR LEFT
Diagram of the five
neighborhoods.

LEFT
View of the new
houses.

Viva White Oak

A Center for Global Health

Greenfield
Urbanism

MONTGOMERY COUNTY, MARYLAND

Master plan.

Rendering of the
new main street at
night.

Our project for Viva White Oak, a former sand and gravel property on the eastern side of Montgomery County, Maryland, offers a counterproposal to the introverted, single-use suburban office park. Owned by Percontee, Inc., which parlayed its gravel business into extensive suburban Maryland real estate holdings, the site is located steps from the headquarters of the U.S. Food and Drug Administration (FDA). Our master plan, developed with Percontee and the county, leverages proximity to the FDA and a proposed new hospital to create a mixed-use, transit-oriented village that will be a center for bio/life sciences and global health. A round-the-clock place to live, work, learn, and play, the project will include office and bio/life sciences research and development space, university-sponsored research facilities, diverse residential uses, a hotel, retail, and civic facilities, including a performing arts center and an elementary school, as well as extensive open spaces incorporating an enhanced regional trail system.

The FDA sees Viva White Oak, with its range of uses and amenities, as a tool to recruit the best scientists, its vitality supported by the 10,000 employees surrounding it. Healthy living was an important theme developed throughout the project, foremost in its multimodal transportation system, which includes a proposed BRT, and in its comprehensive pedestrian system, complete with numerous trails. Also key were the extensive open-space system and emphasis on community, found not only in program elements but also in the planning of discrete neighborhoods around public spaces. A sensitive environmental approach will improve air and water quality, creating a healthy living environment.

©2015 MORRISSEY

Bahçeşehir

ISTANBUL, TURKEY

Sketch of the new
neighborhood.

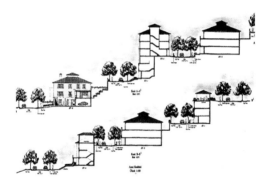

Sections
through the new
neighborhood.

Located in one of the rapidly growing metropolitan areas outside of Istanbul, our project in Bahçeşehir was our first large-scale urban design effort outside of the U.S. Well connected by existing roads and proposed new transit to downtown Istanbul, Bahçeşehir was characterized by vast housing tracts of high- and mid-rise apartments and detached villas. Standard development practice in Istanbul's quickly developing perimeter was to aggressively grade the existing topography, creating segregated platforms of isolated housing types in suburban layouts, eliminating one of the most compelling aspects of Istanbul—the way in which its urban pattern is shaped by the geography of steep hills and deep valleys, as well as by the curves of the Bosphorus.

Commissioned by Emlak Bank to create the master plan for and design the residential types of one of Bahçeşehir's large housing tracts, we approached the project with a single big idea: to revive Istanbul's urban heritage and unite the architecture with the site, inventing residential types that engaged the topography and placing them along streets and spaces to create a viable public realm. We began the project with an on-site, week-long charrette, creating residential types that included uphill and downhill units, as well as single-loaded buildings carved into the hillside. We articulated them with the idiosyncratic massing of towers, loggias, and bays, as well as the red tile roofs and ochre-based palette of traditional Turkish architecture. Key to the master plan was a linked series of open spaces that we thought of as the "spine," beginning with a grand station plaza at the bottom of the site and proceeding upward through an Italian-inspired series of cascades, stairs, and parks, culminating in a summit overlook framed by high-rise towers.

We took the project through design development and, with the exception of the public-space program, the project was built largely to our specifications. Now a mature place, it is characterized by winding, stone-paved roads, luxuriant landscaping, and picturesque streetscapes of villas and apartments.

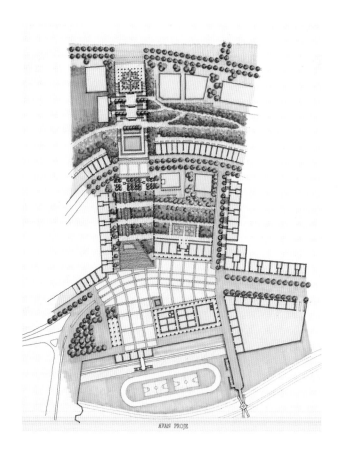

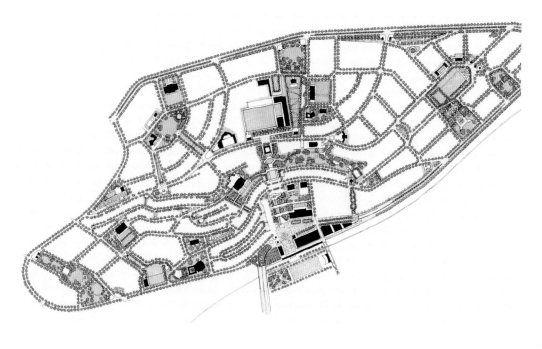

Rendering of the
new neighborhood.

Unionville Main Street

MARKHAM, CANADA

Part of the greater Toronto area, Unionville is a historic village in the city of Markham with a spectacular Main Street, which runs along an elevated ridge adjacent to the Rogue River floodplain. With a fine collection of historic buildings, the street is a popular location for festivals and special events but faces increasing challenges to its continued success, due to limited areas for growth and expansion, inadequate parking, and changing market conditions.

The city of Markham commissioned us to develop a plan to reinvigorate the historic center. An outgrowth of our other work in Markham (pages 108–11), we once again teamed with the architect Michael Morrissey, adding the Gibbs Planning Group to our team as retail consultants. A linchpin of our scheme was the recommendation to increase public parking by building over the existing public parking lot located east of Main Street, adjacent to the floodplain and at its lower elevation. Raised one story above the existing lot, the new parking deck is level with Main Street, providing convenient access and more than doubling the existing parking capacity. Combined with a "Park Once" policy, this additional parking freed up the many small parking lots scattered throughout the village for new development. For new infill, we invented a vocabulary of detached building types with short, gabled fronts and deep masses closely patterned on the character of the existing historic structures. This worked in tandem with a "deep lot" retail strategy, which entailed creating thin fingers of public ways emanating from Main Street to provide access to new retail along fronts and sides, thereby extending and amplifying the retail frontage. Proposed new development along Route 7 will create a new gateway and entrance into the village, and a proposed new community center will provide a terminus to the street on the north. New connections to the Rogue Valley Trail system will link the center to the regional system.

BELOW
Rendering of the
new amphitheater
on Too Good Pond.

OVERLEAF
Master plan with
renderings of
interventions.

RIGHT
Aerial rendering of
the master plan.

HIGHWAY 7

STIVER MILL / MARKET SQUARE

VILLAGE CORE

VILLAGE SQUARE

TOO GOOD POND

Al Wasl

RIYADH, SAUDI ARABIA

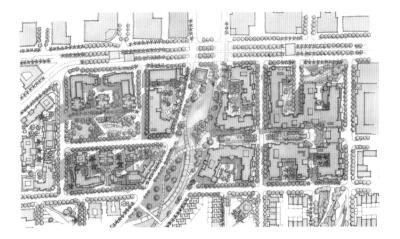

Neighborhood
plan.

Rendering of the
low-rise apartment
buildings.

With a future population of almost 600,000, Al Wasl is a new city northwest of Riyadh founded by Limitless, a global real estate master developer. Our many commissions at the site occurred over several years, and were part of an amazing collaboration between ourselves, Saeed Saeed, the lead client, and Calthorpe Associates, the master planner for the project.

Calthorpe's master plan balanced the traditional organic development pattern of the desert with a contemporary formal urban order. The plan used the valleys, or *wadi*, that crisscrossed the site as major open-space features defining the city and individual neighborhoods, and overlaid their natural forms with a rational street and block grid. The vision was encapsulated in a rendering we referred to as a "Hero Image," with its Central Park–inspired green space surrounded by tiered high-rise development, articulated in a language, at Saeed Saeed's instigation, "of the place."

Our multiple commissions included an early architectural test of a 64-block portion of the plan, detailed conceptual designs for a 5-block area at the retail heart of the city, individual block designs, and architectural and sustainable design codes. A central challenge was to translate strict Islamic traditions of privacy, security, and the separation of male and family space into higher-density residential buildings. We invented typologies across a range of densities, using multiple cores, sensitive block and building arrangements, and layered assemblages of public and private space to produce culturally acceptable living environments. The vernacular architecture of the Saudi region was an important inspiration for the project's image and complex massing, and the use of our Town Information Modeling system, with its capacity to simultaneously link three-dimensional forms with numerical calculations, was essential to reconciling the project vision with our client's financial goals.

Aflaj Al Foah

AL AIN, ABU DHABI, UNITED ARAB EMIRATES

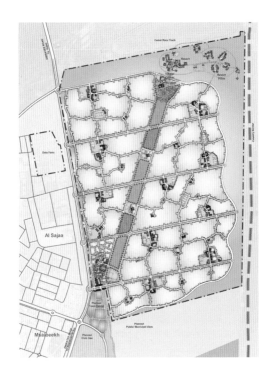

Master plan.

Designed around an existing date farm outside of the historic "Garden City" of the emirate of Abu Dhabi, Aflaj Al Foah will be a compact, mixed-use development. Working in collaboration with Calthorpe Associates for the Al Foah Company, we designed a community that will establish a new paradigm for growth in the region, providing a model for sustainability and independent living that will accommodate Islamic traditions of family growth and expansion. The master plan includes numerous neighborhoods, including a town center, all inspired by traditional Emirati villages. The neighborhood fabric incorporates an elaborate pedestrian network with special spaces tailored to the needs of women, children, and the elderly, creating an animated public realm that respects the Islamic tradition of separating public and family spheres. A unique feature of the open space network will be the date farm, reconfigured to be within easy walking distance of all the neighborhoods.

We developed designs for a series of courtyard homes, which we proposed as an alternative to the freestanding villas and walled compounds of conventional contemporary developments. Based on the concept of a compound, the houses were conceived of as multigenerational dwellings, allowing families to grow and expand over time. Their layouts, composed of multiple courtyards, established layers of private and public spaces, preserving the privacy and integrity of the family unit by separating it from the service/public sphere yet allowing its engagement in the rich communal life fostered in the urban pattern of *sikak* and *barahat* within the blocks. The project aimed for a high level of sustainability in both its urbanism and building designs. Articulated in a language inspired by traditional Islamic architecture, the houses incorporate sustainable features such as thick walls, shading devices, and high-performance roofs.

Aerial rendering of
a Grand Mosque
and the date farm.

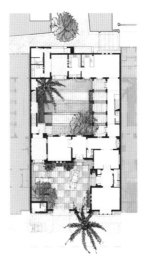

Floor plan of a
courtyard house.

Aerial rendering
of a mosque and
market complex.

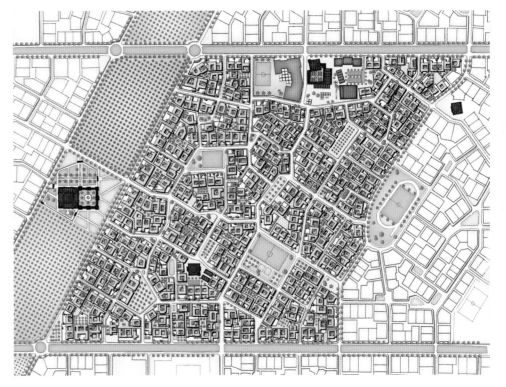

Illustrative
plan of several
neighborhoods.

Umm Al Quwain

UMM AL QUWAIN, UNITED ARAB EMIRATES

Almost at the tip of United Arab Emirates and approximately fifty miles up the coast of the Persian Gulf from Dubai, the emirate of Umm Al Quwain is primarily devoted to oasis farming, pearl diving, and more recently, beach resorts and waterparks. Working once again with Limitless and Calthorpe Associates, we developed a plan for a large, undeveloped parcel just north of the Old Town, offering a counterproposal to the placeless walled compounds and suburban-style resorts proliferating along the coast.

A proposed new ferry line connecting to Dubai sponsored the new development, which we conceived of as an extension of the urban pattern of the Old Town. As in our Arabian Canal City project (pages 146–49), water was a major theme that we exploited in the development of distinct places along the waterfront: a ferry plaza, two fishing villages, a park, and a resort complex. We threaded the water through the plan in a series of canals. The irregular block structure responded to the pattern and was an organic extension of the Old Town. The town edges facing the gulf were reserved for public beaches, new resorts, and a large civic park at the triangular tip of the peninsula, enjoying spectacular views of the Persian Gulf.

RIGHT
Rendering of a courtyard house overlooking the canal.

OPPOSITE TOP
Rendering of the commercial district and ferry plaza, from the harbor.

OPPOSITE BOTTOM
Rendering of the commercial district, looking toward the harbor.

Aerial rendering of
the new develop-
ment and the Old
Town.

Acknowledgments

Torti Gallas + Partners wishes to thank our publisher, Mark Magowan, editor, Jacqueline Decter, and designer, Mark Melnick, for their help and unending support. The entire Vendome team's guidance and expertise made this, our first book journey, a pleasurable one.

To our mentors, Elizabeth Plater-Zyberk and Andrés Duany, thank you for the kind words of assurance and encouragement over the past two decades that permitted us to have the confidence to continue and strive for excellence.

To our friends Gayle Berens, Dhiru Thadani, John Massengale, Gary Brewer, Elizabeth White, and Dean Michael Lykoudis, we thank you for your help and advice in launching this book.

And to the following, for their singular contributions in making this a volume of quality:

ESSAY AUTHORS

John Francis Torti · Thomas M. Gallas · Cheryl A. O'Neill
Neal I. Payton · Sarah Alexander · Atul Sharma
Siva Venkataraman · Erik J. Aulestia

ESSAY AND PROJECT DESCRIPTION AUTHOR AND EDITOR

Cheryl A. O'Neill

BOOK PROPOSAL TEXT AND PROJECT RESEARCH

Robin H. Prater

GRAPHIC DESIGN AND PHOTOGRAPHY ARCHIVIST

Stacy Sutton

PHOTOGRAPHY

Brian Tomaino

BOOK ILLUSTRATION TEAM LEADER

Lester Escobal

BOOK ILLUSTRATION TEAM

Wadiah Akbar · Megan Beveridge · Richard "Will" Deutsch
John Chester Fernando · Gavin Laughland · Russell Regulinski
Yumeng "Mandy" Wang

At Torti Gallas + Partners, planning and architecture is a team effort. Together our teams form segments, and our segments form the firm as a whole. We are indebted to all of the architects, urban designers, planners, and valued support professionals whose leadership, talent, and dedication produced the body of work in this volume.

SENIOR PRINCIPALS

Daniel Ashtary · Charles G. Coleman III · Robert S. Goodill
Neal I. Payton · Sherief Elfar · Robert Wallach

PRINCIPALS

Lawrence V. "Murphy" Antoine Jr. · Erik J. Aulestia · Bruce D. Kennett
Troy E. McGhee · Brian E. O'Looney · Cheryl A. O'Neill

EMERITUS PRINCIPALS

Tunca Iskir · Sylvia Munero · Chaiwat Pilanun

ASSOCIATE PRINCIPALS

Sarah Alexander · Robert E. Jaekel · Scott Welch

SENIOR ASSOCIATES

Mark Bombaugh · Radoslav Brandersky · Felix Deloatch
Nesli Dogrusoz · Ladislav Domen · Lester Escobal · Keith Everhart
Stephanie Farrell · William Fears · Taylora Imes · Jonathan Johnson
Christopher M. Jonick · Tony Lee · Martin P. Leitner
Mauricio Mallea · Michael Parker · Micheal D. Rollison
Elena Marie Romero · Maria Valdivia · Siva Venkataramani

ASSOCIATES

Brandon Boback · Laurence Brady · Seda Candir · Allen Cowling
Alice Enz · Jonathan P. Fisher · Julian Goldman · Greyson Goon
Michael Hennessey · Thomas McManus · Amy T. Mockapetris
Grant A. Saller · Brian Tomaino · Kim Tran-Dyer · Timothy Zork

DIRECTORS

Thomas A. Gilmore · Henry A. Harrell, II · Elizabeth G. MacKillop
Diane McCloskey · Laurie Milligan · Omer Mushahwar
Gilbert Rocca · Sandra Zamaria

We thank you for being members of our family,
John Francis Torti and Thomas M. Gallas

In Memoriam

JACK C. COHEN, FAIA

LEONARD HAFT, AIA

JACK SMITH KERXTON, AIA

On whose foundations we have built.

Richard Abbey · Urban Adams · James Adamson · Tony Ahuja · Wadiah Akbar · Jan Albaum · Sarah Alexander · Wendy Allen · Hang-Ja Allison
Jessica Alston · Yavuz Anahtar · William Andalora · Shenia Anderson · Daniel Anderton · Carlos Andres · Lawrence Antoine, Jr. · Elaine Argiriadis
Loreen Arnold · Emre Aru · Daniel Ashtary · Muhtesem Atasoy · Pelin Atasoy · William Atherton · Christopher Atkinson · Erik Aulestia
Bahram Azabdaftari · Brooke Baker · Wayne Balderson · Matthew Balkey · Andrew Balto · Christopher Balwin · Angela Banks · Kathaleen Barber
Adrianne Barlow · Jean Barnak · Robbie Barrino · Oswaldo Barrio · James Bartlett · Paul Barton · Filiz Basaran · Ricardo Bazan · Leroy A. Beach
Robert Beach · Ronald Beach · Jeffrey Beam · Matthew Bean · Charles Beck · Matthew Bender · Abed Benzina · Mehmet Bereket
Alejandro Bermudez · Cristina Bernardo · Joe Bernardo · Luis H. Bernardo Jr. · Elizabeth Bester · Megan Beveridge · Moni Bhardwaj · Dina Bickel
Kaya Biron · Teresa Bjornes · Jennifer Blair · Brandon Boback · Mark Bombaugh · Pipatana Boonchan · Dirk Bos · Sahnur Bostan
Katherine Bottom · Anne Bowman · Laurence Brady · Radoslav Brandersky · Ron Brasher · Mona Brennan · Adam Bridge · David Bruhnke
Karmala Brunson · Julie Bujnowski · Hector Burga · Thomas Burke · Gene Burnett · Coy Burney · Jermel Burton · Robert Butler · John Byrnes
William Caldwell · Chad Campbell · Reyes Campbell · Seda Candir · Maria Capobianco · Hope Capua · Timothy Carne · Darwin Carre
Margaret Carroll · Bradford Cary · Anna Casey · Anthony Catania · Nese Celebiler · Jose Cerezo · Carlo Cesarie Andres · Scott Chalmers
Eric Chan · Kellie Chaney · Shi Chang · Wayne Chang · Yusuk Chang · Manich Changsuphan · Vic Chao · Rita Chaundy · Lawrence Cherney
Eleanor Choi · Frank Chou · Erin Christensen · Patricia Christenson · Brandon Clear · Jack Cohen · Jerrold Cohen · Max Cohen · Carla Cole
Charles Coleman · Alex Collich · Allison Collins · John Comazzi · Christopher Comeau · Theresa Coolahan · George Cooley · Rebecca Cornell
Omayra Medina Cortes · Wenceslao Cortez · Abigail Courtney · Allen Cowling · Mary Jane Craige · Lawrence Cross · Dena Culbertson
Colleen Cullen · Julie Cunniffe · Michael Curley · Carlos Cusicanqui · Andy Czajkowski · Antonio D'agostino · Linda Dahl · Andrew Dan
Thomas Danco · Kevin Davis · Scott Davis · Henry Dearborn · Oilda del Castillo · Felix Deloatch · Richard Deutsch · Dorita Dixon
Elizabeth Dobozy · Nesli Dogrusoz · Allie Dohrman · Ladislav Domen · Kathryn Donahue · Mary Donlin · Michael Donovan · Stan Dougherty
Seamus Dowling · Mark Drake · Mikhail Dubensky · Roberto Duke · Michael Dulcich · Yildiz Duransoy · Anne Dutton · Chase Eatherly
George Eaton · Thomas Eckert · Bruce Eddy · Stuart Eichler · Janne Einberg · Sherief Elfar · Al Emmons · Samuel Englehart · Wendy Enloe
David Ensor · Alice Enz · Grant Epstein · Karen Erickson · Pipat Esara · Melissa Eschbach · Lester Escobal · Alicia Estrada · Lynnette Etheridge
Matthew Etner · Lydia Evans · Keith Everhart · Natasha Fahim · Richard Fainter · Frank Farls · Mark Farmer · Elizabeth Farrell · Stephanie Farrell
William Fears · John Chester Fernando · Geoffrey Ferrell · John Fetty · Darwin Feuerstein · Chevon File · Dwight Fincher · Jonathan Fisher
Matthew Fitzsimmons · Brian Fletcher · Margaret Flinner · Orlando Flores · AJ Flynn · Glenn Fong · Melissa Ford · Susan Ford · Geoffrey Fowler
Michael Franck · Darlene Frantz · Douglas Frazier · Christopher French · Elizabeth Fribush · Elizabeth Frick · Francisco Fuentes · Don Fulton
Steven Fulwider · Neil Gagliardi · Marianela Gago · Thomas Gallas · Jason Gamache · Stephen Gang · Aaron Garbutt · Enrique Garcia
Amy Gardner · Mwangi Gathinji · Don Gaul · Brian Geib · Brian Gerard · Mary Gerard · Robert Gillcrist · Thomas Gilmore · Diana Gilroy
Sehine Gizaw · Reginald Glenn · Carlos Gles · Christopher Goettge · Julian Goldman · Shri Gondhalekar · Robert Goodill · Greyson Goon
Sue Gosier · Koren Goutos · Ann Graham · David Granovsky · Rafeal Graves · Cynthia Gray · Robert Green · Robert Griffin · Kristen Grim
Tuwase Griner · Peggy Grosswiler · Pablo Guiraldes · Rajesh Gulati · Lalit Gurjar · Marcia Gutierrez · Rita Gutierrez · Carlos Guzman
Robert Hackley · Leonard Haft · Stacie Hahn · Jeffery Hall · Marie Hamilton · Joe Hanbuerger · Gregory Hancock · John Hanley · Carol Harrell
Henry Harrell · Latoya Harrington · Linda Hartman · Ron Hartman · Christina Haskins · Lisa Hawkins · Michael Hawkins · Hao He
Jeffrey Henneman · Michael Hennessey · Holly Hersey · Steve Hickerson · Anthony Hill · Keisha Hill · Reginald Hill · Elza Hisel-McCoy
Halil (Leo) Hiziroglu · Charles Hodge · Shawn Hodge · Jessica Ismart Holmgren · Brad Holtz · David Holtz · William Hopkins · Leslye Howerton
Ming Hu · Howard Huang · Sharon Huang · Diane Hucek · Rogelio Huerta · Rodger Huff · Ming Hui Bon Hoa · Eric Hurtt · Erasmus Ikpemgbe
Taylora Imes · Len Infranca · Miguel Iraola · Meral Iskir · Tunca Iskir · Chanel Jackson · Kevin Jackson · Robert Jaekel · Chandan Jayakumar
Salima Jefferson · Raymond Jenkins · Jonathan Johnson · Michelle Johnson · Robert Johnson · Yvonne Johnson · Kellee Johnston · Brian Jolson
Richard Jolson · Jonathan Jones · Mark Jones · Teresa Isabella Jones · Sumayya Jones-Humienny · Christopher Jonick · Erik Kampman
Elizabeth Kang-Kim · Turgut Karabekir · Michael Karns · Terrance Kean · Patricia Kelleher · David Kendall · Bruce Kennett · Vicky Kennett
Jack Kerxton · Ahmet Kilic · Eun Kim · Hyojung Kim · Jiae Kim · Sami Kirkdil · Navindran Kistan · Donald Klika · Zachary Klipstein
Andrew Kloss · Kara Koch · Yolanda Koh · Julia Koslow · Gerald Kremer · Rebecca Krista · Meghan Kroener · Keith Krueger · Joan Kuckkahn
Robert Kuentzel · Joice Kuo · Barbara Kurtz · Nicholas Kyrus · Joseph Lai · Jeremy Lake · Feliks Lakomeic · Stacy Lancaster · Joseph Landry
Elizabeth Langley · Susan Langley · Gavin Laughland · Manuel Lauzurique-Abiega · Daniel Lawrence · Thongchai Leardprasopsuk · Kyung Lee
Sung Kyun Lee · David Leestma · Michael Lehker · Cynthia Leibman · Martin Leitner · Ivonne Levin · Jeffrey Levine · Kelsey Lew · Dean Lewis
Matthew Lewis · Sarah Lewis · Boyu Li · Sung Lim · Chuenfung Lin · Kele Lin · Wei Shin Lori Lin · Ollie Lincoln · Harrell Little · Chen Liu
Brandi Livoti · Horacio Luvelo · Richard Lydick · Gary Lyon · James Lyons · Michael Mabaquiao · Elizabeth MacKillop · William Madden
Fred Maddox · Diego Magrin · Mauricio Mallea · Patricia Mangus · Isaac Manning · Richard Marietta · Gregory Marinic · Nancy Marsden
Jarry Marshall · Douglas Martin · Gabriela Ochoa Martinez · David Masenten · Georganne Matthews · Michael Mazon · Robert McClennan
Diane McCloskey · Troy McGhee · Patrice McGinn · Thomas McManus · Maggie McNamara · James Meade · Michael Medick · Jeremy Meier
Marcia Lacy Melin · Lucy Mencia · Camille Mendez-Hordatt · Michelle Merriweather · Clyde Messerly · Angelo Messina · Paolina Milasi
Gary Miller · Jeff Miller · Lashawn Miller · Valerie Miller · Laurie Milligan · Sarah Milo · Gertrude Mindlin · Julie Minkunas · Megan Mitchell
Michael Mitchell · Ronald Mizerak · Amy Mockapetris · Jamie Molina · Ivin Moody · Amelia Moore · Catherine Moore · Greg Moore
Daniel Morales · Malcolm Morris · Paul Mortensen · Monique Morton · Mandana Moshtaghi · Susan Moskowitz · Donna Moy · Peter Mullins
Sylvia Munero · Joseph Munroe · Omer Mushahwar · Abdul Muzikir · Timothy Nash · Deborah Neal · Laurie Nesbitt · Dieu Nguyen
Tim Nguyen · Michael Nicolaus · Nikolay Nikolaev · Linda Noll · Charles Obi · Carl Oehrig · Bandele Oguntomilade · Garner Oh · Nuray Okay
Brian O'Looney · Cheryl O'Neill · Andrew Onukwubiri · Resit Orer · Dima Osseiran · David Otieno · Kelvin Page · Robert Palgutt · Delma Palma
Thomas Palmer · Linda Palmerton · Michael Parker · Alison Parks · Sean Parmenter · Jutta Parree · Patricia Parrett · Della Payne
Neal Payton · Jill Pendegraph · Diane Perry · Lawrence Perry · Sharon Perry · Matthew Peters · Milij Petrovic · Luke Petrusic · Mykala Phillips
Chaiwat Pilanun · Alejandra Maria Pineiro · Diana Piotrow · Bruce Pitre · Andrew Pittman · David Pittman · Diane Pittman · Laura Poncelet
Nenad Popovic · Melissa Pouridas · Rewati Prabhu · Susan Presser · Kasey Puls · Rashi Puri · Philip Quintanilla · Edgar Quiroz · Austin Raimond
Raquel Raimundez-Spellacy · Ana Ramos · Deep Randhawa · Simran Randhawa · Satish Rao · Joseph Rapazzo · Kristie Rase · Virendra Rawat
Suzanne Reatig · Russell Regulinski · Dioni Rey · Robert Rhoe · Sharon Richmond · Lindsay Ringwelski · Gilbert Rocca · Limy Rocha
Angel Rodriguez · David Rodriguez · Michelle Rodriguez · Micheal Rollison · Elena Romero · Richard Rosen · Wendie-Ann Rosenbaum
Lois Rosenblum · John Ross · Thomas Ross · Fatemeh Roth · Scott Rouk · Marlon Roxas · Claudia Russell · Grant Saller · Albert Samuel
Manuel Sanchez · Martha Sansaver · Michael Sansaver · Eric Saul · Sarah Sayler · Christopher Schein · Judith Schmidt · James Schrider
Mark Schrieber · Evan Schroeder · Charles Schweickert · Vittorio Sciolli-Claverie · Lillian Scovazzo · Isabel Sebastian-Ramirez · Johathan Seils
Felix Serrano · Juan Carlos Serrano · Jesus Sese · Isaac Sevilla · Marlene Shade · Naresh Shah · Vasu Shah · Patricia Shanley · Atul Sharma
Victoria Shipley · Mark Silva · Sanford Silverman · Janet Simmon · Amanda Simpson · Dionne Sims-White · Anna Simunich · Analak Siwabut
Benjamin Skyles · Melissa Slavin · Angela Smith · Darques Smith · Richard Smith · Murat Soygenis · James Speers · Jason Stabach · Robert Stanton
Janice Stein · Kara Stephenson · Sallie Stewart · Merrill St. Leger · James Stokoe · Taylor Stout · John Stovall · Richard Stutte
Chokchai Suphabphant · Sankar Sur · Deepak Sutaria · Stacy Sutton · Attila Szalay · Dennis Szkotnicki · Catherine Tabor · Robin Tannenbaum
Mehran Tehrani · Ronald Teodoro · Emmett Thomas · John Thomas · Riccardo Thomas · Tyrone Thomas · Lisa Thompson · Michael Thompson
Darius Tirtosuharto · Christopher Todd · Lara Todorov · Brian Tomaino · Denise Tonelli · John Torti · Martin Towles · Kim Tran-Dyer
Junyi Tu · Faik Tugberk · Burak Tuglu · Bulent Tuvalo · Suleiman Umar · Yasuko Usami · Maria Valdivia · Audrey Valente · Jeffrey Vandenburg
Paul Van Riley · Jimmy Vansopark · Telma Vaserman · Carlos Vazquez · Siva Venkataramani · Gilberte Vest · Erikka Vinci · Emily Volz
Rachel Wagner · Clifford Walcott · Darcus Walker · Ronald Walker · Robert Wallach · Jon Wallenmeyer · Maurice Walters · Greg Walton
Ie-Ru Wang · Jesse Wang · Peng Wang · Yumeng Wang · Jennifer Ward · Sarah Warner · Marsha Weaver · Traci Weems · Shelley Weidl
Arthur Weidner · Kenneth Weinstein · Scott Welch · Artensia West · Hildegard White · Peter White · Lisa Wilbanks · Joy Wiles
Michael Wilkerson · Deron Williams · Leon Williams · Darris Wilson · Kris Wilson · Katherine Wohlsen · Julia Woltman · Chun-Hsi Wong
Florence Wong · Sophia Wong · Marc Wouters · Bahadir Yilmaz · Mete Yilmaz · Joyce Yin · Bret Young · Byong Yun · Sandra Zamaria
Daniel Zawadzki · Gary Zickafoose · David Zito · Tim Zork · Bryan Zublick

Contributing
Colleagues, 1953–2016

Timeline

Jack C. Cohen, AIA.
Retires 1989 +
2000.

The suburban house designs range
from traditional to modern.

Al Emmons
joins firm in 1953.
Retires 1993.

Leonard Haft
joins firm in 1953.
Retires 1977.

David A. Holtz joins
firm in 1956 to head
Land Planning Studio.
Retires 1992.

1953 firm founded by Jack C. Cohen, AIA

1956 firm name becomes Cohen and Haft + Architects

Sylvia Munero
joins firm in 1963.
Retires 2014.

Solar-shaded office building,
College Park, Maryland, 1964.

Turgut Karabekir
joins firm in 1963.
Retires 1977.

Town Center Apartments,
Washington, D.C., 1964.

Sligo Creek Apartments,
Silver Spring, Maryland, 1964.

Neighborhood Center,
Columbia, Maryland, 1969.

Summer Village Condominiums,
Bethesda, Maryland, 1971.

Tunca Iskir joins firm
in 1971. Retires 2013.

CHHKK office, 9300 Georgia Avenue,
Silver Spring, Maryland, 1972.

Bentana Woods,
Reston, Virginia, 1974.

Fallswood Condominiums,
North Bethesda, Maryland, 1981.

Somerset Condominiums,
Chevy Chase, Maryland,
1984–1998.

Arlington Plaza
Office Building,
Arlington, Virginia,
1985.

1979 firm name becomes CHHK, Inc.

1982 firm name becomes CHK Architects and Planners

Jack Smith Kerxton, AIA, joins firm in 1959. Becomes CEO in 1981. Retires 1993.

Cohen and Haft + Architects office building, Silver Spring, Maryland, 1960.

Spring Hill Lake Apartments, Greenbelt, Maryland, 1960–1970.

Luis Bernardo joins firm in 1961. Retires 2005.

Paint Branch Unitarian Universalist Church, Adelphi, Maryland, 1963.

Jewish Community Center, Rockville, Maryland, 1968.

Hunters Woods Neighborhood Center, Reston, Virginia, 1968.

Crescent Apartments, Reston, Virginia, 1969.

Synagogue Har Tzeon, Wheaton, Maryland, 1969.

Jack C. Cohen's house, Bethesda, Maryland, 1970.

CHHKK Studio, 1972.

John Torti, AIA, joins firm in 1973.

Montgomery College solar-heated Humanities Building, Germantown, Maryland, 1973.

Montgomery College solar-heated Science Building, Germantown, Maryland, 1973.

1974 firm name becomes CHHKK—Cohen, Haft, Holtz, Kerxton and Karabekir

Thomas M. Gallas, CPA, joins firm in 1985 as Chief Financial Officer.

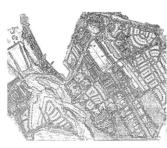

First national design award. South Riding, a new town, receives Progressive Architecture Citation Award, 1994.

Arlington Courthouse Plaza, Arlington, Virginia, 1985–1991.

John Francis Torti, FAIA (right), and Thomas M. Gallas, CPA.

2016 firm principals.

1998 firm name becomes Torti Gallas and Partners · CHK
2004 firm name becomes Torti Gallas and Partners, Inc.

Design
Charter

IN ORDER TO
- CLARIFY the principles that unify our beliefs and guide our practice,
- PRODUCE works that benefit both society and nature—the inhabitants of our communities and the land, the area, and the region,
- CREATE environmentally sustainable places that are socially, economically, and ecologically viable,
- MAKE places of enduring beauty based on the principles of traditional architecture and urbanism,
- ESTABLISH a common accessible language to discuss and critique our work,

WE, THE MEMBERS OF TORTI GALLAS + PARTNERS, DEDICATE OURSELVES TO THE FOLLOWING:

WE ADOPT the Charter of the New Urbanism as a primary set of guiding principles and accept as our mission, with all its attendant challenges, the realization of those principles in built works of architecture and urbanism;

WE EMBRACE our responsibility to the earth and its inhabitants by creating sustainable buildings and communities that will have a minimal impact on the environment and will allow future generations to grow and thrive;

WE ACCEPT our role as civic builders in the creation of diverse communities of sound economy, sensitive ecology, and social equity which balance the direct, private needs of our clients with the larger responsibility to create the public realm;

WE RECOGNIZE the primacy of the role of history in the making of traditional urbanism and thereby embrace creative invention or the transformation of convention and reject the concept of novelty for novelty's sake;

WE COMMIT ourselves to an integrated design process in which we lead the broad range of stakeholders and experts—inside and outside of our offices—involved in the making of the city, thereby creating the interaction necessary to produce sustainable communities;

WE COMMIT to a holistic approach whose aim is both to restore lost connections to nature, history and culture, and to improve the condition of the site, the region and the environment;

WE ACCEPT that the city is composed of a mix of uses—the dwelling, the civic building, and the places of commerce, assembly and worship—and that a formal distinction between public, symbolic uses and utilitarian, private ones is essential to creating urbanism;

WE ACKNOWLEDGE the distinction between the public realm and the private realm as essential to the creation of vital places and accept their respective impacts on building design;

WE ESTABLISH as our primary mission the design of the fabric of the city and accept all attendant responsibilities, specifically:
- *that the major urban role of private buildings is to make the public realm,*
- *that a rich range of building types exists and that their use as a foundation for building design both serves our urban goals and creates regionally appropriate designs,*
- *that value for our clients and our firm involves both the creation of well-designed buildings and economic profits, and we dedicate ourselves to achieving both, recognizing the importance of the public realm to each.*

WE UNDERSTAND that the making of the traditional city necessitates the use of an architecture sympathetic to and supportive of its goals;

WE ACCEPT the principles of traditional architecture as the foundation for all our work and explore their utilization in a broad range of architectural languages, including vernacular idioms, historical styles and principle-based designs;

WE RECOGNIZE the need for stylistic consistency equally in building design and detail;

WE IDENTIFY mass-production techniques and materials as essential to construction and commit ourselves to guiding their use in the creation of well-designed, environmentally sound, finely crafted buildings;

WE EMPLOY materials, techniques and production methods that preserve open space, conserve the earth's natural resources, restore natural hydrology, minimize waste and create a safe and healthy environment for the inhabitants before, during and after construction.

IN ORDER TO REALIZE THE GOALS DESCRIBED IN THE PREFACE OF THIS CHARTER, WE COMMIT TO THE FOLLOWING RULES ON ARCHITECTURE AND URBAN DESIGN:

ON URBANISM

The Charter for the New Urbanism provides a detailed set of principles on all scales of urbanism, from the region to the building, and they govern all urban works. The following principles are in addition to those:

1 Any urban design should begin with an analysis of the context.
   That analysis should look at the site, the neighborhood and the region and at the variety of elements—geography, topography, orientation, climate, hydrology, natural features and habitats, history, cultural and social traditions, streets, spaces and buildings, singularly and in aggregate—that create any environment.
2 Any urban design element, be it community, neighborhood, street or square, should recognize its impact on regional growth patterns and be designed accordingly. Urban designs should recognize and respond to their place in the transect and should be designed to work together to best respond to environmental, social and cultural conditions.
   Infill, transit-oriented and compact development should be promoted over responsible greenfield development. Sustainable strategies and landscape designs should work in concert with urban design concepts, supporting and enhancing them. New development should be designed to conserve the net use of water, energy, and fossil fuels.
3 Neighborhoods should be composed of an appropriate mix of uses, including a range of house types. Their urban design and architectural types, scales and styles should all be consciously designed.
   The programming of a neighborhood is an integral part of the design process. That process should creatively address program requirements (as articulated by the client, the community and the marketplace) in order to develop the best urban and architectural design. Neighborhoods should ideally accommodate a range of populations, including the physically disabled, as well as future uses.
4 Streetscapes should be designed in both their horizontal and their vertical components. The composition of the streetscape should be coordinated with the larger urban design ideas of the project.

ON ARCHITECTURE

We recognize that traditional urbanism is not possible without a building practice based on the principles of traditional architecture. We identify those principles as follows:

Building General:

1 Any building design should begin with an analysis of the context.

That analysis should include urban design, architecture, and the natural environment at the scale of the site, the neighborhood and the region. The analysis should include an evaluation of the strengths and weaknesses of the context. The architecture of the context should be studied in terms of its housing types, existing historic styles and their associated tectonics, and traditional local responses to macro- and micro-climates. Any of these may provide precedents for the project; however, any element so utilized must be derived from the best examples.

2 The design of the building should start with an urban design idea.

Every building should make a positive contribution to the context, either through repairing and improving the urban fabric and/or the natural features of the site or through a sensitive response to positive urban conditions. The primary component of the urban design idea, as articulated in the massing of the building, is the contribution the building makes in defining the public realm. The urban design idea should address the compositional, proportional and scale relationships between the building and the larger context. Particular attention should be paid to projects located in transitional places; in that case a significant component of the urban design idea should be devoted to dealing with those transitions.

3 A building should have both an articulated design *parti* and a sustainability strategy from its inception.

The building parti (defined as the basic scheme or concept for a building as represented in a simple diagram) should recognize the urban design idea, the building type, and the sustainable strategy. The latter shall include a response to local environmental conditions such as solar orientation, prevailing winds, biodiversity and natural hydrology and shall result in an overall improvement in the natural environment. Direct use of a historic type or the transformation thereof should be based on an evaluation of the type and its attributes—architectural and urban—when located in a context similar to that of the project.

4 The life cycle of the building should be considered in its design.

A building intended for long-term use should incorporate durable materials and systems as well as the internal flexibility and adaptability necessary to accommodate various uses and inhabitants. A building or portions of a building intended for short-term use should be designed with deconstruction in mind and include recyclable and reusable materials. Building components, whether structural, partitioning, conditioning or finishing, should be designed for an appropriate life cycle.

5 A building should be designed in either a historic style, a local vernacular or a principle-based language.

The selection of any of these should be reconciled with the building type and building massing. Principle-based design is defined as the use of a language which is not a literal interpretation of a historic style but is derived from a set of principles of composition and character that create their own language based on type, structure, tectonics, performance, and a response to climate.

6 A building should recognize its place in the transect and be designed in concert with it.

7 A building should have a hierarchy of sides, established both by the building's relationship with the public realm and the natural conditions of the site. The articulation of building façades and massing should include an appropriate response to both.

8 A simple building should be composed of a single language. A complex building should be composed of a single language unless a clear and convincing visual argument is made that its mass is composed of a number of buildings, wherein a number of clearly distinct building languages can be utilized.

Internal Spaces:

1 The internal spaces of a building, in their size, location and character, should respond to functional requirements.

Building designs, in their internal and external configuration as well as their siting, should respond to the current and future needs of the population and the environmental conditions of the site for which they are designed. They should simultaneously support and enhance urban design, architectural, and environmental goals.

2 The internal spaces of the building should have a clear hierarchy established by their size, location and character.

3 A space or element (exterior and/or interior) should be located at the building entrance to mediate between the public realm and the private building interior.

4 A clear distinction should be made between public and private spaces; public spaces have a primary relationship with the public realm and should be located accordingly.

5 The internal spaces of a building should have an appropriate connection to nature in order to provide light, ventilation, and external views as well as to minimize energy use.

The building's systems should be designed to provide maximum comfort and control while minimizing the use of energy and natural resources.

External Façades:

1 Building façades should have a *parti*. That *parti* should include:
   a. A rational pattern of elements based on rhythm and hierarchy, including a clear strategy for the use of an odd or an even number of bays.
   b. A hierarchy of windows.
   c. A clear definition of the external surface of the building as wall, frame or skin.
   d. A thinness or thickness of elements appropriate to the external surface.
   e. A response to the environmental conditions and local climate of the site.

2 While the distribution of elements on the building façade should respond to internal conditions, the façade *parti* and its subsequent articulation should primarily relate to the urban design idea, the local climate and the character of the public realm the building abuts.

3 Every building façade should have a base, middle and top.

The base, middle and top of the building should be in the scale of the building. The building top has a specific role in visually terminating the building and helping to protect it from the elements. The building base should be designed to appear to visually support assumed vertical building loads.

4 The language of the exterior façade should be context-based and should be developed according to a coherent set of stylistic principles and an appropriate response to climatic conditions.

These principles may be derived from a local vernacular, a historic style or an appropriate modern language. The selection of the above should be carefully considered in light of the building program, the context and the project budget.

5 Every building façade should be tectonically correct.

Building façades should be designed so that assumed vertical loads are carried to the ground by a reasonable and convincing visible structure. That visible structure should be either a trabeated system, a real or implied gravity-based wall system or a curtain wall system, selected in concert with the expression of the façade as wall, frame or skin. Tectonics should be developed in concert with the building's materials and its language.

6 A building façade should be composed of vertical proportions, whether in part or the whole of the composition. While these vertical proportions are the dominant façade reading, an appropriate balance should be established between both vertical and horizontal readings.

7 Façade elements, including visual structural elements, openings and details should utilize a coherent system of proportion.

8 The ground floor of a building should be scaled to the pedestrian.

The ground floor of a building is the most sensitive area of interaction between the building and the public realm. In conditions where an active street or public space abuts the building, extraordinary care should be given to the design of the ground floor.

9 Every façade should contain sufficient development—in materials, depth and detail—to create a level of visual interest sympathetic to humans.

Building Detail:

1 Building materials should be sustainable, durable and convey the notion of permanence.

Every effort should be made to utilize materials that have low embodied energy, are reused and/or recyclable, and support a healthy indoor environment. Buildings should be designed to decrease energy consumption. reduce waste, and minimize the impact of construction techniques and production methods on the environment.

2 Building materials should be utilized in a manner appropriate to their intrinsic formal properties, including their structural capacities as demonstrated in openings and spans.

3 Architectural elements should respond to regional climate, culture and precedents.

4 The primary architectural elements are walls, openings and roofs, and the configuration of each should first serve to identify building typology. Their character should be consistent with the building's language.

Awards

| 2016 | NAIOP DC | MD Awards of Excellence, Best Multi-Family Project, Park Van Ness, Washington, DC |

2016   NAIOP DC | MD Awards of Excellence, Best Multi-Family Project, Park Van Ness, Washington, DC

Congress for the New Urbanism Charter Award, MetroTowns at Parkside Kenilworth, Washington, DC

2015   Congress for the New Urbanism Charter Award, Wyandanch Transit Oriented Development, Long Island, NY

Congress for the New Urbanism Charter Award, Arise, South Bend, IN

NAHB Pillars of the Industry Awards, Best Workforce Housing Community, MetroTowns at Parkside, Washington, DC

NAHB Pillars of the Industry Awards, Finalist, Best Mid-Rise Community, Monroe Street Market, Washington, DC

2014   Congress for the New Urbanism Charter Award, Westlawn Revitalization, Milwaukee, WI

Builder's Choice Grand Award, Liberty Town Center, Cincinnati, OH

NAHB Best in American Living Award, Gold Award, Woodlawn Village Neighborhood Center, Fort Belvoir, VA

2013   Urban Land Institute, Global Award for Excellence, Finalist, MacArthur Park Apartments, Phase A, Los Angeles, CA

Urban Land Institute, Jack Kemp Excellence in Affordable and Workforce Housing Award, Masonvale, Fairfax, VA

Richard H. Driehaus Charitable Lead Trust, Form-Based Codes Award, Downtown Wyandanch, Long Island, NY

Congress for the New Urbanism Charter Award, Lyon Place at Clarendon Center, Arlington, VA

American Planning Association, National Planning Awards, Crystal City Master Plan, Arlington, VA

2012   Builder's Choice Award, Woodlawn Neighborhood Center, Fort Belvoir, VA

International Property Awards Europe, Architecture Multiple Residence Award, Ormanada, Zekeriyakoy, Turkey

NAHB Pillars of the Industry Awards, Best High-Rise Apartment, Lyon Place at Clarendon Center, Arlington, VA

NAHB Pillars of the Industry Awards, Best Workforce Housing, Masonvale, George Mason University, Fairfax, VA

NAHB Pillars of the Industry Awards, Best Multifamily Community Site Plan, MacDill AFB Family Housing, Tampa, FL

EcoHome Design Award, Salishan Neighborhood Revitalization, Tacoma, WA

Congress for the New Urbanism Charter Award, Georgetown Social Safeway, Washington, DC

Congress for the New Urbanism Charter Award, Wyvernwood Revitalization, Los Angeles CA

2011   NAHB Pillars of the Industry, Best Clubhouse at a Multifamily Community, MCAS Miramar 77, San Diego, CA

ENERGY STAR Leadership in Housing Award, Fort Benning Family Housing, Columbus, GA

NAHB Best in American Living Award, Neighborhood Design Gold Award, Janie's Garden, Sarasota, FL

International Council of Shopping Centers, Gold Sustainable Design, Georgetown Social Safeway, Washington, DC

Multi-Housing News, Multi-Housing Community of the Year Award, Pacific Beacon, San Diego, CA

Builder's Choice Award, Courtyard Homes at Asbury Methodist Village, Gaithersburg, MD

Builder's Choice Award, The Chapman at Peninsula Town Center, Hampton, VA

2010   NAHRO Journal of Housing & Community Development, Living Above the Station Award, Metro Pointe, Wheaton, MD

NAHB Pillars of the Industry Awards, Best Mid-Rise Apartment, Park Place Apartments, Washington, DC

GreenGov Presidential Award, Fort Belvoir Military Family Housing, Fairfax County, VA

Builder's Choice Award, MacDill Air Force Base Housing Revitalization, Tampa, FL

Builder's Choice Award, George Mason University Faculty and Staff Housing, Fairfax, VA

Urban Land Institute Global Award for Excellence, Columbia Heights Neighborhood, Washington, DC

2009   NAHB Pillars of the Industry Awards, Best Mid-Rise Apartment, Highland Park, Washington, DC

Design-Build Institute of America, National Design-Build Award, Private Sector Building over $25 Million, Pacific Beacon, San Diego, CA

Multi-Housing News Excellence Award, Pacific Beacon, San Diego, CA

AIA/HUD Secretary's Award, Bridgeton HOPE VI, Bridgeton, NJ

Congress for the New Urbanism Charter Award, Baldwin Park Town Center, Orlando, FL

Congress for the New Urbanism Charter Award, Crystal City Vision 2020, Arlington, VA

Congress for the New Urbanism Charter Award, Columbia Heights Neighborhood, Washington, DC

2008   Builder's Choice Award, Columbia Heights Neighborhood, Washington, DC

Builder's Choice Award, Fort Irwin Family Housing, Mojave Desert, CA

Builder's Choice Award, The PATH Concept Home, Omaha, NE

Builder's Choice Award, Gilbert Court at the Greene, Beavercreek, OH

Charles L. Edson Tax Credit Excellence Award, New Desire Phase I, New Orleans, LA

Charles L. Edson Tax Credit Excellence Award, Belmont Heights Estates, Tampa, FL

National Association of Housing and Redevelopment Officials, Merit Award, Horizon Village, North Charleston, SC

NAHB 50+ Housing Council Awards, Gold Award, Victory Heights, Washington, DC

2007   NAHB Best in American Living Awards, Best Suburban Smart Growth Community, The Village at Camp Parks, Dublin, CA

International Council of Shopping Centers (ICSC), Certificate of Merit, Town Center at Fort Belvoir, VA

Builder's Choice Award, Herryford Village, Fort Belvoir, VA

Builder's Choice Award, Martin Luther King Plaza Revitalization, Philadelphia, PA

Builder's Choice Award, Salishan Neighborhood Revitalization, Tacoma, WA

Congress for the New Urbanism Charter Award, Salishan Neighborhood Revitalization, Tacoma, WA

Congress for the New Urbanism Charter Award, Cooper's Crossing, Camden, NJ

Congress for the New Urbanism Charter Award, The Ellington, Washington, DC

American Institute of Architects Housing Award, Salishan Neighborhood Revitalization, Tacoma, WA

American Institute of Architects Housing Award, Bridgeton HOPE VI, Bridgeton, NJ

AIA/HUD Secretary's Award, Salishan Neighborhood Revitalization, Tacoma, WA

Multi-Housing News Design Excellence Award, Quantico MCB Family Housing, Quantico, VA

NAHB Pillars of the Industry Awards, Best Mixed-Use Community Site Plan, Fort Belvoir
 Family Housing, Fairfax, VA

NAHB Pillars of the Industry Awards, Best Affordable Neighborhood Revitalization, Military
 Housing, Monterey, CA

2006 American Planning Association, Outstanding Federal Planning Project, Fort Belvoir
 Communities, Fairfax, VA

NAHB Best in American Living Awards, Gold Award, Fort Belvoir Military Family Housing,
 Fairfax County, VA

NAHB Best in American Living Awards, Silver, Best Urban Smart Growth Community,
 Gateway Village, San Diego, CA

NAHB Best in American Living Awards, Silver, Best Smart Growth Community, Historic
 Apartments, Quantico MCB, VA

NAHB Best in American Living Awards, Silver, Best Rural Exurban Smart Growth Community,
 Military Housing, Fort Irwin, CA

Multifamily Executive Awards, Project of the Year—Military, Gateway Village Family Housing,
 San Diego, CA

Congress for the New Urbanism Charter Award, Fort Belvoir Military Family Housing,
 Fairfax, VA

Congress for the New Urbanism Charter Award, Martin Luther King Plaza Revitalization,
 Philadelphia, PA

Residential Architect Design Awards, Project of the Year, Martin Luther King Plaza
 Revitalization, Philadelphia, PA

American Institute of Architects Honor Award in Regional and Urban Design, Martin Luther
 King Plaza, Philadelphia, PA

NAHB Multifamily Pillars of the Industry Awards, Best Mid-Rise Rental Apartment, The
 Clarendon, Arlington, VA

2005 NAHB Best in American Living Awards, Gold Award, Fort Belvoir Military Family Housing,
 Fairfax County, VA

Builder's Choice Award, City West Revitalization, Cincinnati, OH

Builder's Choice Award, Centergate Baldwin Park, Orlando, FL

American Institute of Architects IDP Outstanding Firm Award, Large Firm Category

Multifamily Executive Awards, Grand Award, Project of the Year—Military, Quantico Family
 Housing, Quantico, VA

Multifamily Executive Awards, Grand Award, Best Use of Technology, Monterey Bay Military
 Housing, Monterey, CA

NAHB Pillars of the Industry Awards, Alban Towers/Alban Row, Washington, DC

NAHB Pillars of the Industry Awards, Centergate Celebration, Orlando, FL

NAHB Pillars of the Industry Awards, The Ellington, Washington, DC

NAHB Pillars of the Industry Awards, The Garlands at Barrington, Barrington, IL

Residential Architect Design Award, City West, Cincinnati, OH

American Institute of Architects Housing PIA Award, LeMoyne Gardens, Memphis, TN

American Institute of Architects Housing PIA Award, The Garlands of Barrington,
 Barrington, IL

2004   Builder's Choice Award, LeMoyne Gardens, Memphis, TN
         NAHB Pillars of the Industry Awards, 1225 13th Street, Washington, DC
         Congress for the New Urbanism Charter Award, Commercial Corridor Study,
              Charlottesville, VA
         Congress for the New Urbanism Charter Award, The Neighborhood Model,
              Albemarle County, VA
         Congress for the New Urbanism Charter Award, City West Revitalization, Cincinnati, OH
         Congress for the New Urbanism Charter Award, Twinbrook Commons, Rockville, MD
         American Institute of Architects Housing PIA Award, Belmont Heights Estates, Tampa, FL
         American Institute of Architects Housing PIA Award, City West, Cincinnati, OH

2003   US Environmental Protection Agency, Smart Growth Achievement Award, Village at NTC,
              San Diego, CA
         US Department of Housing and Urban Development, New Face of America's Public Housing,
              City West, Cincinnati, OH
         US Department of Housing and Urban Development, New Face of America's Public Housing,
              Martin Luther King Plaza, Philadelphia, PA
         American Institute of Architects Honor Award in Urban Design, Commercial Corridor Studies,
              Charlottesville, VA

2002   American Institute of Architects Honor Award in Urban Design, Development Area Initiatives
              Study, Albemarle County, VA

2001   American Institute of Architects Honor Award in Urban Design, Flag House Courts
              Revitalization, Baltimore, MD
         Congress for the New Urbanism Charter Award, Flag House Courts Revitalization,
              Baltimore, MD
         Congress for the New Urbanism Charter Award, King Farm, Rockville, MD

2000   American Institute of Architects Honor Award in Urban Design, Town of Bahçeşehir, Istanbul,
              Turkey
         Residential Architect Design Award, Kentlands Cottages, Gaithersburg, MD

1999   Builder's Choice Award, Kentlands Cottages, Gaithersburg, MD

1997   American Institute of Architects Honor Award in Urban Design, Lafayette Courts,
              Baltimore, MD
         National Association of Home Builders and Builder Magazine Silver Award, The Visitor's
              Center at South Riding, VA
         National Association of Home Builders and Builder Magazine Silver Award, Community of the
              Year, Town of South Riding, VA
         National Association of Home Builders "Best of Seniors' Housing Award," Maplewood Park
              Place, Bethesda, MD

1996   NAHB National Commercial Builder's Council Merit Award, Town Hall, South Riding, VA
         American Society of Landscape Architects Awards Program, Honorable Mention, Lafayette
              Courts, Baltimore, MD

1994   Progressive Architecture Citation Award, The Town of South Riding, VA

BUILDINGS
Urban Buildings

Columbia Heights

WASHINGTON, D.C.

2002–2008

Kenyon Square: 153 condominiums, 20,000 sf of ground-floor retail

Victory Heights: 75-unit affordable senior building

Highland Park: 229 rental apartments, 19,000 sf of ground-floor retail

Project Client: Donatelli Development

Project Team: Brian O'Looney, Tunca Iskir, Thomas Danco, Maurice Walters, Sarah Alexander, Chevon File, Filiz Basaran, Dioni Rey, Virendra Rawat, Thomas Persch, Laurence Brady, Urban Adams, Elizabeth Bester, Daniel Lawrence, Elizabeth Kim, Sidette Latta, Howard Hill, William Madden

Landscape Architect: Parker Rodriguez

Interior Design: Hickock Cole Architects

Park Triangle: 131 rental apartments, 18,000 sf of ground-floor retail

Project Client: Park Triangle Development

Project Team: Sherief Elfar, Marc Wouters, Feng Xiao, Sylvia Munero, Stephanie Farrell, Scott Welch, Maria Valdivia, Dima Osseiran, Vasu Shah, Angela Smith, William Madden

Interior Design: Forma Design

The Ellington

WASHINGTON, D.C.

1999–2004

186 rental apartments, 15,000 sf of ground-floor retail

Project Client: Donatelli Development

Project Team: Maurice Walters, Charles Coleman, Sylvia Munero, Feng Xiao, Susan Langley, Laurence Brady, Elizabeth Kim, Chevon File, Urban Adams, Andrew Balto, Filiz Basaran, Thomas Gilmore, Michael Dulcich

Interior Design: Design Works Interiors

The Bentley

WASHINGTON, D.C.

2011–2015

53 rental apartments, 4,135 sf of ground-floor retail, 20 below-grade parking spaces

Project Client: Richard Dubin and Irwin Edlavitch

Project Team: John Torti, Sarah Alexander, Sherief Elfar, Sylvia Munero, Maria Valdivia, Charles Coleman, Tyng Gulick, Joice Kuo, Diane Pittman

Interior Design: HapstakDemetriou+

360° H Street

WASHINGTON, D.C.

2005–2013

212 rental apartments, 43,000 sf grocery store, 5,000 sf of retail, 270 below-grade parking spaces

Project Client: Steuart Investment Company

Project Team: Sarah Alexander, Sherief Elfar, Stephanie Farrell, Ladislav Domen, Maria Valdivia, Felix Deloatch, Michael Hennessey. Kim Tran-Dyer, Laurence Brady, Mary Yagi, Carlos Guzman, Susan Langley, Tyng Gulick, Dioni Rey, Thomas Gilmore

Landscape Architect: Parker Rodriguez

Interior Design: SR/A Interior Design

8th + H Street

WASHINGTON, D.C.

2006–PRESENT

384 rental apartments, 52,000 sf of ground-floor retail, 405 below-grade parking spaces

Project Client: The Rappaport Companies and WC Smith

Project Team: Sarah Alexander, John Torti, Cheryl O'Neill, Sherief Elfar, Robert Jaekel, Kim Tran-Dyer, Laura Poncelet, Michael Hennessey, Carlos Guzman, Aaron Garbutt, Julie Bujnowski, Charles Coleman, Felix Deloatch, Thomas Gilmore, David Leestma, Abraham Murrell, Taylor Stout, Dioni Rey, Tyng Gulick

Landscape Architect: Studio 39 Landscape Architecture

Interior Design: SR/A Interior Design

City Vista

WASHINGTON, D.C.

2004–2009

685 mixed-income rental apartments and condominiums, 55,000-sf grocery store, 24,000-sf fitness club, 50,000 sf of additional retail, 800 below-grade parking spaces

Project Client: Lowe Enterprises

Project Team: Sherief Elfar, Stephanie Farrell, Maurice Walters, Maria Valdivia, Ladislav

Domen, Felix Deloatch, Tunca Iskir, Feng Xiao, Dima Osseiran, Ming Hu, Mandana Moshtaghi, Michael Parker, Hector Burga, Vasu Shah, Meaghan Kroener, Emre Aru, Carlos Guzman, Anne Bowman, Thomas Gilmore, Scott Welch
Associated Architect for Rental Apartment Design: Marshall Moya Design
Landscape Architect: Lee and Associates
Interior Design: Hartman Design Group

Georgetown Safeway

WASHINGTON, D.C.

2007–2013

71,000-sf grocery store, 6,800 sf of liner retail, 268 parking spaces
Project Client: Safeway
Project Team: Brian O'Looney, Sherief Elfar, Sylvia Munero, Michael Parker, Ladislav Domen, Michael Hennessey, Chris McCabe, Patrick Cheek, Dioni Rey, Thomas Gilmore
Store Architect: Rounds VanDuzer Architects
Landscape Architect: Freeland & Kauffman

Park Place, Petworth Safeway, and the Swift

WASHINGTON, D.C.

2003–2008

Park Place: 148 rental apartments, 17,000 sf of ground-floor retail, Metro entrance, 7 townhouses, 188 above- and below-grade parking spaces
Petworth Safeway and the Swift: 220 rental apartments, 57,000-sf grocery store, 180 below-grade parking spaces
Project Client: Donatelli Development, Safeway and Duball, LLC respectively
Project Team: Brian O'Looney, Maurice Walters, Sarah Alexander, Tunca Iskir, Robert Wallach, Sylvia Munero, Mary Yagi, Chevon File, Sharon Huang, Carlisle Bean, Filiz Basaran, Laurence Brady, Kalinda Brown, Thomas Gilmore, Yildiz Duransoy, Mehran Tehrani, Mark Peterson, Virendra Rawat, Gray Wilson
Landscape Architect: Parker Rodriguez
Interior Design: Hickok Cole Architects

Alban Towers and the Residences at Alban Row

WASHINGTON, D.C.

1998–2001

Alban Towers: 226 rental apartments in renovated landmark building, partially buried garage for 240 cars
The Residences at Alban Row: 15 fee simple duplexes
Project Client: Charles E. Smith Company, Encore Development, respectively
Project Team: Bruce Kennett, Maurice Walters, Michael Hennessey, Pablo Guiraldes, Rebecca Krista, Diana Piotrow, Mark Silva, Sherief Elfar, Luis Bernardo, Charles Coleman, Robert Wallach, Tunca Iskir, Seda Candir, Paul Barton, Maria Valdivia, Darcus Walker, Douglas Martin, Mehran Tehrani, Susan Langley
Historic Renovation: Martinez + Johnson Architecture
Landscape Architect: Lee and Associates
Interior Design: Hartman Design Group

Park Van Ness

WASHINGTON, D.C.

2011–2016

272 rental units, 10,000 sf of ground floor retail, 225 below-grade parking spaces
Project Client: B. F. Saul Company
Project Team: John Torti, Sarah Alexander, Sherief Elfar, Tunca Iskir, Sylvia Munero, Carlos Guzman, Kim Tran-Dyer, Michael Parker, Diane Pittman, Zachary Klipstein, Thomas Gilmore, Ladislav Domen, Jose Cerezo, Julie Bujnowski, Kiley Wilfong, Salima Jefferson, Amanda Simpson
Landscape Architect: Michael Vergason Landscape Architects
Interior Design: RD Jones & Associates

Suburban Repair

Shirlington Village

ARLINGTON, VIRGINIA

2003–2006

Three buildings, comprising 241 rental apartments, 28,000-sf grocery store, 24,000 sf of ground-floor retail, 795-space above-grade parking garage
Project Client: Federal Realty Investment Trust

Project Team: John Torti, Daniel Ashtary, Sherief Elfar, Maurice Walters, Andrew Czajkowski, Tunca Iskir, Feng Xiao, Maria Valdivia, Michael Parker, Ladislav Domen, Charles Beck, Lalit Gurjar, Ming Hu, Sharon Huang, Meaghan Kroener, Elizabeth Kim, William Madden, Patricia Shanley
Landscape Architect: Parker Rodriguez

Upstairs at Bethesda Row
BETHESDA, MARYLAND
2001–2008
180 rental units, 44,000 sf of ground-floor retail, 249 below-grade parking spaces
Project Client: Federal Realty Investment Trust
Project Team: John Torti, Maurice Walters, Thomas Danco, Tunca Iskir, Charles Coleman, Sylvia Munero, Robert Wallach, Elizabeth Bester, Yildiz Duransoy, Thomas Gilmore, Douglas Martin, Thomas Persch, Susan Langley, Virendra Rawat, Sidette Latta

Gables Pike District
ROCKVILLE, MARYLAND
2011–2016
455 residential units, 31,000 sf of ground-floor retail, 818-space above-grade parking garage, including 250 public parking spaces
Project Client: Gables Residential
Project Team: Daniel Ashtary, Robert Jaekel, Scott Welch, Charles Coleman, Thomas Danco, Nesli Dogrusoz, Jonathan Johnson, Julian Goldman, Lester Escobal, Thomas Gilmore, Dominic Aello, Brandon Boback
Landscape Architect: Mahan Rykiel Associates
Interior Design: Marly + Co

The Upton at Rockville Town Center
ROCKVILLE, MARYLAND
2005–2015
140-room hotel, 485 rental apartments, 23,1000 sf of ground floor retail,1,156 above- and below-grade parking spaces
Project Client: Duball, LLC
Project Team: Daniel Ashtary, Robert Jaekel, Tunca Iskir, Andrew Czajkowski, Thomas Danco, Sylvia Munero, Robert Wallach, Jonathan Johnson, William Fears, Michael Parker, Lester Escobal, Thomas Gilmore, Yildiz Duransoy, Mary Yagi, Carlos Guzman, Chevon File, Mercideli Mesa, Vicky Lee, Mark Rivetti,

Joice Kuo, Jeffrey Pollack, Lindsay Ringwelski, Christina Park, Patricia Vaz de Carvalho, Florence Wong
Landscape Architect: Parker Rodriguez
Interior Design: Hartman Design Group

Lyon Place at Clarendon Center
CLARENDON, VIRGINIA
2004–2010
South Block: 244 rental apartments, 83,580 sf of office, 11,000-sf grocery, 27,333 sf of ground-floor retail, 471 below-grade parking spaces; North Block: 97,860 sf of office, 15,725 sf of ground-floor retail, 129 below-grade parking spaces
Project Client: B. F. Saul Company
Project Team: Sherief Elfar, Maurice Walters, Sarah Alexander, Sylvia Munero, Tunca Iskir, Stephanie Farrell, Ladislav Domen, Maria Valdivia, Radoslav Brandersky, Scott Welch, Felix Deloatch, Thomas Gilmore, Michael Hennessey, Yildiz Duransoy, Chris McCabe, Mandana Moshtaghi, Ming Hu, Carlos Guzman, Dioni Rey, Patricia Shanley, Dima Osseiran, Susan Langley, Carol Beach, Vasu Shah, Amanda Tiani, Mehran Tehrani, Juan Serrano, Julie Peter, Thomas Persch, Nese Celebiler
Interior Design: RD Jones & Associates

The Nannie Helen at 4800
WASHINGTON, D.C.
2009–2013
70 mixed-income rental apartments, including 23 low-income units, 7,600 sf of retail and community space, 41 parking spaces
Project Client: A.Wash & Associates, DCHA, DMPED
Project Team: Stephanie Farrell, Sherief Elfar, Sarah Alexander, Sylvia Munero, Cheryl O'Neill, Felix Deloatch, Thomas Gilmore, Tyng Gulick, Christina Haskins
Landscape Architect: Parker Rodriguez
Interior Design: Kreative Ways & Solutions

Notch 8
ARLINGTON, VIRGINIA
2011–2015
253 rental apartments, 65,000-sf grocery, 295 below-grade parking spaces
Project Client: JBG
Project Team: Brian O'Looney, Robert Wallach, Yildiz Duransoy, Jonathan Johnson, Grant

Saller, Brandon Boback, Charles Coleman,
Thomas Gilmore, Sylvia Munero, Kasey Puls,
Florence Wong
Entitlement Architect: SK + I
Store Architect: JCA Architects
Landscape Architect: Studio 39 Landscape
Architecture

The Bartlett

ARLINGTON, VIRGINIA

2011–2016

699 rental apartments, 40,800 sf of ground-
floor retail, including urban grocery store
Project Client: Vornado Realty Trust
Project Team: Sherief Elfar, Sarah Alexander,
Stephanie Farrell, Mauricio Mallea, Andrew
Czajkowski, Robert Wallach, Sylvia Munero,
Ladislav Domen, Felix Deloatch, Radoslav
Brandersky, Nesli Dogrusoz, Dioni Rey, Mary
Yagi, David Leestma, Kiley Wilfong, Zachary
Klipstein, Brian Tomaino, Alexander Collich,
Michael Lehker, Abraham Murrell, Jose Cerezo,
Tyng Gulick
Associated Architect: Maurice Walters
Architect
Landscape Architect: Studio 39 Landscape
Architecture
Interior Design: Hartman Design Group

Residences at the Greene

BEAVERCREEK, OHIO

2004–2006

152 rental apartments, 18 townhouses, 70,000 sf
of specialty retail, 350 spaces in shared garage
Project Client: Steiner + Associates, Mall
Properties
Project Team: Daniel Ashtary, Brian O'Looney,
Andrew Czajkowski, John Torti, Mark Drake,
Susan Langley, Tunca Iskir
Landscape Architect: Michael Vergason
Landscape Architects
Landscape Architect of Record: The Edge
Group
Interior Design: RD Jones & Associates

4665 Steeles Avenue

MARKHAM, CANADA

2013–2014

600 apartments, 300-room hotel, 100,000 sf of
office/amenity space, 210,000-sf retail galleria,
1,120 below-grade parking spaces

Project Client: Global Fortune Real Estate
Development Corporation
Project Team: Robert Goodill, Daniel Ashtary,
Robert Jaekel, Laurence Brady, Julian Goldman,
Laura Poncelet, Margaret McNamara
Associated Architect: Michael Morrisey
Architect

NEIGHBORHOODS
Neighborhoods

The Garlands of Barrington

BARRINGTON, ILLINOIS

1997–2005

256 independent-living apartments, 26 villas,
60 skilled nursing beds, 60-room country inn,
amenities including health club with indoor
pool, beauty salon, and convenience retail
shops, 700 below-grade parking spaces
Project Client: Barrington Venture
Project Team: John Torti, Daniel Ashtary,
Sherief Elfar, Robert Goodill, Erik Aulestia,
Luis Bernardo, Rick Jolson, Sylvia Munero,
Ladislav Domen, Scott Welch, Mauricio Mallea,
Greyson Goon, Michael Hennessey, Thomas
McManus, Thomas Gilmore, Don Gaul,
Vasu Shah, Lydia Evans, Margaret Carroll,
Patricia Shanley, Dima Osseiran, James Lyons,
Dina Bickel, Shelley Weidl, Emre Aru, Chad
Campbell, Darcus Walker, Angela Smith,
Brooke Baker, Anthony Hill, Elizabeth Kim,
Daniel Lawrence, Douglas Martin, Satish Rao,
Richard Rosen, Phillip Quintanilla
Landscape Architect: Joe Karr & Associates
Interior Design: Kenneth E. Hurd & Associates

Centergate at Celebration

ORLANDO, FLORIDA

1999–2001

726 rental housing units, integral garage and
surface parking
Project Client: Pritzker Residential
Project Team: John Torti, Robert Goodill,
Maurice Walters, Thomas Danco, Bruce
Kennett, Tunca Iskir, Scott Welch, Nesli
Dogrusoz, Mary Yagi, Richard Smith, Reginald
Glen, Daniel Lawrence, Ronald Teodoro,
Emmit Thomas, Michael Dulcich, Anthony
Hill, Yildiz Duransoy
Town Architect: Geoffrey Mouen

Centergate at Baldwin Park and Baldwin Park Town Center

ORLANDO, FLORIDA

2002–2003

Centergate: 214 rental apartments over flex; Town Center: 1,120 residential units, 225,000 sf of office, 75,000 sf of commercial, 80,000 sf of flex space, 45,000-sf grocery store
Project Client: Pritzker Residential
Project Team: John Torti, Robert Goodill, Maurice Walters, Troy McGhee, Scott Welch, Thomas Danco, Daniel Lawrence, Yildiz Duransoy

Masonvale

FAIRFAX, VIRGINIA

2011–2014

157 transitional rental housing units
Project Client: George Mason University, Masonvale, Inc.
Project Team: Murphy Antoine, John Torti, Sylvia Munero, Taylora Imes, Allen Cowling, Michael McGrattan, Katherine Kepferle, Adrienne Bicknell, Jeffrey Beam, Jenny An, Juan Serrano
Landscape Architect: Parker Rodriguez

Merwick Stanworth

PRINCETON, NEW JERSEY

2011–PRESENT

72 apartments, 254 stacked flats
Project Client: Princeton University, American Campus Communities
Project Team: John Torti, Murphy Antoine, Robert Goodill, Bruce Kennett, Allen Cowling, Brian Tomaino, Taylora Imes, Siva Venkataramani, Michael McGrattan, Jeremy Lake, Eric Joerdens
Landscape Architect: Arnold Associates
Interior Design: Sixthriver Architects

Ormanada

ZEKERIYAKOY, TURKEY

2008–2012

199 single-family homes, 114 townhouses and apartments, social club, convenience retail
Project Client: Eczacibasi Group
Project Team: John Torti, Thomas Gallas, Robert Goodill, Daniel Ashtary, Tunca Iskir, Andrew Czajkowski, Thomas Danco, Keith Everhart, Michael Hennessey, Laurence Brady,

Timothy Zork, Abdul Muzikir, Rachel Cohen-Stevens, Elizabeth Bester, Vicky Lee, Robert McClennan

Kemer Country

ISTANBUL, TURKEY

1994–1996

180 residential units, including townhouses and flats, 500-acre golf course
Project Client: Esat Edin
Project Team: John Torti, Tunca Iskir, Sami Kirkdil, Daniel Ashtary, Abed Benzina, Marty Towles, Valerie Miller

Arabian Canal Courtyard Neighborhood

DUBAI, UNITED ARAB EMIRATES

2007–2008

Neighborhood, prototypical block of 40 courtyard homes
Project Client: Limitless
Project Team: John Torti, Daniel Ashtary, Robert Goodill, Troy McGhee, Scott Welch, Keith Everhart, Siva Venkataramani, Lester Escobal, Elizabeth Bester, Leslye Howerton, Rachel Cohen-Stevens, Chris McCabe, Robert McClennan, Ahmet Kilic, Peter Korb, Juan Serrano, Darwin Feuerstein, Hao He
Master Planner: Calthorpe Associates

Devanhalli

BENGALURU, INDIA

2013–2014

187 villas and townhouses, 20,000-sf clubhouse
Project Client: Tata Housing Development Company
Project Team: Thomas Gallas, Murphy Antoine, Erik Aulestia, Mark Bombaugh, Siva Venkataramani, Atul Sharma, Alex Salazar, Greyson Goon

Community Centers (2004–2014)

Fort Stanton and Barry Farm Recreation Centers

WASHINGTON, D.C.

Project Client: District of Columbia Department of Parks and Recreation, Regan Associates
Project Team: Shereif Elfar, Maria Valdivia ,

Sarah Alexander, Mark Bombaugh, Stephanie Farrell, Radoslav Brandersky, Marianela Gago

Woodlawn Village Community Center

FORT BELVOIR, VIRGINIA

Project Client: Clark Realty Capital
Project Team: Bruce Kennett, Allen Cowling, Thomas Gilmore

Addison Terrace Community Center

PITTSBURGH, PENNSYLVANIA

Project Client: KBK Enterprises
Project Team: Murphy Antoine, Andy Czaikowski, Greyson Goon, Lindsay Ringwelski

Capper/Carrollsburg Community Center

WASHINGTON, D.C.

Project Client: District of Columbia Housing Authority
Project Team: Robert Wallach, Taylora Imes, Evan Schroeder, Brandon Clear, Cheryl O'Neill, Thomas Palmer, Jeffrey Beam, Sahnur Bostan. Thomas Gilmore
Landscape Architect: Parker Rodriguez
Canal Park Pavilion Architect: Studios Architecture

Miramar Community Center

SAN DIEGO, CALIFORNIA

Project Client: Clark Builders Group
Project Team: Bruce Kennett, Marianela Gago, Mark Bombaugh, Abdul Muzikir, Juan Uehara, Jose Cerezo

San Diego Naval Training Center Community Center

SAN DIEGO, CALIFORNIA

Project Client: Clark Builders Group
Project Team: Marianela Gago, Jose Cerezo, Felix Serrano, Juan Uehara, Mark Bombaugh

MacDill Air Force Base Community Center

TAMPA, FLORIDA

Project Client: Clark Builders Group
Project Team: Murphy Antoine, Chase Eatherly, Robert McClennan, Greyson Goon, Tony Lee, Gregory Boll

Centennial Hill Community Center

MONTGOMERY, ALABAMA

Project Client: The Michaels Development Company
Project Team: Murphy Antoine, Scott Welch, Chase Eatherly, Seda Candir, Allen Cowling

Mixed-Income Housing

Martin Luther King Plaza

PHILADELPHIA, PENNSYLVANIA

1998–2006

128 mixed-income units on-site and 121 in Hawthorne, 8,000 sf of retail, ½-acre urban park
Project Client: Pennrose, Universal Companies, Philadelphia Housing Authority
Project Team: Thomas Gallas, Cheryl O'Neill, Murphy Antoine, Patrice McGinn, Robert Wallach, Jan Albaum, Mehran Tehrani, Shenia Anderson, Margaret Carroll, Ronald Teodoro, Thomas Gilmore, Paul Mortensen, Loreen Arnold, Emre Aru, Jeremy Meier, Barry Jackman
Local Architect: Walden-Holland Architects
Hawthorne Park Landscape Architect: Ground Reconsidered

City West

CINCINNATI, OHIO

2000–2003

585 mixed-income units, 23,000 sf of commercial, 5,000-sf community center
Project Client: The Community Builders, Cincinnati Metropolitan Housing Authority
Project Team: John Torti, Murphy Antoine, Thomas Gallas, Jeffrey Beam, Cynthia Gray, Paul Mortensen
Architect of Record: glaserworks

Salishan

TACOMA, WASHINGTON

2002–2010

1,278 mixed-income units, village center with retail, community center, and senior building
Project Client: Lorig Associates, Tacoma Housing Authority
Project Team: Thomas Gallas, John Torti, Keith Everhart, Theresa Coolahan, Kevin Davis, Cynthia Gray, Thomas Gilmore, Christopher French, Elza Hisel-McCoy, Jeremy

Lake, Patrice McGinn, Paul Mortensen, David
Rodriguez, Charles Moore
Local Architect: McGranahan Architects

College Park

MEMPHIS, TENNESSEE
2000–2004
269 mixed-income units, 80-unit senior
building, 25,000-sf community building
Project Client: Urban Atlantic, The Integral
Group, Memphis Housing Authority
Project Team: Cheryl O'Neill, Murphy
Antoine, Chaiwat Pilanun, Tunca Iskir, John
Torti, Thomas Gallas, Seda Candir, Nesli
Dogrusoz, Taylora Imes, Anthony Hill, Ronald
Teodoro, Chad Campbell
Landscape Architect: Pickering Firm

Belmont Heights

TAMPA, FLORIDA
1999–2005
860 mixed-income units, 76 affordable senior
duplexes, 4 community centers
Project Client: The Michaels Development
Company, Tampa Housing Authority
Project Team: Thomas Gallas, Neal Payton,
Erik Aulestia, Patrice McGinn, Thomas
McManus, Seda Candir, Chaiwat Pilanun, Elza
Hisel-McCoy, Barry Jackman, Hector Burga,
Mark Jones, Feliks Lakomiec, Jeremy Meier,
Shenia Anderson, Mehran Tehrani
Landscape Architect: Glatting Jackson Kercher
Anglin

Westlawn

MILWAUKEE, WISCONSIN
2008–PRESENT
865 affordable rental units, including
apartments, townhouses, and flex units, 12,500
sf of commercial/incubator retail space, 13,000-
sf management building
Project Client: Housing Authority of the City
of Milwaukee
Project Team: Murphy Antoine, William
Fears, Greyson Goon, Brian Tomaino, Charles
Moore, Jeremy Lake, Alexander Kacur, Thomas
Gilmore
Associated Architect: KINDNESS architecture
+ planning
Landscape Architect: Schreiber Anderson
Associates

Military-Family Housing

San Diego Naval Facilities Command

SAN DIEGO, CALIFORNIA
1999–2002
500 military-family housing units, 11,000-sf
community center
Project Client: Clark Builders Group
Project Team: John Torti, Thomas Gallas,
Robert Goodill, Maurice Walters, Tunca Iskir,
Nesli Dogrusoz, Yildiz Duransoy, Elizabeth
Bester, Roberto Duke, Kara Lawrence, James
Meade, Margaret Carroll, Grant Epstein
Landscape Architect: Rick Engineering

Fort Belvoir

FAIRFAX COUNTY, VIRGINIA
2002–2009
1,630 military-family housing units, renovation
of 178 historic homes, 5 neighborhood centers,
town center with 14,000 sf of retail and 45 live/
work units
Project Client: Clark Realty Capital
Project Team: John Torti, Thomas Gallas, Neal
Payton, Robert Goodill, Bruce Kennett, Troy
McGhee, Chaiwat Pilanun, Robert Wallach,
Mark Bombaugh, Radoslav Brandersky, Seda
Candir, Taylora Imes, Michael Hennessey,
Greyson Goon, Keith Everhart, Elizabeth
Hesler, Marianela Gago, Leslye Howerton,
Thomas Gilmore, Shenia Anderson, Darwin
Carre, Theresa Coolahan, Horacio Luvelo,
Harrell Little, Jeremy Meier, Abdul Muzikir,
Maria Pineiro, Julia Koslow, Jeremy Lake,
Virendra Rawat
Landscape Architect: Parker Rodriguez

MacDill Air Force Base

TAMPA, FLORIDA
2006– 2013
337 military-family housing units, 6,000-sf
welcome center
Project Client: Clark Builders Group
Project Team: Murphy Antoine, Troy McGhee,
Tony Lee, Taylora Imes, Allen Cowling, Chase
Eatherly, Jeremy Lake, Virendra Rawat, Robert
McClennan, Florence Ho, Emmett Thomas,
Suzanne Lillis, Sarah Milo, Gregory Boll

Fort Irwin

2002–2012

715 military-family housing units, 200 senior units, 664 renovated homes, community clubhouse

Project Client: Clark Realty Capital
Project Team: Thomas Gallas, John Torti, Neal Payton, Robert Goodill, Luis Bernardo, Robert Wallach, Troy McGhee, Tunca Iskir, Chaiwat Pilanun, Greyson Goon, Keith Everhart, Siva Venkataramani, Michael Hennessey, Christopher Jonick, Juan Rafael Espinosa, Mwangi Gathinji, Carlton Davis, Kevin Davis, Theresa Coolahan, Hector Burga, Roberto Duke, Darwin Carre, Darius Tirtosuharto, Robert Stanton, Felix Serrano, Erik Kampmann, Lalit Gurjar, Jason Gamache, Emre Aru, Shenia Anderson, Robert McClennan, Harrell Little, Cynthia Gray, Chase Eatherly, Hyojung Garland, Adrienne Bicknell
Associated Architect: Bennett Frank McCarthy Architects
Landscape Architect: DeLorenzo International

PLACES
Catalysts for Transformation

Capper/Carrollsburg

WASHINGTON, D.C.
2001–2006

Neighborhood revitalization

Project Client: Urban Atlantic, Forest City Enterprises, District of Columbia Housing Authority
Project Team: Cheryl O'Neill, Thomas Gallas, Sherief Elfar, Robert Goodill, Luis Bernardo, Dina Chin-Bickel, Elizabeth Kim, John Ross, Patricia Shanley, Vasu Shah, Angela Smith, Jeffrey Beam, Sahnur Bostan
Townhouse Architect: Lessard Design
Landscape Architect: AECOM
Canal Park Landscape Architect: David Rubin while equity partner at OLIN Studios

Camana Bay

GRAND CAYMAN ISLAND
2009–2016

Town center and neighborhood

Project Client: Dart Realty
Project Team: John Torti, Erik Aulestia, Daniel

Ashtary, Bruce Kennett, Murphy Antoine, Robert Wallach, Tunca Iskir, Thomas Danco, Lester Escobal, Elena Romero, Timothy Zork, Chaiwat Pilanun, Thomas Gilmore, Jonathan Johnson, Allen Cowling, Greyson Goon, Scott Welch, Michael Hennessey, Michael McGrattan, Chase Eatherly, Dioni Rey, Carlos Guzman, Weiqing Feng, James Han, Charles Moore, Mark Rivetti, Lindsay Ringwelski, Vicky Lee, Tyng Gulick, Joshua Eckert, Elizabeth Farrell, Dominic Aello, Rachel Cohen-Stevens, Julie Bujnowski
Town Architect: Michael Watkins Architect

The Parks at Walter Reed

WASHINGTON, D.C.
2013–PRESENT

Master plan for the revitalization of historic campus with new neighborhoods and town center

Project Client: Urban Atlantic, Hines, Triden
Project Team: Thomas Gallas, John Torti, Erik Aulestia, Daniel Ashtary, Elena Romero, Timothy Zork, Gabriela Martinez
Landscape Architect: Michael Vergason Landscape Architects

National Cathedral Close Master Plan

WASHINGTON, D.C.
1995–2000

Master plan for historic site

Project Client: Protestant Episcopal Cathedral Foundation
Project Team: John Torti, Cheryl O'Neill, Robert Goodill, Grant Epstein, Matthew Bell, Dina Chin-Bickel
Landscape Architect: Michael Vergason Landscape Architects

Monroe Street Market

WASHINGTON, D.C.
2006–2009

Town center

Project Client: Abdo Development, Bozzuto
Project Team: Thomas Gallas, Cheryl O'Neill, Sarah Alexander, Maurice Walters, Cynthia Gray, Abdul Muzikir, Mark Bombaugh, Chris McCabe
Arts Walk Architect: Maurice Walters Architect

Architect of Record: KTGY

Landscape Architect: Oehme, van Sweden & Associates

Crystal City Master Plan
ARLINGTON, VIRGINIA
2006–2010

Retrofit of suburban district, increasing density from 21 to 40 million sf

Project Client: Arlington County, Virginia

Project Team: John Torti, Robert Goodill, Elena Romero, Laurence Brady, Timothy Zork, Paul Mortensen, Kalinda Brown

Landscape Architect: AECOM

MacArthur Park Apartments
LOS ANGELES, CALIFORNIA
2006–2012

172 affordable rental units, 30,000 sf of retail, 244 parking spaces

Project Client: McCormack Baron Salazar

Project Team: Neal Payton, Christopher Jonick, Charles Coleman, Robert Wallach, Scott Welch, Feng Xiao, Navindran Kistan, Joice Kuo, Jose Cerezo, Florence Wong, Tom Louie, Jamie Molina

Collaborating Architect: Roschen Van Cleve Architects

Landscape Architect: Fong Hart Schneider & Partners

Coast Highway Vision Plan
OCEANSIDE, CALIFORNIA
2008–2009

Town center and retrofit of suburban arterial

Project Client: City of Oceanside, CA

Project Team: Neal Payton, David Cutler, Amber Hawkes, Georgia Sheridan, Brad Lonberger, Jacob Kerin, Bonnie Gonzalez

Real Estate Economics Advisor: RCLCO

Transportation Consultant: Nelson\Nygaard

Form-Based Codes

Downtown Wyandanch Master Plan
TOWN OF BABYLON, NEW YORK
2012–2016

Town center

Project Client: Town of Babylon, NY

Project Team: John Torti, Erik Aulestia, Daniel

Ashtary, Laurence Brady, Timothy Zork, Lester Escobal, Julian Goldman

Santa Monica Downtown Community Plan
SANTA MONICA, CALIFORNIA
2011–2016

Downtown plan

Project Client: City of Santa Monica, CA

Project Team: Neal Payton, Georgia Sheridan, Kelsey Lew, Alison Collins, Bonnie Gonzalez, Jamie Molina, Andrew Petrovsky

Real Estate Economics Advisor: RCLCO

Transportation Consultant: Nelson\Nygaard

Downtown Westminster
WESTMINSTER, COLORADO
2013–2015

Retrofit of regional mall into town center

Project Client: Westminster Economic Development Authority

Project Team: Neal Payton, Martin Leitner, Daniel Ashtary, Jamie Molina, Alison Collins, Radoslav Brandersky

Transportation Consultant: Nelson\Nygaard

New Wyvernwood Master Plan
LOS ANGELES, CALIFORNIA
2006–2010

Neighborhood

Project Client: Fifteen Group

Project Team: Neal Payton, David Cutler, Vinayak Bharne, Lillian Scovazzo, Brad Lonberger, Jacob Keirn, Leslye Howerton, Amber Hawkes, Bonnie Gonzalez, Myranda Sims, Georgia Sheridan

Landscape Architect: Melendrez

Greenfield Urbanism

The Neighborhood Model
ALBEMARLE COUNTY, VIRGINIA
1997–2000

Smart growth

Project Client: Albemarle County, VA

Project Team: Neal Payton, Elizabeth Hesler

Landscape Architect and Renderers: Dodson Associates

Environmental Engineer: Center for Watershed Protection

King Farm

ROCKVILLE, MARYLAND
2001–2004

Five neighborhoods and a town center

Project Client: The Penrose Group, Pritzker Residential

Project Team: Cheryl O'Neill, Robert Goodill, John Torti, Erik Aulestia, Troy McGhee, Siva Venkataramani, Steven Gang, Elizabeth Hesler

Town Architects: Matthew Bell, Ralph Bennett, Larry Frank

Landscape Architect: LandDesign

Viva White Oak:
A Center for Global Health

MONTGOMERY COUNTY, MARYLAND
2004–PRESENT

Town center

Project Client: Percontee

Project Team: Thomas Gallas, Robert Goodill, Keith Everhart, Elena Romero, Brian Tomaino, Grant Epstein, Paul Mortensen, Hao He, Lindsay Ringwelski

TransNational Urbanism

Bahçeşehir

ISTANBUL, TURKEY
1995–1997

Neighborhood

Project Client: Emlak Bank

Project Team: John Torti, Tunca Iskir, Robert Goodill, Daniel Ashtary, Jim Stokie, Lester Escobal, Matthew Bell, Michael Franke, Daniel Anderton, Chun Hsi Wong, Tony D'Agostino, Melissa Wilfong

Unionville Main Street

MARKHAM, CANADA
2012–2014

Revitalization of town center

Project Client: Town of Markham

Project Team: Robert Goodill, Daniel Ashtary, Erik Aulestia, Elena Romero, Atul Sharma, Lindsay Ringwelski

Associated Architect: Michael Morrisey Architect

Landscape Architect: Ferris + Associates

Al Wasl

RIYADH, SAUDI ARABIA
2007–2009

Town center and neighborhoods

Project Client: Limitless

Project Team: John Torti, Daniel Ashtary, Erik Aulestia, Laurence Brady, Lester Escobal, Siva Venkataramani, William Fears, Stephanie Farrell, Michael Parker, Taylora Imes, Felix Deloatch, Radoslav Brandersky, Chaiwat Pilanun, Bruce Kennett, Murphy Antoine, Sarah Alexander, Maria Valdivia, Rachel Cohen-Stevens, Natasha Fahim, Florence Wong, Patricia Vaz de Carvalho, Lindsay Ringwelski, Chris McCabe, Mercideli Mesa, Elizabeth Farrell, Anne Bowman, Lillian Scovazzo, Dioni Rey, Michael Dulcich, Tyng Gulick, Michael Mitchell, Andrew Czajkowski, Jeffrey Pollack

MASTER PLANNER: Calthorpe Associates

Aflaj Al Foah

ABU DHABI, UNITED ARAB EMIRATES
2009–2010

Town center and neighborhoods

Project Client: Al Foah Company

Project Team: Thomas Gallas, John Torti, Daniel Ashtary, Robert Goodill, Lester Escobal, Greyson Goon, Henry Harrell, Elizabeth Farrell, Greg Moore, Lindsay Ringwelski

Master Planner: Calthorpe Associates

Umm Al Quwain

UMM AL QUWAIN, UNITED ARAB EMIRATES
2008–2009

Extension of Old Town with new neighborhoods and town center

Project Client: Limitless

Project Team: John Torti, Daniel Ashtary, Elizabeth Farrell, Ahmet Kilic

Master Planner: Calthorpe Associates

Additional Projects

1993
South Riding Town Plan, Trafalgar House, Loudoun County, VA
Rock Springs Town Plan, Davis & Camalier, Bethesda, MD
Germantown Town Center and Town Plan, Germantown Town Center, LLC, Germantown, MD
Veterans Affairs Loch Raven Nursing and Rehabilitation Center, US Department of Veterans Affairs, Baltimore, MD
Fort Myer Child Development Center, US Army Corps of Engineers, Fort Myer, VA
Shot Tower Plaza, Maryland Mass Transit Administration, Baltimore, MD
Southern Maryland Higher Education Center, St. Mary's County, MD

1994
Lafayette Courts HOPE VI Revitalization, Housing Authority of Baltimore City, Baltimore, MD
Hearthstone Mews High-Density Townhomes, Hearthstone Communities/Madison Homes, Old Town Alexandria, VA
Brighton Gardens Senior Assisted Living, Marriott International, Friendship Heights, MD
West Farm Bus Maintenance Facility, Montgomery County Public Schools, Silver Spring, MD

1995
Lexington Terrace HOPE VI Revitalization, Struever Bros. Eccles & Rouse/Housing Authority of Baltimore City, Baltimore, MD
Parc Somerset Luxury Condominiums, Somerset House, Inc., Chevy Chase, MD
333 + 419 Russell Avenue Senior Living, Asbury Methodist Village, Gaithersburg, MD

1996
Brambleton Town Plan, Brambleton Land Corporation, Loudoun County, VA
Portner's Landing Historic Re-Use and Townhomes, Madison Homes, Alexandria, VA
Ingleside High-Density Single Family Homes, Madison Homes, McLean, VA
Grosvenor Metro Village, Potomac Investment Properties, Inc., Bethesda, MD
Ispartakule New Town Plan, Korkmaz Yigit, Istanbul, Turkey
Richmond Highway Revitalization Plan, Robert Charles Lesser & Company, Fairfax County, VA
Rivercreek Homes, Michael Harris Builders, Leesburg, VA
The Gramercy at Town Center Apartments, The Bozzuto Group, Columbia, MD
Bolling Air Force Base Family Housing, Harkins Builders, Washington, DC
Belle Point Office Townhouses, HLA Connecting Point, Greenbelt, MD
Center for Military History, US Army Corps of Engineers, Fort McNair, Washington, DC
Walter E. Washington Estates Townhouse Neighborhood, HR Crawford Associates, Washington, DC
Stamp Student Union Renovation, University of Maryland, College Park, MD
Honor Guard Bachelor Enlisted Quarters, Naval Support Facility Anacostia, Clark Construction Group, LLC, Washington, DC
Stratford at Reston Town Center Luxury High and Mid-Rise Condominiums, Renaissance Housing Corporation, Reston, VA
Ashburn Village Apartments, Encore Development Corp., Ashburn, VA

1997
Maryland State House Dome Restoration, Maryland Department of General Services, Annapolis, MD
Har Shalom Synagogue Renovation & Expansion, Congregation Har Shalom, Potomac, MD
Old Town Green, Centex Homes, Alexandria, VA
Whittier Park Townhouses, The Holladay Corp., Falls Church, VA
Wellington Ridge HOPE VI Revitalization, Pennrose Properties/Chester Housing Authority, Chester, PA
Reisterstown Plaza Metro Police Substation and Child Care Center, Mass Transit Administration, Reisterstown, MD
Clarksburg Post Office, Glen Construction, Inc., Clarksburg, MD
Lexington Park Post Office, Glen Construction, Inc., Lexington Park, MD
Kentlands 2 Over 2, Centex Homes, Gaithersburg, MD
Kentlands Live/Work Townhouses, Mitchell & Best, Gaithersburg, MD
Woodmont Neighborhood Plan, Arcadia Land Company, Montgomery County, PA

1998   Montgomery Lane Townhouses, Greenhill Capital Corp., Bethesda, MD

Norfolk 5 Communities Master Plan, Norfolk Redevelopment and Housing Authority, Norfolk, VA

1515 N. Courthouse Road Office Building, The Holladay Corp., Arlington, VA

St. Paul's Senior Living, The Bozzuto Group, Capitol Heights, MD

Lamokin Senior Living, Pennrose Properties, Chester, PA

Air Rights Center New Hotel and Apartments, Lowe Enterprises Mid Atlantic, Inc., Bethesda, MD

Frederick Douglass/Stanton HOPE VI Revitalization, Urban Atlantic/District of Columbia Housing
    Authority, Washington, DC

Avalon at Arlington Square Apartments, Townhomes and Live/Work Neighborhood, AvalonBay
    Communities, Inc., Arlington, VA

Ridgecrest Community Center, H. R. Crawford, Washington, DC

Henry Adams House, LCOR, Washington, DC

Asbury Solomons Island Senior Villas, Asbury Methodist Village, Solomons Island, MD

Russett Townhouse Neighborhood, The Bozzuto Group, Laurel, MD

Omerli Yapi Ve Turizm, A.S. Hamlets + Village, Seferusta Ciftligi, Istanbul, Turkey

King Farm Boulevard Condominiums, The Bozzuto Group, Rockville, MD

Kumkoy Evleri Resort, Enternasyonel Turizm, Istanbul, Turkey

Flag House Courts HOPE VI Revitalization, Urban Atlantic/Integral/Housing Authority of Baltimore
    City, Baltimore, MD

Centergate King Farm Apartments, Townhomes, Manor Homes, and Charleston Rental Types, Pritzker
    Residential, Rockville, MD

Desire HOPE VI Revitalization, The Michaels Development Co., New Orleans, LA

West Harlem Park Revitalization, Bank of America CDC, Baltimore, MD

Russett Site Feasibility Study, Pritzker Residential, Laurel, MD

Eagleview Apartments, The Hankin Group, Chester County, PA

Rosborough Wellness & Cultural Arts Center, Asbury Methodist Village, Gaithersburg, MD

Millbrook II Apartments, The Mark Winkler Company, Alexandria, VA

Visualizing The Planned Regional Center, State of New Jersey

Hudson Pointe Apartments, Lincoln Property Co., Jersey City, NJ

The Mews at Collingwood Park, The Ingerman Group, Farmingdale, NJ

Ingleside Townhomes Phase 2, Madison Homes, McLean, VA

1999   Belmont Town Center Plan and Townhomes, EFO Capital Management, Prince William County, VA

Chelton Terrace Affordable Housing, The Ingerman Group, Camden, NJ

14th & N Street Luxury Apartments, Raymond C. Brophy, Inc., Washington, DC

Perry Homes HOPE VI Revitalization, Atlanta Housing Authority, Atlanta, GA

Washington Ridge HOPE VI Revitalization, TCG Development Services, LLC/Lakeland Housing
    Authority, Lakeland, FL

Downingtown Keystone Opportunity Zone Master Plan, Borough of Downingtown, PA

Charlottesville Commercial Corridors Study, City of Charlottesville, Charlottesville, VA

2000   Harborview HOPE VI Grant Application, TCG Development Services, LLC, Duluth, MN

Asbury Manor House Independent Living, Asbury Methodist Village, Gaithersburg, MD

Asbury Carriage Houses, Asbury Methodist Village, Gaithersburg, MD

The Hudson Apartments, Clark Realty Capital, LLC, Arlington, VA

Melwood Townhouses, The Bozzuto Group, Bowie, MD

Mason Run Community, Crosswinds Communities, Detroit, MI

New Haven Planning, Phillips Preiss and Shapiro, Inc., New Haven, CT

Miramar Mixed-Use Town Center, City of Miramar and The Related Group of South Florida,
    Miramar, FL

Germantown Transit Center, Bellemead Development Corp., Germantown, MD

Silver Spring Transit, Montgomery County, Silver Spring, MD

Eastlake HOPE VI Revitalization, Leon N. Weiner & Associates/Wilmington Housing Authority, Wilmington, DE

Brookland Manor Workforce Housing, Ford, Mid-City Financial Corp., Washington, DC

Germantown Town Center Apt. Bldgs 13–20, Beazer Homes, Germantown, MD

Pentagon Hospital Site Luxury Apartments, KSI Services, Inc., Arlington, VA

Fort Meade Housing, Lincoln Property Co., Fort Meade, MD

The Landings, Mystic Harbor Corp., Berlin, MD

Congressional Plaza Greyfield Housing, Federal Realty Investment Trust, Rockville, MD

Jeffrey Square Mixed-Use Neighborhood Plan, Concorde Communities, Columbus, OH

Wayne Place Apartments, St. Paul's Community Development Corporation, Washington, DC

Shirlington Plaza Neighborhood Plan, Federal Realty Investment Trust, Arlington, VA

Bolling Family Housing 2000, Harkins Builders, Inc., Washington, DC

Strathmore Park Luxury Condominiums at Grosvenor-Strathmore Metro, Eakin-Youngentob Associates, North Bethesda, MD

Stonelake Townhouses, Miller and Smith, Howard County, MD

Navy Yard Master Plan Study, William C. Smith & Co., Washington, DC

13th & M Street Luxury Rental Apartments, Jefferson Apartment Group, Washington, DC

Fairlee Neighborhood Master Plan, Clark Realty Capital, LLC, Vienna, VA

1225 13th Street Complete Apartment Building Remake, MDC, Washington, DC

Harrison Commons TOD Neighborhood and Mixed-Use Design, The Pegasus Group, Harrison, NJ

Detroit Opera House Redevelopment Design, Crosswinds Communities, Detroit, MI

2001   Meadows Town Center Town Plan, Castle Rock Development Co., Castle Rock, CO

Daytona Beach HOPE VI Revitalization, TCG Development Services, LLC/Daytona Beach Housing Authority, Daytona Beach, FL

Bethesda Row Mixed-Use Entitlement and Design, Federal Realty Investment Trust, Bethesda, MD

Victory Terrace Senior Housing, Victory Housing Inc., Potomac, MD

Grosvenor IV Apartments, AvalonBay Communities, Inc., North Bethesda, MD

Western Bus Garage Mixed-Use Redevelopment Plan, Clark Realty Capital, LLC, Washington, DC

Van Dorn Metro Site Mixed-Use, KSI Services, Inc., Alexandria, VA

New Brunswick Redevelopment, New Brunswick Development Corp., New Brunswick, NJ

Shirlington Library & Theater Plaza, Federal Realty Investment Trust, Arlington, VA

Four Corners New Village Master Plan, WCI Communities, Inc., Fishkill, NY

Kimberly Park HOPE VI Revitalization, TCG Development Services, LLC, Winston-Salem, NC

Owings Mills Apartments Site Plan, Pritzker Residential, Owings Mills, MD

Cabrillo Planning and Residential Architecture, Clark Realty Capital, San Diego, CA

Monrovia Nursery Master Redevelopment Plan, City of Azusa, Azusa, CA

Woodmont Townhomes, Rocky Gorge Communities, Inc., Bethesda, MD

Colonial Terrace Condo, Greystar, Arlington, VA

Blackwell Revitalization Plan, TCG Development Services, LLC, Richmond, VA

Claremont Homes, Housing Authority of Baltimore City, Baltimore, MD

Bridgeton HOPE VI Revitalization, The Ingerman Group/Bridgeton Housing Authority, Bridgeton, NJ

Parc Dulles Apartments, Lerner Corporation, Dulles, VA

Villages at Balk Hill, Rocky Gorge Communities, Inc., Landover, MD

Camden Westwinds Apartment Community, Camden USA, Inc., Sterling, VA

Meadowlands Residential Design, Encap, LLC, Meadowlands, NJ

2002   Indefinite Delivery Contract, District of Columbia Housing Authority, Washington, DC

King Farm Phase III, Mitchell & Best, Rockville, MD

Celia Saxon HOPE VI Revitalization, TCG Development Services, LLC/Columbia Housing Authority, Columbia, SC

Horizon Village HOPE VI Revitalization, TCG Development Services, LLC, North Charleston, SC

Wayne Place Traditional Neighborhood Design, Arcadia Land Company, Washington, DC

Arthur Capper/Carrollsburg Senior Building I, Urban Atlantic, Washington, DC

Happy Hills HOPE VI Revitalization, TCG Development Services, LLC/Winston-Salem Housing
     Authority, NC

Monterey Military-Family Housing, Clark Realty Capital, LLC, Monterey, CA

Fort Campbell Military-Family Housing, Clark Pinnacle Family Communities, LLC, Fort Campbell, KY

Manor Houses at Balk Hill, Rocky Gorge Communities, Inc., Landover, MD

Hanson-Taney HOPE VI Revitalization, TCG Development Services, LLC/Frederick Housing
     Authority, Frederick, MD

Lansdowne Town Center Master Plan, Lansdowne Town Center, LLC, Lansdowne, VA

Perkins Homes, Housing Authority of Baltimore City, Baltimore, MD

Water's Edge Master Plan, Mystic Harbor Corp., Ocean City, MD

MetroPointe TOD Apartments, The Bozzuto Group, Wheaton, MD

Moffett Field Military-Family Housing, Clark Realty Capital, LLC, Mountain View, CA

Camp Parks Military-Family Housing, Clark Realty Capital, LLC, Dublin, CA

Gateway Military-Family Housing, Clark Builders Group, LP, San Diego, CA

Admiral Hartman Military-Family Housing Renovations, Clark Builders Group, LP, San Diego, CA

Murphy Canyon Military-Family Housing Renovations, Clark Builders Group, LP, San Diego, CA

Twinbrook Commons TOD Master Plan, The JBG Companies, Rockville, MD

Grosvenor TOD High Rise, Potomac Capital Investment Corporation, Rockville, MD

Porter Street Duplex Homes, Encore Development Corp., Washington, DC

Chevy Chase Mansionization Code, Town of Chevy Chase, Chevy Chase, MD

400 M Street Affordable Senior Housing, Urban Atlantic, Washington, DC

Silver Spring Gateway Site Redevelopment Plan, The JBG Companies, Silver Spring, MD

Woodland Terrace HOPE VI Revitalization, The Ingerman Group, Pleasantville, NJ

2003   Harborview Revitalization Plan and Residential Design, TCG Development Services, LLC, Duluth, MN

Quantico Military-Family Housing, Clark Realty Capital, LLC, Quantico, VA

Encore Haverstraw Village Master Plan and Urban Design, WCI Communities, Inc., Haverstraw, NY

Monument Place Apartment Community, Camden USA, Inc., Fairfax, VA

Maple Lawn Farm Luxury Townhomes, Mitchell & Best, Fulton, MD

Center Court HOPE VI Revitalization, Rosenberg Housing Group, Niagara Falls, NY

Redlands Downtown Master Plan, City of Redlands, Redlands, CA

Collins Park HOPE VI Revitalization,, TCG Development Services, LLC, Spartanburg, SC

Downtown Temple Terrace Revitalization Plan and Urban Design, City of Temple Terrace,
     Temple Terrace, FL

Hopewell Crossing Neighborhood Revitalization and Residential Architecture, WCI Communities,
     Inc., Bridgewater, NJ

Casey Property Neighborhood Design and Residential Design, Rocky Gorge Communities, Inc.,
     Washington, DC

2004   Fort Benning Military-Family Housing, Clark Pinnacle Family Communities, LLC, Fort Benning, GA

Dulles Baseball Town Plan, Lansdowne Town Center, LLC, Dulles, VA

Northwest One Neighborhood Revitalization Plan, McCormack Baron Salazar, Inc./District of
     Columbia, Washington, DC

Crystal Houses III Infill TOD Residential, Archstone, Arlington, VA

SW Greenleaf Master Plan Study, The John Buck Co., Washington, DC

North Bethesda Master Plan and Urban Design, The JBG Companies, Rockville, MD

Paddington Square Apartments, Housing Opportunities Commission, Silver Spring, MD

One Loudoun Center Town Design and Master Plan, Miller & Smith, Loudoun County, VA

Gaithersburg Olde Towne District Master Plan, City of Gaithersburg, Gaithersburg, MD

Lionsgate at Woodmont Corner Luxury Condominiums, Duball, LLC, Bethesda, MD

Coopers Crossing Mixed-Use Master Plan and Urban Design, Steiner + Associates, Inc., Camden, NJ

Zona Rosa Master Plan Update, Steiner + Associates, Inc., Kansas City, MO

San Diego Phase III Navy Family Housing, Lincoln/Clark San Diego, LLC, San Diego, CA

Capper Community Center, District of Columbia Housing Authority, Washington, DC

Bayshore Mixed-Use Study, Steiner + Associates, Inc., Milwaukee, WI

2005   Johnson & Johnson, Mixed-Use Transit Village, Garden Homes, South Brunswick Township, NJ

Path Concept Home Development, Low-Energy Research Home, Newport Partners, LLC, Omaha, NE

Brookview Master Plan and Town Code, The Commonwealth Group, Ltd., Claymont, DE

Capital Metro Oak Hill Mixed-Use Neighborhood, Martinez Wright & Mendez, Austin, TX

Capital Metro TOD South Congress, McKinney Architects, Inc., Austin, TX

Crisfield Strategic Revitalization, Crisfield Associates, Crisfield, MD

Pacific Beacon Navy BEQ, Clark Realty Builders, LP, San Diego, CA

Barry Farm Neighborhood Revitalization Plan, District of Columbia/District of Columbia Housing
    Authority, Washington, DC

Morningside Neighborhood Revitalization Plan, Graham Development, Charlotte, NC

Asbury Methodist Village Master Plan, Asbury Methodist Village, Gaithersburg, MD

Patriot's Landing, Tunnell Companies, LP, Millsboro, DE

Seacrest Village, Intown Development Group, Boynton Beach, FL

Taylor Yard Master Redevelopment Plan, McCormack Baron Salazar, Inc., Los Angeles, CA

Mississippi Renewal Charrette, Duany Plater-Zyberk & Company, Gautier, MS

Town Center Plaza Apartments Renovation, Bernstein Companies, Washington, DC

Vantaggio of Baldwin Hills Condominium, MSA Development, LLC, Los Angeles, CA

Villages at Mont Luzerne Resort Design and Concept Architecture, Homeworks, Inc.,
    Mont Luzerne, NY

Glenmont Metro Planning, The JBG Companies, Wheaton, MD

Seaside Main Gate Flag Officer Homes, Clark Realty Capital, LLC, San Diego, CA

New York Avenue Gateway Brownfields Mixed-Use Town Center, Abdo Development, Washington, DC

Silver Place Mixed-Use TOD Plan and Conceptual Architecture, The Bozzuto Group, Silver Spring, MD

Privatization of Army Lodging, AAFES Clark Army Lodging, various locations throughout US

Clarksburg Charrette, Town Plan and Conceptual Architecture with DPZ, Inc., Newland
    Communities, Clarksburg, MD

Smiley Heights Neighborhood Revitalization, McCormack Baron Salazar, Inc., Baton Rouge, LA

Savage MARC Station, Liberty Property Trust, Savage, MD

2006   Upland Downtown Plan, CIM Group, Upland, CA

California State University at Monterey Bay Faculty Housing, California State University at Monterey
    Bay, Monterey, CA

Winkler Redevelopment Master Plan, The JBG Companies, Alexandria, VA

Master Plan Consultant, City of Ventura, Ventura, CA

Poplar Point TOD, Energy Zero Master Plan, Clark Realty Capital, LLC, Washington, DC

Newark Mixed-Use Development, RBH Group, LLC, Newark, NJ

Andrews Air Force Base Family Housing, Clark Realty Capital, LLC, Camp Springs, MD

Kenilworth Avenue MPD Fleet Shop, Abdo Development, Washington, DC

Janie's Garden Mixed-Use Affordable Neighborhood Plan and Residential Design, Michaels
    Development Co., Sarasota, FL

Peninsula Town Center Mall Redevelopment, Steiner + Associates, Inc., Hampton, VA

Scaleybark Neighborhood Plan, McCormack Baron Salazar, Inc., Charlotte, NC

The Traditions at Huron Crossing, Charter Real Estate, Ltd., Ann Arbor, MI

Peninsula Waterfront Plan, The Commonwealth Group, Ltd., Wilmington, DE

West Rock Redevelopment, Michaels Development Co., New Haven, CT

Biscuit Run, Newland Communities, Charlottesville, VA

Coolfont Resort Plan, Carl M. Freeman Associates, Inc., Berkeley Springs, WV

Dover Knolls Mixed-Use Master Plan and Code, Benjamin Companies, Dutchess County, NY

Rolling Hills Southside Revitalization, McCormack Baron Salazar, Inc., Durham, NC

Four Corners Retail, City of Farmers Branch, Farmers Branch, TX

Downtown Redlands Specific Plan, City of Redlands, Redlands, CA

Patrick Square Town Plan, JMC Communities, Clemson, SC

Easton Town Center Master Plan Update and Expansion, Steiner + Associates, Inc., Columbus, OH

Leander TOD Master Planning, Leander Partners/American Realty Corp., Leander, TX

National Conference Center, Oxford Capital Partners, Inc., Leesburg, VA

Ventura Urban Design Review, City of Ventura, Ventura, CA

Umbria Street Entitlement Process, Stubbs Enterprises, Inc., Philadelphia, PA

Monmouth TOD, Somerset Development, LLC, Aberdeen, NJ

2007   New Cairo New Town Design, Al Oula Real Estate Development, Cairo, Egypt

San Diego Navy Family Housing Phase IV, Clark Realty Builders, LLC, San Diego, CA

Metro Westside Extension, Parsons Brinckerhoff, Los Angeles, CA

George Mason Square East Site Planning, City of Fairfax, Fairfax, VA

Parkside Neighborhood Center, CityInterests, LLC, Washington, DC

North Summit and Girard Street Master Plan, Hearthstone Communities, LLC, Gaithersburg, MD

Enhanced Use Lease Andrews Air Force Base, Clark Realty Capital, LLC, Camp Springs, MD

Bowie State MARC Station Sector Plan, Maryland National Capital Park & Planning Commission, Bowie, MD

Spring Hill Lake Apartments Master Plan and Densification Update, AIMCO, Greenbelt, MD

City of Falls Church Zoning Re-Write, Clarion Associates, Inc., Falls Church, VA

Courts at Monte Vista, Bowden Development, Inc., Claremont, CA

Babcock Ranch Master Plan and Design Codes, Kitson & Partners, Charlotte County, FL

Ridge Avenue Parcel, Ball Street Fund, LLC, Philadelphia, PA

Fort Sam Houston Lifestyle Center, Army and Air Force Exchange Service, San Antonio, TX

Skyland Town Center, Mixed-Use Town Center with Big Box Retail, Rappaport Companies/WC Smith, Washington, DC

C. J. Peete HOPE VI Revitalization, McCormack Baron Salazar, New Orleans, LA

Front Beach Master Plan, City of Ocean Springs, Mississippi, Ocean Springs, MS

Loudoun Metro Master Plan and Design Guidelines, DuPont Fabros Development, LLC, Loudoun County, VA

Downtown Jebel Ali Urban Design and Code, Limitless, LLC, Dubai, UAE

South Capitol Street Mixed-Use Center, CityInterests, LLC, Washington, DC

Fort Lewis Lifestyle Center, Army and Air Force Exchange Service, Fort Lewis, WA

Safeway at Tenleytown Mixed-Use Design, Safeway Grocery Stores and Clark Realty Capital, LLC, Washington, DC

Lake Zurich Village Plan and Concept Architecture, Equity Services Group, LLC, Lake Zurich, IL

Codorus Homes, York Housing Authority, York, PA

19Nineteen Clarendon TOD Apartments, ZOM, Inc., Arlington, VA

Cottonwood, General Growth Properties, Inc., Holladay, UT

2008   Round Rock Downtown Master Plan, City of Round Rock, Texas, Round Rock, TX

Waterfront Apartments, Norstar Development, Buffalo, NY

Wilson School Site, Arlington County Department of Planning, Arlington, VA

New Braunfels Downtown Master Plan, City of New Braunfels, New Braunfels, TX

Tilcon Quarry Neighborhood Plan, Lynmark Group, Suffern, NY

Brookside Town Center, Brookside Communities, LLC, Warrenton, VA

Safeway Palisades MacArthur Boulevard Mixed-Use Design, Safeway Grocery Stores, Washington, DC

Ventura View Corridor Analysis, City of Ventura, Ventura, CA

Route 108 School Site Hamlet Design, Land Design & Development, Inc., Clarksville, MD

Bermuda Affordable Housing, Clark Construction Group, King's Wharf, Bermuda

Glenn Dale-Seabrook-Lanham Sector Plan, Maryland National Capital Park and Planning Commission, Prince George's County, MD

Warrior in Transition Barracks, Clark Builders Group, LLC, Fort Belvoir, VA

2009   White Oak Apartments, Housing Opportunities Commission, Silver Spring, MD

Family Housing Revitalization, Naval Air Station Fallon, Clark Builders Group, LLC, Fallon, NV

Architectural Design Guidelines, El Cajon, City of El Cajon, El Cajon, CA

Fort Stanton Recreation Center, District of Columbia Department of Parks and Recreation, Washington, DC

Barry Farms Recreation Center, District of Columbia Department of Parks and Recreation, Washington, DC

Mauka Area Form-Based Code, Hawaii Community Development Authority, Honolulu, HI

Lake Mann HOPE VI Revitalization, Norstar Development, Orlando, FL

Parkway Overlook Apartments, KBK Enterprises, Washington, DC

Rêve de la Mer High-Density Waterfront Neighborhood, KAT Tourism Real Estate Inc., Istanbul, Turkey

10-Year Plan for Houston Housing Authority, Houston Housing Authority, Houston, TX

Victor Tulane Neighborhood Revitalization, Michaels Development Co., Montgomery, AL

Somerville TOD Redevelopment, Somerset Development, LLC, Somerville, NJ

Webb Tract Master Planning, Montgomery County Department of General Services, Montgomery County, MD

Wheaton New Downtown Master Plan and Neighborhood Consensus Plan, B. F. Saul Company, Wheaton, MD

2010   Bayside Master Plan, Carl M. Freeman Associates, Inc., Ocean City, MD

Yizhuang Town Center Design, Master Plan, Senior Apartment Design and Town Welcoming Building Design, Beijing Yuan Sheng Development Limited, Beijing, China

North Bethesda Market II & III Master Plan, The JBG Companies, Rockville, MD

Happy Meadows Urban Design and Architectural Imaging, Calthorpe Associates, Jeddah, Saudi Arabia

Markham TOD Master Plan and Code, Michael Morrissey, Markham, Ontario, Canada

Ivy City/Trinidad and Anacostia Assessments, National Community Reinvestment Coalition, Washington, DC

Kaka'ako Streetscape, Kamehameha Schools (Endowment), Honolulu, HI

Twinbrook Metroplace, High-Density Mixed-Use Neighborhood, Hotel, Office Building, Retail and Residential, Northwestern Mutual Life Insurance Co., Rockville, MD

Skyline Terrace Neighborhood Revitalization, KBK Enterprises, Pittsburgh, PA

Parkside/Kenilworth Choice Neighborhood, District of Columbia Housing Authority, Washington, DC

Vint Hill Village Master Plan, Vint Hill Economic Development Authority, Vint Hill, VA

2011   Santa Monica Downtown Specific Plan, City of Santa Monica, Santa Monica, CA

Alice Griffith Revitalization and Workforce Residential Buildings, McCormack Baron Salazar, Inc., San Francisco, CA

Beacon Center Revitalization of Existing Historic Church and Affordable Housing, Northern Real Estate Urban Ventures, Washington, DC

White Oak Master Plan, Saul Centers, Inc., White Oak, MD

Saudi Affordable Housing, Parsons, Kingdom of Saudi Arabia

2nd & H Street NE Revised Planned Unit Development, Louis Dreyfus Property Group, Washington, DC

Naval Air Station Fallon Planning and Residential Design, Clark Builders Group, LP, Fallon, NV

Aertson Midtown Mixed-Use, Apartments, Hotel, and Retail, Buckingham Companies, Nashville, TN

Windmill Parc Residential Neighborhood at Dulles Town Center, Lerner Enterprises, Dulles, VA

Liberty Town Square, Steiner + Associates, Inc., Liberty Township, OH

2012
Ashby Apartments, Washington Real Estate Investment Trust, McLean, VA

Ward 7 and 8 Community Meetings, America Speaks/District of Columbia, Washington, DC

Creighton Court/Nine Mile Road Revitalization, The Community Builders, Inc., Richmond, VA

Oxford Apartments, Lerner Enterprises, Dulles, VA

Poughkeepsie Waterfront Redevelopment Master Plan and Urban Design, Stantec, Poughkeepsie, NY

White Flint Sector Redevelopment Plan and Design, Saul Centers, Inc., Rockville, MD

A.D. Price Phase 3 Residential Workforce Neighborhood, Norstar Development, Buffalo, NY

Twin Rivers Redevelopment, McCormack Baron Salazar, Inc., Sacramento, CA

LA Zoning Ordinance ReWrite, Code Studio, Los Angeles, CA

Hilton Homewood Suites Hotel Façade Design, B. F. Saul Company, Arlington, VA

Twinbrook Master Plan, Zoning and Concept Architecture, Saul Centers, Inc., Rockville, MD

DCHA Architectural and Engineering Services, District of Columbia Housing Authority,
    Washington, DC

365 W San Jose Avenue, Neptune Investment Group, Inc., Claremont, CA

University of Southern California Housing, University of Southern California Capital Construction
    Development, Los Angeles, CA

Short Pump Multifamily, Eagle Construction of VA, LLC, Richmond, VA

Moorefield Station, Comstock Partners, LC, Vienna, VA

Loudoun Station TOD Master Plan and Architecture, Comstock Partners, LC, Ashburn, VA

10Eleven M Luxury Condominiums, Community Three Development, Washington, DC

Galatyn Park Project, Expedition Capital Partners, Richardson, TX

2013
Markham Precinct Plan, ARUP, Markham, Ontario, Canada

Stanton Square Workforce and Supportive Housing, Horning Brothers, Inc., Washington, DC

Montgomery Village Golf Course Redevelopment, Monument Realty, LLC, Montgomery Village, MD

Singer Island Gateway Site Design and Multifamily Housing, Singer Island Gateway LLC,
    Singer Island, FL

Meridian Hill Historic Site Condominium Design, Streetscape Partners, LLC, Washington, DC

Tower Oaks Apartments, The Tower Companies, Dulles, VA

Capitol Quarter Community Center, District of Columbia Housing Authority, Washington, DC

28 Main Street Condominiums, Global Fortune Real Estate Development Corporation, Markham,
    Ontario, Canada

Bethune Cookman University Student Housing Master Plan and Architecture, Hensel Phelps Con-
    struction/Quantum Capital, Daytona Beach, FL

Banner Hill Apartment Design, ZOM, Inc., Baltimore, MD

Westchester Bio-Science and Technology Center Master Plan, Fareri Associates, LP, Valhalla, NY

West Side Corridors Master Plan, City of South Bend Department of Community Investment,
    South Bend, IN

Laureate Park Village Center Neighborhood Design, Tavistock Development Company, Orlando, FL

Rainbow Village Master Planning Services, Norstar Development, Largo, FL

Plaza Saltillo, Endeavor Real Estate Group, Austin, TX

Yorktown Center Mixed-Use Master Plan, Continuum Development Company, LLC, Lombard, IL

Prince George's Plaza Transit District Plan, The Maryland-National Capital Park and Planning
    Commission, Hyattsville, MD

Gaziosmanpasa Urban Regeneration Project, Soyak Yapi Insaat Sanayi ve Ticaret A.S., Istanbul,
    Turkey

Festival Square Mixed-Use TOD, Global Fortune Real Estate Development Corporation, Toronto,
    Canada

Embassy of Bahrain Renovations, Embassy of the Kingdom of Bahrain, Washington, DC

Grosvenor-Strathmore WMATA Joint Development, TOD Mixed-Use Master Plan, Streetscape
    Partners, LLC, Rockville, MD
Benning Stoddert Recreation Center Modernization, Government of the District of Columbia,
    Washington, DC
River House Mixed-Use, 900-unit Addition to Existing 1,500-unit Apartment Complex, Vornado/
    Charles E. Smith, Arlington, VA
3912 and 3928 Highway 7, Re/Max Excel Realty, Ltd., Toronto, Canada

2014   East Pleasanton Design Advisory Services, Legacy Partners, East Pleasanton, CA
        Spring Valley, K. Hovnanian Homes, Leesburg, VA
        Hillandale Shopping Center Master Plan, The Duffie Companies, Silver Spring, MD
        Park Morton Redevelopment, Workforce Housing and Park, The Community Builders/District of
            Columbia, Washington, DC
        301 H Street NE TOD Mixed-Use Residential, Foulger-Pratt Contracting, LLC, Washington, DC
        Adams County Housing Authority Properties at Westminster, Denver Regional Council of
            Governments, Westminster, CO
        Lincoln Heights, District of Columbia Housing Authority, Washington, DC
        Westridge Commons Master Plan, Continuum Development Company, LLC, Midland, TX
        Kazliçesme Mixed-Use Development, Ozak-Yenigun-Ziylan Adi Ortakligi, Istanbul, Turkey
        Twinbrook Phase 1 Residential Building, Saul Centers, Inc., Rockville, MD
        Grosvenor Heights Townhouse Neighborhood, Community Three Development, Rockville, MD
        Mayor Wright Homes, PBR Hawaii, Honolulu, HI
        Kenilworth Courts, Michaels Development Co./District of Columbia Housing Authority,
            Washington, DC
        Deanwood Hills, Pennrose Properties, LLC, Washington, DC
        Highway 7 Master Plan, Wyview Group, Markham, Ontario, Canada
        Roger Williams Homes Master Planning, Hunt Development Group, LLC, Mobile, AL
        Las Palmas Senior Housing, McCormack Baron Salazar, Inc., Los Angeles, CA
        South Bend Downtown Mixed-Use, Supermarket, Residential, Garage on Century City Parking Lot,
            City of South Bend Department of Community Investment, South Bend, IN
        Great Pond Neighborhood Plan and Residential Design, Hirschfeld Properties, Windsor, CT
        301 N Street NE Mixed-Use Residential/Retail Design, Foulger-Pratt Contracting, LLC,
            Washington, DC

2015   Belcrest Plaza/Alterra Residential Community, Contee Company, LLP, Hyattsville, MD
        405 San Fernando, Fifteen Group, LLC, Los Angeles, CA
        Leander Apartment Study, Transit Village Investments, Ltd., Leander, TX
        Bergen Square Master Plan and Residential Design, Builders of Hope, Camden, NJ
        Progressive National Baptist Convention, Progressive National Baptist Convention, Inc./
            Atlantic-Pacific/UrbanMatters, Washington, DC
        Iberville Planning Study, McCormack Baron Salazar, Inc., New Orleans, LA
        Waikiki Design Guidelines, Waikiki Improvement Association, Waikiki, HI
        Al Sulaimania Development Master Plan, HAK Architectural and Engineering Consultants, Jeddah,
            Saudi Arabia
        Greater Cheverly Sector Plan Analysis, The Maryland-National Capital Park and Planning
            Commission, Cheverly, MD
        Waterfront Station Parcel TOD Mixed-Use Apartments, Retail, and Theatre, PN Hoffman,
            Washington, DC
        Gateway Redevelopment Area Plan, Miller-Valentine Group, Montgomery, OH
        WMAL Transmission Site Infill High-End Residential Neighborhood, Toll Brothers, Bethesda, MD
        Herndon Homes Redevelopment and Revitalization, Hunt Development Group, LLC, Atlanta, GA

Shady Grove New Town Center Mixed-Use Master Plan and Architectural Imaging, 1788 Holdings,
    Gaithersburg, MD
Herndon Town Center Infill, TOD, Mixed-Use Master Plan, Comstock Partners, LC, Herndon, VA
Hanson Property Master Plan Hamlet, Toll Brothers, North Potomac, MD
Destiny USA Development Master Plan, MSK2, LLC, Syracuse, NY
Scottish Rite Masonic Temple Site and Concept Design, PN Hoffman, Washington, DC
Southern Towers Property Master Plan and Densification, Caruthers Properties, Alexandria, VA
Chapman Lot 14B Master Plan and Concept Design, Hines, Rockville, MD
Falkland Chase Mixed-Use Redevelopment, Retail and Residential, The JBG Companies,
    Silver Spring, MD
South Gate Affordable Housing, PATH Ventures, South Gate, CA
Mellody Farm Concept Design, Focus Development, Lake Forest, IL
Lake Nona Mixed-Use Prototype, Tavistock Development Company, Orlando, FL
Sacramento Downtown Specific Plan, ESA | Community Development, Sacramento, CA
Glendale Senior Housing, Integral Group, Glendale, CA
The Resort Village at Bodrum, TT Gayrimenkul ve Ticaret A.S., Bodrum, Turkey
Cornell University Maplewood Graduate and Professional Student Housing, EdR Trust, Ithaca, NY
Parcel 42 Residential Competition, Donohoe Construction Company, Washington, DC
Northlake, Crescent Communities, LLC, Charlotte, NC
Burnet Avenue Condominium, Steiner + Associates, Inc., Cincinnati, OH
The Ladybird Mixed-Use Infill Development, Valor Development, LLC, Washington, DC
Syosset Park Concept Design of Seven Residential Types, Simon Property Group, Oyster Bay, NY
300 8th Street NE Condominium, Community Three Development, Washington, DC

2016   Rancho Cucamonga Consulting, City of Rancho Cucamonga, Rancho Cucamonga, CA
Brookhaven National Laboratories TOD Planning Study, Suffolk County Government,
    Farmingville, NY
The Grove at Shoal Creek, ARG Bull Creek, Ltd., Austin, TX
Woodbridge Neighborhood Design, Duball, LLC, Woodbridge, VA
Frisco Square Pattern Book, Arcadia Development Company, Frisco, TX
Brookland Manor Mixed-Income Revitalization Neighborhood, Mid-City Financial Corp.,
    Washington, DC
Reid Temple Active Living Senior Housing Master Plan and Concept Design, Reid Temple AME
    Church, Glenn Dale, MD
Vine City Atlanta Neighborhood Urban Design, Thadani Architects + Urbanists, Atlanta, GA
Station Square Apartment Design, Washington Property Company, Silver Spring, MD
Kelly Hamilton Architecture Design, KBK Enterprises, Pittsburgh, PA
Woodlawn East Neighborhood, Clark Realty Capital, LLC, Fort Belvoir, VA
Eckington Planned Unit Development, Foulger-Pratt Contracting, LLC, Washington, DC
Al Zahia Master Plan, Majid Al Futtaim Properties, LLC, Sharjah, UAE

Index

First published in the United States of America by

THE VENDOME PRESS

www.vendomepress.com

ISBN 978-0-86565-336-8

Editor: Jacqueline Decter
Production Director: Jim Spivey
Production Color Manager: Dana Cole
Designer: Mark Melnick

Library of Congress Cataloging-in-Publication Data

Names: Duany, Andrés, writer of foreword. · Plater-Zyberk, Elizabeth, writer of foreword.
Torti, John Francis, writer of introduction. · Gallas, Thomas M., writer of introduction. · O'Neill, Cheryl A., editor.
Title: Torti Gallas + Partners : architects of community / foreword by Andrés Duany and Elizabeth Plater-Zyberk ;
introduction by John Francis Torti and Thomas M. Gallas ; essays and descriptions edited by Cheryl A. O'Neill.
Description: New York : Vendome, 2017.
Identifiers: LCCN 2017001097 · ISBN 9780865653368 (hardback)
Subjects: LCSH: Torti Gallas + Partners. · Architecture, Modern—20th century. · Architecture, Modern—21st century.
BISAC: ARCHITECTURE / Urban & Land Use Planning. · ARCHITECTURE / Buildings / General.
ARCHITECTURE / Individual Architects & Firms / General.
Classification: LCC NA737.T558 A4 2017 · DDC 724/.7—dc23
LC record available at https://lccn.loc.gov/2017001097

This book was produced using acid-free paper, processed chlorine free, and printed with soy-based inks.

Printed in China by OGI
First printing

Page 1: Rooftop terrace at 360° H Street, Washington, D.C.
Pages 2–3: Night view of 14th Street in the Columbia Heights neighborhood of Washington, D.C., looking south.

Illustration Credits

All photographs and drawings are by Torti Gallas + Partners with the exception of the following. Numbers refer to page numbers.

Photographs

Hedrich/Blessing © Steve Hall: 16, 19 top, 20, 23, 26–28, 29 bottom, 33, 39, 47 top right, 52–53, 55, 73, 75, 80–84, 106–7, 112, 117–20, 121 top,
123–27, 131, 132 (with TG+P adaptations), 133, 157 center right, 160, 163, 168–70, 173–75, 181–85, 187 top, 189, 191–92, 207, 260–61, 263
Dioni Rey: 1, 37 bottom · Getty Images: 2–3, 50–51 · Joel Shlabotnik via flickr: 18 top · Everett Historical via shutterstock: 18 bottom
Permission granted from The Baltimore Sun. All rights reserved: 29 top · Bacci Filippo/istock.com: 30 · ErmakovaElena/istock.com: 31
From the Collections of the Museum of the City of New York: 43 top · Warren K. Leffler/Library of Congress: 45, 46 top center
From the Collections of the Historical Society of Washington, D.C.: 46 top left · Lindsay Ridgwelski: 48
Max MacKenzie: 66–67 top · With the permission of the Charles E. Smith Company: 74 · Cameron Davidson: 115, 129
With permission from the Eczacibasi Group: 141 · Ersin Alok: 142–43, 145, 212–13, 267 · Courtesy of HABMC: 179 center right
Ben Kracke for Studios Architecture: 217 bottom · Compassion over killing via flickr: 218 right · Jnthogs via flickr: 218 left
RMA Photography: 242 bottom · Matt Robinson: 243

Watercolor and Pencil Renderings

Vladislav Yeliseyev: 24, 33, 61, 147–48, 208, 221–23, 241, 274–76, 279 top, 280–85 · Mongkol Transantisuk Architectural Presentations, p. 27
Michael Vergason: 78, 227 bottom right · Dariush Vaziri: 144–45, 194, 268–69 · Chaiwat Pilanun: 206, 244 · Studio Yves: 256–57
Dodson Associates: 259 · Jeff McSwain: 264, 265 top · Michael Morrissey: 265 bottom

Digital Renderings

Beijing Visual Yuanjing Figures Science & Technology: 39, 87, 200–201 (with TG+P adaptations), 202–3, 224–29, 248–49, 252–53, 254
bottom, 255 · Radoslav Brandersky: 150–53 · Michael Morrissey Architect: 108–11, 270 · Studio AMD: 279 bottom

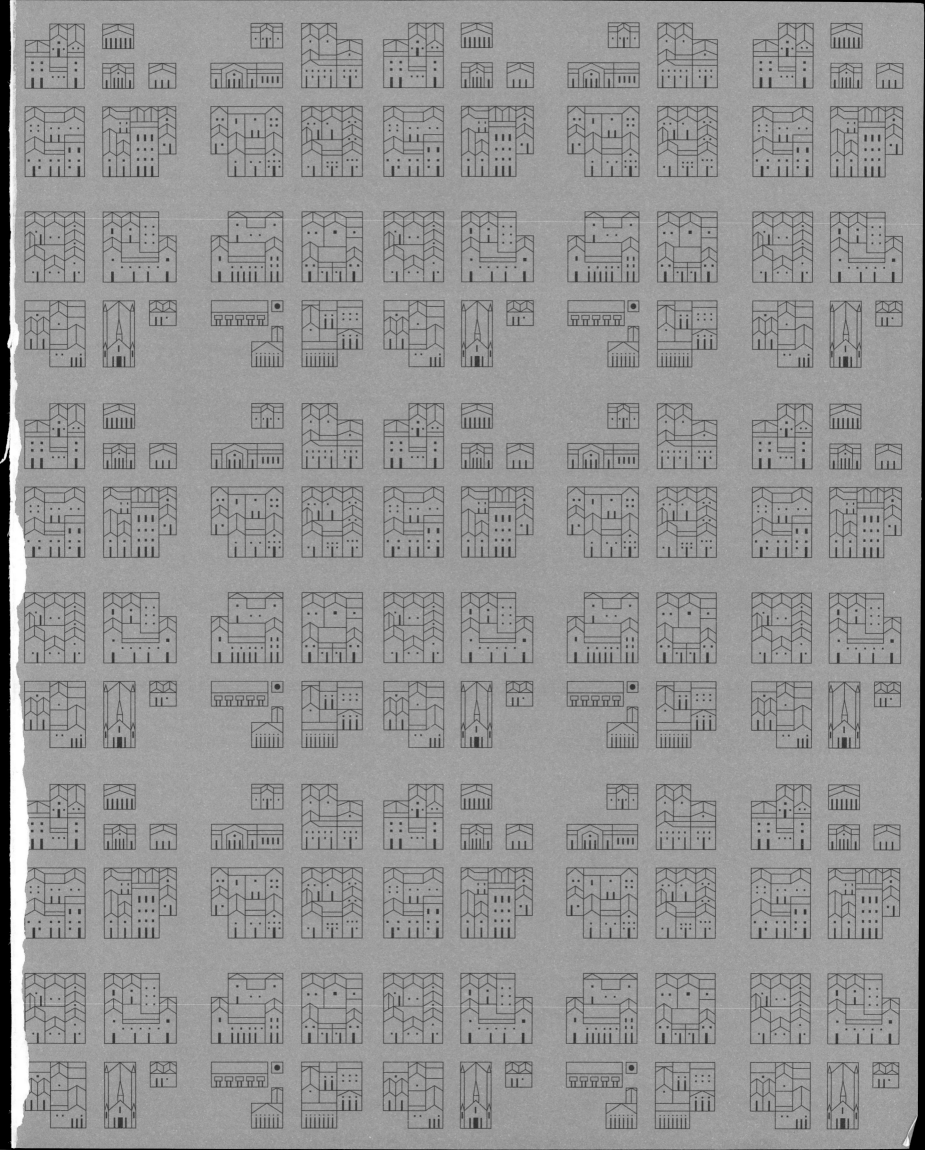

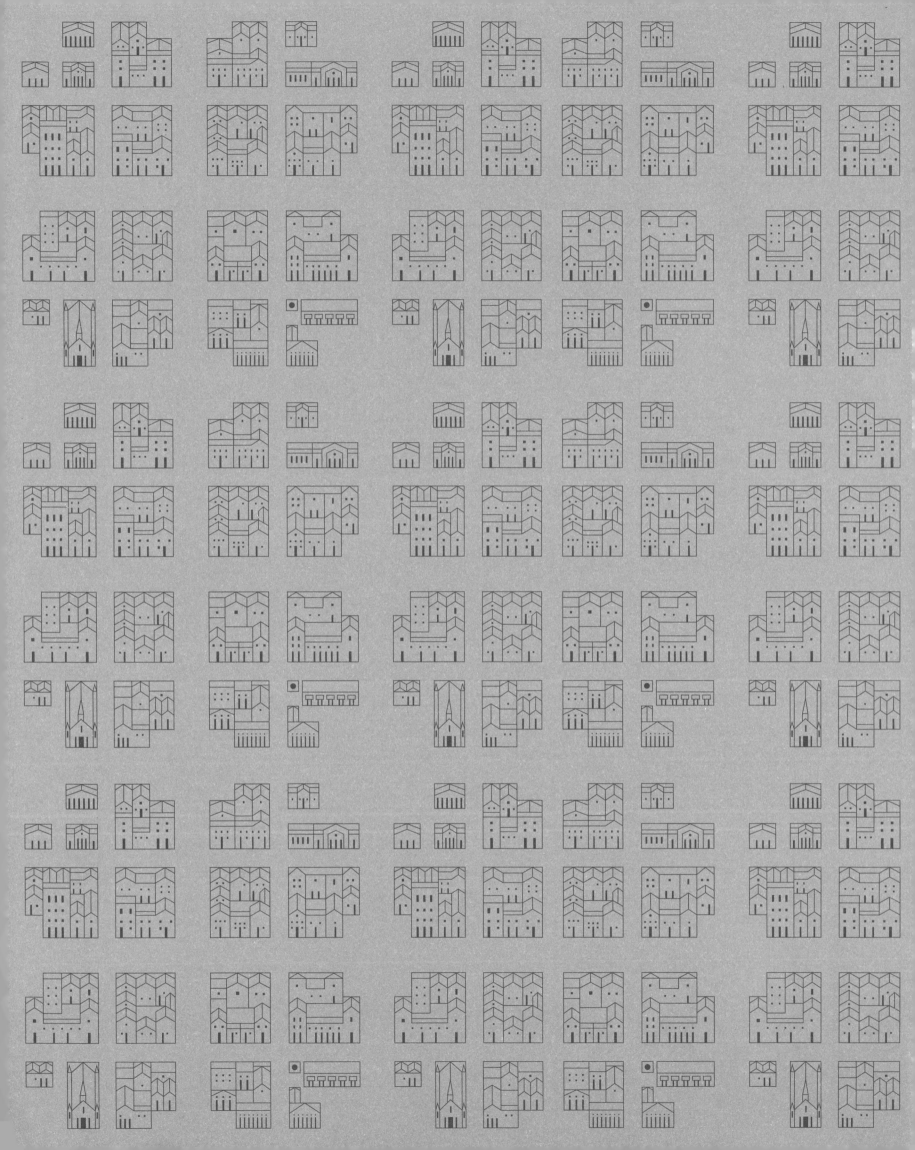